**W9-ADF-446**

WITHDRAWN

Gramley Library
Salem College
Winston-Salem, NC 27108

WITHDRAWN

# Robert Musil's 'The Man without Qualities'

Robert Musil's *The Man without Qualities* is perhaps the most important novel in German written this century – certainly it is among the most brilliant, puzzling and profound. This, the first comprehensive study of the work to appear in English, guides the reader towards Musil's central concerns.

It examines how Musil laboured through draft after draft to produce material that would pass his own strict literary 'quality control', and traces major themes through different layers of narrative with the aid of close textual analysis. It details how Musil subjects leading figures of *fin-de-siècle* Vienna to intense ironic scrutiny, and how, by drawing on his extensive knowledge of philosophy, psychology, politics, sociology and science, he works into his novel essayistic statements which record the state of contemporary European civilisation. It follows through an extraordinary literary experiment in which Musil immerses Ulrich, his hero, in the inner experiences of a murderer, and identifies Ulrich's determination, despite many entanglements (one with a flirtatious nymphomaniac, another with a frenzied female follower of Nietzsche, another with a campaign to assert the cultural supremacy of moribund Imperial Austria over upstart Prussia), to fulfil his primary task, namely to find the vital link between thinking and doing, and so discover the right way to live. Through a disturbing, and deeply serious, liaison with his own sister, Ulrich is shown to struggle through to the brink of self-discovery and enlightenment.

# CAMBRIDGE STUDIES IN GERMAN
*General editors*: H. B. NISBET *and* MARTIN SWALES

Also in the series
### S. S. PRAWER
*Frankenstein's Island: England
and the English in the writings of Heinrich
Heine*

### BENJAMIN BENNETT
*Hugo von Hofmannsthal:
The Theatres of Consciousness*

forthcoming:
### ANNA KUHN
*Christa Wolf's Utopian Vision:
From Marxism to Feminism*

Robert Musil in his study (Rasumofskygasse 20,
Vienna, 1935), by courtesy of
the Robert-Musil-Archiv Klagenfurt,
A-9020, Austria

90-322

PT
2625
.U8
M415
1988

# Robert Musil's
# 'The Man without Qualities'

## A Critical Study

### PHILIP PAYNE

*Lecturer in German Studies,*
*Department of Modern Languages,*
*University of Lancaster*

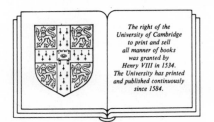

The right of the
University of Cambridge
to print and sell
all manner of books
was granted by
Henry VIII in 1534.
The University has printed
and published continuously
since 1584.

## CAMBRIDGE UNIVERSITY PRESS

*Cambridge*
*New York   New Rochelle   Melbourne   Sydney*

Gramley Library
Salem College
Winston-Salem, NC 27108

Published by the Press Syndicate of the University of Cambridge
The Pitt Building, Trumpington Street, Cambridge CB2 1RP
32 East 57th Street, New York, NY 10022, USA
10 Stamford Road, Oakleigh, Melbourne 3166, Australia

© Cambridge University Press 1988

First published 1988

Printed in Great Britain
at the University Press, Cambridge

*British Library cataloguing in publication data*
Payne, Philip
Robert Musil's 'The man without qualities':
a critical study. – (Cambridge studies in German).
1. Musil, Robert. Mann ohne Eigenschaften, Der
I. Title
833'.912    PT2625.U8z/
*Library of Congress cataloguing in publication data*
Payne, Philip, 1942–
Robert Musil's 'The man without qualities'.
(Cambridge studies in German)
Bibliography
Includes index.
1. Musil, Robert, 1880–1942. Mann ohne
Eigenschaften. I. Title. II. Series.
PT2625.U8M415   1988   833'.912   87-33746

ISBN 0 521 34032 2

CE

To Anne

# CONTENTS

# PREFACE

Robert Musil's reputation has grown steadily since his death in 1942; if experts were asked to list the major figures in German literature since the turn of the century, there is little doubt that they would rank Musil with Thomas Mann, Franz Kafka, Bert Brecht and Rainer Maria Rilke as being one of the most important. His work is a central contribution to twentieth-century Austrian and German culture and is frequently quoted by historians who value the irony and succinctness of his formulations and the accuracy and depth of his insights. In view of Musil's importance within the context of European literature, it is not necessary to apologise for the present book which is concerned primarily with the interpretation of Musil's incomplete masterpiece, *Der Mann ohne Eigenschaften* (*The Man without Qualities*). However, I am conscious, of course, that this is not the only study of Musil's work written particularly with English-speaking readers in mind. Anglo-Saxon scholarship can be proud of the collective contribution of Burton Pike, Frederick Peters, David Luft and Hannah Hickmann to our understanding of Musil's literary work, for they were all inspired, not only with enthusiasm for Musil but with a desire to be intermediaries between the reader, whether expert or not, and the given text. This study is, however, the only one published in English which offers a general introduction to *The Man without Qualities*.

Not only is the contribution of Musil to German literature itself worthy of continuing re-evaluation, but the huge growth in critical work on Musil means that our knowledge of the author requires constant up-dating. A single example will illustrate this. Musil's literary portraits are almost invariably drawn from life. Of all the major figures in his literary works, only one seemed to be entirely of Musil's making: Moosbrugger, the murderer in *The Man without Qualities*. Here, it appeared, Musil had allowed his imagination to take flight and to produce a magnificent monster. Karl Corino demolished this illusion in a recent paper in which he argued conclusively that Musil had based the Moosbrugger-theme on a murder which had preoccupied the newspaper-reading public in Austria before World War I – indeed the post mortem on the victim in *The Man without Qualities* is taken almost verbatim from a paragraph in one of these newspaper reports!

As far as the reception of Musil is concerned, the most important events of recent years have been Adolf Frisé's editions of Musil's *Tagebücher* (*Diaries*) (1976), *Gesammelte Werke* (*Collected Works*) (1978) and *Briefe* (*Correspondence*) (1981). Just as the original Frisé 'readers' edition' of *The Man without Qualities* ushered in the post-war era of interest in Musil, so it is already clear that these later contributions mark not only a new phase in Musil scholarship but also, and more significantly, a deepening appreciation of Musil among the general public. The effect of these editions is only now starting to be seen in research publications.

It is quite impossible to record fully my debt to Musil scholarship – though some indication of this will be found in my text and notes – but it would be equally wrong not to thank those to whom I owe so much, in particular Adolf Frisé who not only furnished the textual basis for Musil-scholars to work with – an astonishing achievement, combining indomitable energy with painstaking accuracy – but who has provided me personally with invaluable advice about Musil's life and work, with support in my research, and generous hospitality; I should also like to mention Professor Marie-Louise Roth and her colleagues, Frau Militzer, Frau Daigger and Frau Chevalier, who have made the *Robert-Musil-Arbeitsstelle* in Saarbrücken not only an indispensable store of research material but a delightful place to work in. Martin Swales first suggested this book and then followed it up with advice, criticism and encouragement; Graham Bartram, a colleague at Lancaster University, has laboured patiently and precisely through draft after draft of my work, helping me to reshape much of what I originally said; Eric Harber provided considerable intellectual stimulation and explained how some of the problems which Musil faced are similar to those of his contemporaries in English literature; Iain White of Cambridge University Press has guided me with patience, skill and good humour through the final stages of preparing the manuscript; my oldest and deepest debt is to Peter Stern, who supervised my post-graduate studies on Musil and who has continued to keep a critical eye on the progress of my work since.

I am most grateful to the Canada Council for a scholarship to

*Preface*

pursue my work in Europe, to the Austrian Cultural Institute for a grant for a summer's study in Vienna, to the University of Toronto for providing study leave for my research and to the University of Lancaster for a research grant to help me complete this book. I also wish to extend my thanks to the editors of *Forum for Modern Language Studies*, *Literatur und Kritik*, *Musil-Forum*, *New German Studies*, *Sprachkunst* and *wirkendes wort* for permission to make use of articles of mine which first appeared in their journals, and to the Director of the Germanic Institute in London for allowing me to include part of my paper from *Musil in Focus*, edited by Lothar Huber and John White.

I would like here to thank Bill Pobjoy whose teaching provided a stimulus whose force has not diminished with the passage of time, to express my gratitude to Chris Campos for his undergraduate supervisions and to Wolf and Erika Meyer-Erlach for their friendship and support during the earlier stages of my work on Musil, and to remember Stan Wilkinson who passed on his deep involvement in literature and life to so many of his pupils.

My family has learned to live with this obsession with Musil's work: my wife did not know me at the time when I contracted it; Emma, Tom and, more lately, Harry have grown up with Musil, but perhaps Jack will be less seriously affected since his birth has coincided almost precisely with the completion of this book.

Lancaster, June 1987

## A note on the translation of quotations and on references

In most cases, quotations from Musil's works are given in my English translation. Musil's style, word-play, antitheses, fluent transition from one subject or idea to another, and subtle matching of literary and scientific terminology present a formidable challenge to the translator. I have tried to be faithful to the original, even though this often results in English which sounds rather stilted. Where a word in Musil's text implies a range of meaning for which there is no adequate synonym in English, I have sometimes added the original German word in brackets. All quotations from German originals other than Musil's works are given only in my translation, with the exception of references to titles of books and articles in German.

In the text below, page references given in brackets after quotations from Musil's works are to the following German editions:

*Gesammelte Werke* (*Collected Works*), edited by Adolf Frisé, 2 vols (Reinbek bei Hamburg, 1978)

*Tagebücher* (*Diaries*), edited by Adolf Frisé, 2 vols (Reinbek bei Hamburg, 1976)

*Briefe* (*Correspondence*), edited by Adolf Frisé, 2 vols (Reinbek bei Hamburg, 1981)

Quotations followed by a simple page reference are to *Der Mann ohne Eigenschaften* (*The Man without Qualities*) which is Volume I of *Gesammelte Werke*. (In the endnotes this volume is identified by the abbreviation 'MoE'.) Otherwise, page references are preceded by one of the following abbreviations or titles: 'GWII' for *Gesammelte Werke* II, 'TbI' or 'TbII' for '*Tagebücher* I' or 'II', and '*Briefe* I' or '*Briefe* II'.

# Part I

# ASPECTS OF MUSIL'S LIFE AND WORKS

# I

# IMPRESSIONS OF ROBERT MUSIL SEEN FROM WITHIN

In 1939 Musil's head was modelled in clay by the sculptor, Fritz Wotruba. Wotruba was thus in a unique position to study him, at least from without. These are his impressions: '[He was] a handsome man with a powerful and well-proportioned body [...]. His manner was that of an Austrian gentleman of the old school, his skull and build were typically Slavic, his fine head, set on a thick neck, had an air of fatigue.'[1] Others were less struck by physical attributes – for them the charm of old Austria, the fastidiousness of the man in matters of dress and hygiene, were only superficial. What mattered was more the special psychic signature. Hans Mayer wrote: 'In discussion, as in every movement he made, Musil conveyed a sense of strain. Every verbal exchange with him was forced.'[2] A close friend, the psychologist Johannes von Allesch, records the 'enormous [...] intensity which Musil expended in attempts to grasp both things and events firmly in his mind'.[3] Wolfdietrich Rasch, too, registers 'the vibrations of a highly responsive sensibility [...], sceptical, tensed [...] to register answers to passionate questions, ceaselessly on the alert'.[4] Rasch takes us from objective to subjective mode, from Musil seen from without to Musil seen from within. The evidence of Musil's inner life is to be found in his *Tagebücher*.

Musil's diaries are records of the 'subject' in the sense in which Schopenhauer talks about the world as being 'object-for-the-subject', in other words a place which only exists in so far as a consciousness is there to observe it.[5] Musil is extraordinary in his self-awareness, his awareness of himself as subject. This subject has many aspects: it is, by turn, husband, lover, political observer, intellectual, creative writer, scientist, or simply a consciousness that registers what it is like to be alive. Below, we shall examine a few sketches from Musil's continuing self-portraiture in his *Tagebücher*. Although we can identify recurrent concerns and attitudes, the overriding impression we receive of Musil's self-perceptions is

3

of bewilderment and disorientation. The following entry is characteristic of his self-questioning: 'In the morning a spontaneous thought: it really belongs to the 40th or 50th, but not to the 60th year of a life: who and what manner of man are you? What are your principles? How are you proposing to round things off?' (Tb1, 946). Thus, only a short while before his death, Musil's vision of himself remains unclear. It would therefore be inappropriate, in what follows, to offer much more than impressions.

It is 30 March 1930. Musil is working desperately hard on *The Man without Qualities*. He has to serve two masters: his own obsession with getting the work right so that it will be intellectually watertight and formally perfect, and his publisher whose patience has been stretched almost to breaking point by Musil's repeated failures to meet deadlines. To add to this Musil's health is not good. He decides to take bromide and, with that constant fascination for himself as the human being whom he knows best, then sets down in writing what effect this has on him: 'a [...] certain [...] excitement [...] A convulsion in the head like blood suddenly being drained away. Expected an unpleasant final moment as with an anaesthetic' (Tb1, 711) – as if it were not enough to feel these things, to know this anxiety, Musil anticipates them and makes a record of them, holding on to them for posterity, for the sake of understanding. (This sense of the intellect as a fascinated but helpless onlooker at the spectacle of life is present in much of Musil's work.) The next morning on waking, the watching mind makes a discovery about this curious body with which it is fused: it experiences 'an uncharacteristic laziness, a reluctance to get up' (Tb1, 712). 'Aha!', says Musil, 'so that is what it feels like to wake from a good night's sleep, to feel relaxed.' The sense of feeling different from usual provides an awareness of a tension so constant that it is imperceptible, it becomes the measure of how Musil usually feels: 'because I feel so different (I recognise) that I am normally in a state of nervous tension' (Tb1, 712). Musil looks in the mirror of the mind and – meets Musil.

Musil often observes himself observing. Looking further back we find an entry in his diary from 1913, the time when Musil was precisely the age of the hero of *The Man without Qualities*; he has been married for just two years: 'Towards the end of November. I have gone to bed early, I feel I have caught a slight cold, indeed I'm perhaps running a temperature. The electric light is switched on; I

4

see the ceiling or the curtain over the door of the balcony. You began to get undressed after I had already finished doing so; I am waiting. I simply listen to you. Incomprehensible walking to and fro' (Tbɪ, 286). We begin with a succinct record of actions and sense impressions; then comes the evidence of the mental effort involved with the words: *'incomprehensible* walking to and fro' (Tbɪ, 286) (my emphasis). From here on, the sense of the mind straining to understand merges with the descriptive detail: Musil's perceptive apparatus is wide awake, registering sensory data, but he also takes account of the activity of the mind as it shapes impressions into images of specific actions: 'You come to put something on your bed; what can it be[?] You open the cupboard, put something in or take something out, I hear it shut again. You put hard objects on the table, others on the marble top of the chest of drawers. You are constantly in motion. Then I hear the familiar sounds of hair being let down and brushed' (Tbɪ, 286).

On one level, the diary here is recording the tension which is generated as a man waits for a woman to undress and get into bed; on another we have a quite technical account of the interplay of perceptual apparatus and sensory data, namely Musil diverting his irritation into an *ad hoc* attempt to grasp how the psyche tries to come to terms with the uninterrupted onslaught of experience. This is mind trying to master matter:

Water rushing into the wash-basin. Before that, clothes being slipped off; now more of them; it is incomprehensible to me how many clothes you are taking off. The shoes. Then your stockings move to and fro constantly just as the shoes did before. You pour water into glasses, three, four times, one after the other. In my visualisation I have long exhausted every conceivable possibility, whereas you, in reality, clearly still have things to do. I hear you putting on your nightdress. But still you are far from finished.

(Tbɪ, 286)

Musil never, to my knowledge, used these lines in any literary work. They seem to have been just a kind of exercise, a training of the mental faculties – what else would have made him take the trouble to record all these thoughts, to which he adds, as a final flourish, the 'mark' of himself as observer?

Again a hundred small actions. I know you are hurrying; so clearly all this is necessary. I understand: we observe the behaviour of dumb animals and are astonished how, in beings which are not supposed to have a mind, action succeeds action from morning till night. It is precisely the same now. You have no awareness of the countless movements your hands perform.

5

You have no awareness of all the things which seem necessary to you and which yet are quite insignificant. But they emerge in sharp relief on the profile of your life. *I, as I wait, happen to feel it* (Tb1, 286–7) (my emphasis).

The impressions set down here confirm both the 'vibrating sensibility' which Rasch recognised – the unceasing watchfulness which finds relaxation difficult even on the threshold of sleep – and the inveterate note-taking, the obsessive writing-up of existential data. (Incidentally, Musil disliked being observed himself; in his favourite coffee-house in Vienna he would remain standing until a table became available from which he could watch others, but which gave others no opportunity to watch him undetected!)[6]

Observation was the precondition for his literary production; the diaries tell us even more about Musil's work than about his life. Frisé's superb edition gives us overwhelming evidence of the way in which the roots of Musil's works reach right back into his life, his reading and his times.[7] We know that characters from his works are based on real people: the successive heroes of the various novel drafts which led to *The Man without Qualities* – Achilles, or Anders, or Ulrich – were based on Musil himself; Walter, the hero's friend, on Musil's friend, Gustav Donath; Clarisse, Walter's wife, on Gustav's wife, Alice Donath; Agathe on Martha Musil. But this edition of the *Tagebücher* also demonstrates how Musil captured the spirit of each character in the novel by going back from the moment when he was working on the relevant section of the text to the source material he had noted down in one of his notebooks when his impressions of Alice, or Gustav, or whoever, were still fresh in his mind (which might be ten, twenty or even thirty or more years in the past). The evidence of this recapitulation of experience is to be found in the many later notes which Musil made in the margin of his diaries.[8] It is not only within the circle of his friends and acquaintances that this is so – it works, too, for other real people around whom Musil created some of his characters. Frisé's edition provides details of this process, reaching in many cases beyond his notes through to the appendix where material from other sources among Musil's papers is reproduced. Thus we are able to reconstruct something of the creative process from its source in Musil's day-to-day experience, through the slow transformations in the author's imagination to the final formulation in a literary work. We watch, for example, the real Prinz Alois von und zu Liechtenstein, one of the co-founders of the Austrian 'Christlich-Soziale Partei', gradually changing into the only-a-couple-of-degrees-less-than-real Graf Leinsdorf;[9] we follow Ellen Key's ideas from their origin in her essay, 'Die Entfaltung der Seele durch Lebenskunst' ('The Unfolding of the Soul through the Art of Living')[10] to the point where they issue sweetly from the charming mouth of Diotima, Ulrich's cousin in *The Man without Qualities*;[11] and we wonder what Martha Musil must have made of her idealised literary self, Agathe, when she breaks with her precept-spouting educationalist husband, Georg Kerschensteiner (who was renamed 'Gottlieb Hagauer' in the novel), only to become emotionally embroiled with another pedagogue, Friedrich Wilhelm Foerster (dubbed August Lindner in *The Man without Qualities*).[12] Frisé identifies the source of countless excerpts from articles and books from the field of science, or psychology, or education, or music, or philosophy, or religion, and shows where an idea taken from one of these sources has found its way into Musil's published *œuvre*. The authenticity of tone of *The Man without Qualities* derived in part from the unique skill with which Musil worked material which he had borrowed from a living author into his account of the words or thoughts of a fictional character.[13] *The Man without Qualities* is, among many other things, an anthology of some aspects of con-temporary[14] intellectual history. But, even so, the reader does not ever quite become lost in the reconstruction of another's ideas because he or she remains conscious of the critical awareness of the author as a hyper-sensitive, insatiably curious and sceptical observer.

Musil would have published far more if he had not spent so much time writing and rewriting in preparation for publication. The matching of the real to the fictional is an extraordinarily time-consuming process in Musil's hands, involving personal psychologi-cal experimentation: Musil lived for a considerable period with the ideas of each intellectual he portrayed, getting the feel of what it was like to think this way. Seen from this inner perspective, *The Man without Qualities* has the quality of a vast research project moving almost imperceptibly forward through innumerable stages. It involves not only acts of creative imagination but also slow and sometimes tedious sifting through, and reshaping of, the accumu-lated manuscript pages in which authentic existential data – the stuff of Musil's experiences – are recorded.

Why did Musil write this way? I think that the reason was that, for the material to be embodied in his literary work, Musil laid down standards of 'quality control' which were unusually stringent. The satirist, Franz Blei, caught this sense of striving for perfection when he greeted Musil one day with the words 'And how many pages did this gentleman strike out last night?'[15] As far as possible Musil chose material which he had experienced himself; where that was not possible he worked with material until he felt he had taken possession of it psychically whether it was an Austrian aristocrat making a speech, a Viennese lady enthusing about the 'Soul', or a murderer about to be hanged.[16] To meet Musil's requirements the finished text, in position in a narrative, had to keep faith with that original lived or re-lived experience and so bring the reader into the closest possible contact with the world from which it was originally taken. But this was only the first requirement, the second was to make the reader reflect intensely on that world.[17]

Why then did Musil become a writer of fiction at all? Was he not rather cut out to be a philosopher? The diaries help to explain this choice of career. In his late twenties Musil was asking himself precisely the same question. In 1905 he 'interviewed' himself in an attempt to sort out his ideas:

Let us have a short talk with ourself, Herr Musil. So you know days when you have no sympathy with artists?
Yes.
And also days when you go out of your way to avoid philosophers?
Indeed. There are times when the former are too lacking in philosophical sophistication, and there are times when the latter are too lacking in humanity.
What about today?
Today I'm on the side of the artists. I felt irritated at the Institute and, by way of contrast, spent the evening next to a table where artists sat, delighting me with their harmless merriment. (TbI, 149)

But, of course, Musil cannot leave it at that; the two sides have to be analysed precisely. 'Artist-Musil' rests his case on the way in which he is able to situate a particular idea in a living human context, showing its effect on human relations; this, he suggests, is beyond the powers of the philosopher. 'Philosopher-Musil' counters quickly: 'Certainly; but the creative author has no grasp of ideas. He cannot imbue an idea with the fine flavour which the philosopher's palate demands' (TbI, 150). In 1908, when he writes to a professor at Graz turning down the academic post he has been offered there, the conflict seems unresolved even though an important decision has been taken; he is conscious of the honour attached to such an invitation, he writes, 'but my love for creative literature is no less strong than that for academic research and, because of it, a decision which may seem straightforward became one of existential significance for me' (Tbı, 893).[18]

So the decision is taken; Musil becomes a creative writer. But he has a serious 'handicap' – an unusually critical and probing mind. He wants not only to describe the things he studies, but, as we have seen, to comprehend them, and he obliges the reader to follow the path of reflection which he has taken. There is a touch of envy mixed with scorn when he says of Balzac: 'his types are only meaningful because he believes in the meaningfulness of the atmosphere in which they live' (Tbı, 342). The message hidden in this remark about Balzac is that Musil is not content to leave the task of trying to make sense of things to other men; he spends his waking life trying to find some sense. Creative writers are often satisfied when they can say of a passage: 'Yes, that is precisely the experience I wished to convey, I have captured it exactly!' Musil is not content with that; he is consumed with Faust's desire to know more than common men – to reach a pitch of self-knowledge and knowledge about others that will help to transform civilisation.

In 1913, by now committed to creative writing but still fascinated by 'Wissenschaft', Musil meets a professor of anthropology in Rome: '[The Professor] works about 14 hours a day [...] Has published a great deal. Looks like a smart young Roman coachman, but has a very finely-worked forehead which is at once beautiful and ugly'(Tbı, 277). Then comes the Musilian sting: 'Psychically he seems like a seventeen-year-old. His scientific work has not the slightest effect on the way he lives' (Tbı, 277). This, for Musil, is a most serious charge, for he, as 'Wissenschaftler' and writer, wants to influence the way that we live in this century. The Italian anthropologist, this expert on mankind, is 'as naive as a blithe monk' (Tbı, 277) – he knows next to nothing about what it is to be alive. Musil, by contrast, subsumes everything – his creative energy, his scientific approach, his wide knowledge – to a critical, as well as creative, study of life today. This is his individual contribution to the collective enterprise of all those of like mind, who want society to be internally coherent and consistent. His contribution will take on many different forms: the attempts to overturn convention in *Die Schwärmer* (*The Enthusiasts*), for example, or the probing of aspects of mystical experience in *Drei Frauen* (*Three Women*), or the sometimes gentle, sometimes virulent satire, in *The Man without Qualities*, directed against social inertia. Musil's understanding of his function as creative author can be illustrated by his account of the role of the hero of *The Man without Qualities* in an interview in 1926: '[I introduce] a young man [. . .] who has been schooled in the best of contemporary knowledge, in mathematics, physics, technology. [. . .] He [. . .] realises to his astonishment that reality is at least one hundred years behind what is happening in the realm of thought' (GWII, 940). Implicit in this statement is Musil's wish to change the world, to bring it up to date.

In an immediate historical context, however, Musil's desire for objectivity, coupled with the mood of intense reflection in his writing, may appear as culpable inactivity. On a visit to Berlin he watched the effects of the Nazi 'Machtergreifung' on those around him, among them his landlady:

March 1933. Three days ago the Reichstag burned. Yesterday the emergency regulations to exterminate the Communist and Socialist Parties appeared. The new men are throwing their weight about. In the circles with which I came in contact, there was first a general feeling of outrage, an instinctive response to this blow in the face for truth, for freedom and the like. It is the reaction of the liberal education which these people have grown up with. Yesterday, after Goering has expounded the reasons for these measures in a calm, friendly, masculine voice, Frau Witte is already visibly wavering. 'If it's true, what the Communist Party was preparing, then it's really bad!' The hypothetical element in this statement is already shrinking. (TbI, 722)

Here too, Musil gives the impression of not being directly involved in what is happening; it is as if he were not a member of contemporary society at all, but outside, looking in. At a time when other authors were actively resisting Nazism he seems to adopt the attitude of a later historian who, in a great leap of creative imagination, has projected himself into the past and is now looking about him, in impotent astonishment, at what the Nazis are doing in 1933:

Freedom of the press, of expression of any kind, freedom of conscience, respect for the individual, [. . .] etc., all the basic liberal rights are now set aside without even one single person getting extremely annoyed, indeed by and large without people being particularly bothered at all. They all simply let it pass over them like a fierce storm. The average individual does not yet feel affected. It would be possible to be most deeply disappointed by this, but it would be more correct to draw the conclusion that all the things which have been done away with here do not much concern them any longer. This was indeed the case. Has the individual human being made any use, for example, of his freedom of conscience? (TbI, 723)[19]

When Musil wrote this, he was only a visitor to Germany, but the sense of non-participation is nevertheless disturbing. He was involved whether he liked it or not, and, five years later, was to have his books banned in Austria as well as Germany by these 'new men'. With hindsight we can recognise here a form of 'inner emigration' and, though Musil seems to have put himself in personal danger by protesting about the actions of the Nazis in Vienna in 1938,[20] he did not display the political courage in the fight against Fascism of, for example, Thomas Mann or Bert Brecht. Musil may have been wrong in this, but he knew precisely where he stood, he had thought out his position carefully and was ready to defend it: he insisted that the creative author had an obligation to his work to keep aloof from practical politics.[21] Creative writing left no room for any other commitment, no time or energy should be spared for other things, but the works which grew from this private commitment, once made public, would alter readers' perceptions of the world and thus shape the future. Politically-committed colleagues dismissed this attitude as naive; the journalist, Egon Erwin Kisch, a Communist, having listened to Musil's defence of his views at a writers' conference in Paris in 1935, called him an 'asozialer Problematiker' ('asocial poser of problems').[22] But Musil was firmly convinced that an author who became involved in politics was compromising his work. He felt that Thomas Mann's *Der Zauberberg* (*The Magic Mountain*) would have benefited from a longer period of gestation and greater personal commitment from its creator. As it stood it was neither well-researched nor properly finished but merely 'in its "intellectual" sections [...] like a shark's maw' (Briefe I, 504)!

Musil's attitude towards the external world explains his isolation. Michael Hamburger argues that this was typical of many figures in German literature in the first decades of this century: 'To an extent almost inconceivable in any other age, each considerable writer seemed then, and still seems, to move within his own orbit, a law unto himself. Whether large or small, his readership did not constitute a public, far less the public.'[23] With Musil this sense of isolation is accentuated by his own natural predisposition and by the unusual range of his interests, which spread so much wider than those of his fellow-writers that their concerns often seemed to him to be shallow and parochial. He did have a small circle of literary friends and acquaintances in Vienna (including Franz Blei, Alfred Polgar, Franz Theodor Csokor and Oskar Maurus Fontana) whom

Gramley Library
Salem College
Winston-Salem, NC 27108

he could rely on to advance his reputation in the periodicals to which they contributed. His relations with major literary figures, however, were characterised by a public show of courtesy but a private lack of respect.

Musil felt that other writers made lesser demands on themselves than he did, yet were rewarded by a response from the public that was much greater than for his work. Hearing that an admirer had built a house for Hermann Hesse in Switzerland where the author lived sheltered from unwelcome visitors by a doting young third wife, Musil muttered darkly to himself in a diary entry: '[Hesse] can't stand any noise at home, nor any irregularities in the daily round of work, reading, walk, meal and sleep. All of this is perfectly comprehensible; the only strange thing about it is that he has the foibles of a greater man than he can lay claim to be. Today one can have the status of a major writer without producing major works' (Tb1, 973–974). If fellow-authors like Hesse, and Thomas Mann, too, were more demanding fewer people would grasp what they were trying to express and that would affect their popularity; Musil has to console himself with the prospect of posthumous fame since the significance of his work will take time to emerge fully: '[Thomas Mann and] others like him write for those who are here now; I write for people who are not here' (Tb1, 880). Karl Kraus, too, has found a place within the 'system', albeit a more eccentric one. Musil writes tartly: 'Kraus is positively on the way to becoming a complex' (Tb1, 634). This, Musil, argues, has something to do with the nature of contemporary journalism which Kraus pursued with his relentless criticisms: 'Sloppiness of style and lack of morality in the profession are projected, so to speak, into the external world by the journalist. Kraus is the redeemer-figure; the fact that Kraus is there to curse and criticise, makes everything right again. Objectified bad conscience' (Tb1, 634). Musil is suggesting here that a symbiotic relationship exists between Kraus and every journalist he attacks; each is indispensable to the other. Kraus perpetuates the practices he condemns because he is part of the system. Since society has no essential coherence and no moral backbone, no action within society can be taken to be what it is intended to be. Not intentions but effects are decisive; Kraus hurls his thunderbolts down on the journalistic landscape but, despite the noise, nothing changes. Journalists write as they have always written.

Musil praised few writers: Franz Werfel he satirised in the portrait of Feuermaul, the Expressionist poet; his few remarks on

Stefan George were cool and critical; Hermann Broch he accused of plagiarism. Hugo von Hofmannstal and Alfred Döblin he did admire, as he did Franz Kafka; of all his contemporaries, Rainer Maria Rilke was closest to his heart. Even these writers, however, seem to have had little direct influence on his actual writing. As he explained in a letter to the literary historian, Joseph Nadler, he owed most to dead authors, including Dostoevsky, Emerson, Novalis, Maeterlinck and Nietzsche.[24]

With such mentors Musil was more aware than most of his contemporaries of the crisis of confidence within contemporary culture. At the end of the nineteenth century there was a movement away from a concern with palpable reality. The sturdy pragmatism and materialism which marked the age of technological and industrial growth on the continent of Europe was countered in the last decade of the century by symbolism and aestheticism – the real was met by the spiritual (though this was often distorted by decadence and even satanism). Musil, who grew up at the time of this ideological confrontation within culture, seems to present a synthesis of both broad movements: he has the empiricism of the scientist and the fine, perhaps overrefined sensitivity of the aesthete; he can be blunt and sceptical, but he remains open to mysticism; he reads Ernst Mach's positivistic *Die Analyse der Empfindungen*, but also enjoys Ricarda Huch's soulful *Blütezeit der Romantik*; he reasons, but does not let reasoning entirely inhibit what he feels.[25] Accordingly, he is equally at his ease – or equally out-of-place – in different literary traditions: on the one hand, in Naturalism with its strong foothold in the mainstream of nineteenth-century realism and, on the other, in Expressionism with its exultant and incoherent messages from the beyond. This helps to explain why his work is, by turns, earth-bound and ecstatic.

This central paradox of Musil can be seen in his constant concern with the question of morality. At first, he accepted Nietzsche's diagnosis of the moral condition of contemporary mankind. Nietzsche's view might be summarised thus: morality grew up originally with religion, deriving its energy from belief – and belief, itself, was mere invention. With the loss of belief, morality became merely a cast-off shell of orthodox behaviour, bereft of inward conviction and outward legitimacy. Under Nietzsche's influence, Musil felt that all his contemporaries were disorientated by lack of any guidance: which criteria could shape their actions when the only principles available were not upheld, as they had once been, by living belief but only by the inertia of tradition? Actions derived from such principles – which had no grounding in views which were held in common by the majority of the members of society – were like a complex structure which floated free without support. Much of Musil's effort in his literary works is directed towards discovering modes of action which were authentic – which are not suspended in the void. But where Nietzsche sought an answer in the self-assertion of wilful individuals (through the evolution of the 'Übermensch'), Musil went his own more contemplative way which took him, albeit tentatively and sceptically, towards mysticism. Nietzsche believed that through intense psychological investigation he had exposed man's religious concerns as elaborate and intricate counterfeits. Musil's more diffident version of Nietzsche's 'Übermensch' is not muscle-bound from an excess of intellectual exercise; he knows how to relax the will. His mind is contemplative as well as active, self-assertive but also spiritually receptive. Musil was fascinated by the literature of religious experience[26] – in this respect he is close to the psychologist, William James, a man firmly rooted in the academic tradition, who explored with scientific objectivity but also with undisguised enthusiasm and excitement the literary evidence for the transports of religious experience.

Musil's fundamental allegiance was not to the tradition of realism but to that of idealism. In an interview in 1926 he said that he wanted to contribute to the 'geistige [...] Bewältigung der Welt' (GW$_{II}$, 942) ('mind taking charge of the world'). I believe he meant this literally. And if he had expressed his fundamental view in a couple of sentences – which he would never have done since it involved too great a simplification, too glib a summary of a life-time of struggle to understand the universe – he might have said something like this: the world is the struggle of light and darkness, the interaction of God, the Creator, and matter which is clay in His hands – both yielding and resistant to His fingers. Dark is the realm of matter, ignorance and distance from the divine; Light is the realm of 'ratio', love and the closeness of God.[27]

# 2
# MUSIL FROM YOUTH TO MATURITY

Robert Musil was born in 1880 in Klagenfurt, a town in Southern Austria. His father, Alfred (1846–1924), a distinguished mechanical engineer, whose services were rewarded with a patent of nobility a year before the dissolution of the Empire, later settled in Brünn (a city which, as Brno, is now in Czechoslovakia but which was then still part of the province of Moravia and under direct rule from Vienna) where he held a professorship at the Technical University. Alfred Musil was a rather shy, reserved man and was dominated by his wife, Hermine, a woman of nervous unpredictability; a third adult made up the household, Heinrich Reiter, the constant companion of Hermine Musil and possibly Musil's natural father.[1] Even as a child Musil was puzzled by the relationship between his mother and her two male companions. Musil grew up in the shelter of this family of means; his contact with the lower classes was restricted to short but brutal encounters with other boys in the moments when the attention of his nursemaid had strayed.

Musil showed from early childhood that, in addition to a brilliant intellect, he possessed his mother's intensity and will-power; he continually fought with her until he got his own way and was sent to a boarding-school at Eisenstadt in the Burgenland which prepared its pupils for a military career. He was not happy there, but his next school, another military college, at Mährisch-Weißkirchen in Moravia, was worse. Here he was to undergo some of the experiences that are recorded in *Die Verwirrungen des Zöglings Törleß* (*Young Törless*).

He graduated from the college in 1898 but then, after a short and intensely depressing spell at a military academy in Vienna, decided that he wanted a civilian career. He enrolled as a student of mechanical engineering in his father's department at the University of Brünn. This gave him the freedom to take stock of his environment; Musil's awareness that other young men of his age who had attended grammar schools, like his friend Gustav Donath, knew far more than he did about literature and culture sharpened his ambition. He began to read poets, novelists, essayists and philosophers such as Goethe, Novalis, Dostoievsky, Nietzsche, Emerson, Ellen Key, Jacobsen and many others, whom he had not had the opportunity to study before. Sibylle Mulot has investigated the cultural experiences that were available to Musil over the period 1898–1901 in Brünn: he read the *Wiener Rundschau* which had contributions by Baudelaire, Maeterlinck, D'Annunzio, Altenberg, Wilde, Verlaine, Poe, Rilke and Chekhov; at the theatre in Brünn during this period he had the opportunity to see plays by Ibsen, Hofmannsthal, Hauptmann, Sudermann, Bahr and Schnitzler; he may also have attended some of the current lectures and exhibitions in Brünn which covered such subjects as the Pre-Raphaelites, the 'modern' school in Vienna, Impressionism and the Symbolists.[2] As a well-to-do young man-about-town who had not yet settled into a career Musil began to write literary essays and sketches and kept a diary. In *Die Welt von Gestern*, Stefan Zweig captures the excitement of such activity for young men who, having spent their adolescence in schools which seemed designed to stifle all interest in living culture, became aware in their late teens of the appeal of current developments in the arts.[3]

This 'escape' from the influence of their elders was in fact a triumph of official policy. The authorities in the Empire had decided to encourage activities which both channelled youthful energies away from politics and also positively helped to foster an Austrian culture which, by transcending the distinctions of race, nationality and class, might help to bind the disintegrating Empire together. Even a movement like the 'Sezession', in which young painters and artists around Gustav Klimt proclaimed a break with the past and with what they saw as sterile Austrian traditionalism, was given official backing. The 'Sezession' building, which is still in use as an art gallery in Vienna today, is a monument to that policy. In the view of officials in the Habsburg Empire, 'art nouveau' was obsessed with the aesthetic and saw only the surface of objects. But leading figures like Klimt and Otto Wagner saw the movement quite differently; they believed that it worked from the surface through to the essence of things. Klimt's designs for the ceiling of the new University building had, as the dominant figure of a painting representing jurisprudence, a naked old man with bowed head drawn with Naturalistic exactness. Those who commissioned the picture probably wanted conventional images of truth and justice, but Klimt's intention was evidently to provoke discussion about the law, by presenting the point of view of the defendant rather than that of the lawyer.[4] Otto Wagner was not just the designer of façades to new buildings on the 'Ringstraße' in Vienna; in later work he pioneered the practice of exposing supporting structures, exemplifying in iron and concrete the engineering principles in his designs.

Likewise in literature, the watchword was 'modern' and this, too, involved a paradox. To be 'modern' was, by the turn of the century, to prefer a cult of feeling to all forms of practical activity, to be intensely introverted and intellectual rather than out-going and energetic. This attitude prompted young intellectuals to leave political issues alone (which was precisely what the establishment wanted), but it also disposed them to penetrate the surface of life as presented by those in authority, to see through the language of ideals, through the gloss of progress and culture, to the ugliness, the falsehoods, the fears and the pressures that were hidden beneath.

Thus what appeared at the time as a movement of narcissistic and self-indulgent young people was to prove in retrospect to have been a school for critical intellects. Some members of the movement would later – in the case of Musil, much later – turn their attention away from their own private predicaments to consider the whole world in which they lived; they would help to break the 'frame' round nineteenth-century man.

Dolf Sternberger shows that young Musil's contemporaries were indeed confined within a frame: he describes as symbolic of nineteenth-century attitudes the phenomenon of the 'panorama', a huge painting done by a popular artist in which a scene from contemporary life was displayed life-size on an enormous canvas.[5] Each member of the public mounted a platform and, from that perspective, could imagine himself or herself to be almost literally 'in the picture', seeing that his or her proportions were in scale with those of even the greatest contemporary figures depicted on the canvas, thereby fusing the private and the public and indulging in the illusion that there existed a continuum of feeling and thinking common to all humans. The Naturalist movement, though it was stronger in Germany than Austria, may be seen as an extension of this: in their works the Naturalists tried to represent the forces that shaped the lives of individuals as part of the objective nexus of creation. Such forces could all be identified by the diligent observer and ultimately traced to the operation of the laws which science had identified. But from within the 'modern' movement – despite the influence which Naturalism had on some of its members, such as Schnitzler and Musil – came a counter-current. Here the individual was no longer part of the total public and external 'picture'. He or she still felt the pressures to become a stereotyped member of a community, to behave in conformity with social expectations, to allow the mind to be filled until it overflowed with the public thoughts and public utterances; but the 'modern' man or woman resisted this, said 'No!' to outer pressure, defending an inner realm within which it was possible to be private, to indulge in esoteric experiences, to taste the subtle pleasure of being a backwater which life, the biological imperative of the will to assert oneself, had pushed aside and, having renounced the world (at least the world as the robust and competitive nineteenth century conceived the world), contemplate the chaos around from the vantage point of a sensibility refined by intellectual musings. It was a generation which enthused about Nietzsche, the philosopher of will and self-assertion, but which was secretly guided by Schopenhauer, the philosopher of renunciation – and where was it more appropriate to renounce the world than in Austria, the country that had surrendered German hegemony to Prussia?

Arthur Schnitzler gives the theme of the disjunction of inner and outer worlds a special twist in his story, *Leutnant Gustl*.[6] His central character is an insensitive and rather brutal young officer for whom tactical considerations of his standing with his peers and his superiors outweigh any stirrings of conscience or sympathy. The narrative is a stream of consciousness composed exclusively of this young man's thoughts and feelings. Gustl is primarily concerned with his social image, the dashing and stylish 'persona' which he presents to the world. Schnitzler, however, examines Gustl not from his public but his private side – he looks out with Gustl through the 'persona' at the world. Schnitzler's choice of perspective is in itself a declaration of allegiance: his work is 'modern'. Schnitzler provides no commentary because this is not necessary – Gustl is condemned out of his own mouth and mind. Schnitzler knew that the most sensitive members of the reading public whom he was addressing, with their emotional refinement and aesthetic sensitivity, would feel an intense alienation from the central character. They would need no prompting to ask the questions that Gustl's behaviour implied: what is a man's public standing worth when it is upheld by thoughts like these? Of what value is a show of bravery when it conceals a confusion of apprehensions and anxieties such as those that are revealed to the reader with his or her privileged vantage point? The work turns on the gulf between the consciousness of the central character, with his concern about appearances and about his progress in society, and that of sensitive readers with their predisposition to look behind the world of appearances to the principles that shape them.

Musil had escaped the world of the Leutnant Gustls by switching to a career in engineering. Here he hoped to be with men whose scientific training led them beyond the contemporary world with its anachronistic patterns of behaviour, its out-dated codes of honour, its hypocrisy and obsession with externals. But he discovered that their education had not touched them personally. By profession they were engineers; by convention and conviction they remained nineteenth-century gentlemen. So it was that Musil turned to literature as the realm in which he could pursue his search for an authentic life. When, in 1902, after completing a year of voluntary military service in Brünn, he moved to Stuttgart to do postgraduate research at the Technical University, he began work on the novel, *Young Törless*, which was to be his first piece of lasting value; but before we examine this work we should briefly review some of the intellectual influences that helped to shape his attitude to the world.

Austria–Hungary was a confluence of *Weltanschauungen*: Catholic orthodoxy met Marxism, psychoanalysis, liberalism and many minor movements. By upbringing and conviction Musil was a liberal.[7] In the Jewish civil servant, Leo Fischel, in *The Man without Qualities* Musil was to provide an image of the liberal ethos in its Habsburg context. Fischel is both deferential and mildly sceptical; he is an intelligent man who can see many of the flaws of a dissolving Empire but is evidently content to allow the tide of history to correct the flaws. His superiors value him for his rational, well-informed counsels. Musil himself is more sharply critical in his observations than Fischel; but, like Fischel, Musil is an evolutionist and not a revolutionary; he sees it as his task to point up an institutional or social anachronism, to focus on some typical inconsistency of contemporary conduct and then to step back and allow the process of self-correction to take its own slow course.

For Musil 'Geist' ('intellect', 'force of mind' and 'spirit') is not Reason as an Enlightenment deity; he is opposed to all forms of dogma, even one which places reason at the centre of creation. 'Geist', from one perspective, is presented as the psychic potential which can be harnessed by the will and directed towards specific goals; from another perspective, it is awareness of the extent to which the real is found wanting when measured against the ideal. In Musil's inner world there is free competition of ideas, a kind of parliamentary approach to intellectual questions where, as we shall see, all factions can argue their case and win in turn the endless sequence of debates. In this liberal debating-chamber of the psyche, intolerance and fanaticism have no place.

The dominant intellectual force in Musil's formative period was, of course, Friedrich Nietzsche,[8] all of whose works testify to the intensity of his childhood faith. Nietzsche's loss of belief as a young man made him acutely aware of the void at the heart of a society which paid only lip-service to Christianity, the main force that had shaped it. Through the energy and anguish of Nietzsche's writing Musil was made profoundly aware of this void and became convinced that it was the first duty of intellectuals like himself to find ways to fill it. Evidence of the influence of Nietzsche's ideas is found throughout Musil's work[9] – indeed Ulrich, Musil's 'alter ego' in *The Man without Qualities* gives a woman-friend, Clarisse, Nietzsche's collected works as a wedding present. (The gift is clearly an expression of his interests rather than her list of desiderata!)

Having turned away from Christianity, Nietzsche found a spiritual home in Ancient Greece – indeed the experience of Greek culture was so powerful that it coloured his perception of contemporary Germany. Nietzsche was not impressed by the citizens of the new German Empire of 1871, their faith in technology and science seemed perhaps more of a myth to him than Homer's accounts of the interventions of the Gods in the lives of men. In taking the measure of contemporary civilisation, Nietzsche disregarded the 'official' yardsticks of productive capacity, social harmony, scientific advance and the smug conviction that this was the most moral of communities – he looked upon it not in its own terms but almost as if he were a stranger from another culture whose criteria were different, and who asked the 'wrong' kind of questions: not 'Are these people good?' but 'Are they – physically and spiritually – strong?'; not 'Is this society productive?' but 'Is it beautiful?'; not 'Do men and women here live in comfort?' but 'Does this culture gain its strength from the dynamic interaction of profoundly distressing insights which can only be prevented from stifling Life itself by supreme artistic activity?' Musil, like Nietzsche, often appeared to be a stranger within contemporary civilisation; but Musil was a stranger who examined the world through the alienating medium of 'Geist' – and here he and Nietzsche follow different paths. For where Nietzsche sees 'Geist' as a force that is derived from the innate biological energy of the human organism, for Musil it appears to float free of the individual, transforming itself into a permanent perspective to which mankind can always have access.

To understand something of the genesis of this point of view we must reconsider the phase in Musil's early adulthood when, having started out on a career in engineering, he set about making good the gaps in an education in which the humanities had been neglected. His reading at this time included, as we have seen, essays by Ellen Key and R. W. Emerson.

Emerson, whose popularity reached its peak in Germany around 1900, seems almost like an extroverted nineteenth-century incarnation of the spirit of Musil stripped of all his intellectual doubts and scepticism.[10] In an essay entitled 'Self-Reliance' Emerson gives almost ecstatic expression to his conviction that each one of us, though an individual, has access to a principle working through the whole of creation. Each individual must surrender to 'that source [which is] the essence of genius, of virtue and of life, which we call Spontaneity or Instinct [...]. In that deep force, the last fact, behind which analysis cannot go, all things find their common origin.'[11] How are we to 'tune in' to the universe? Emerson is more enthusiastic than specific: 'The relations of the soul to the divine spirit are so pure, that it is profane to seek to interpose helps. It must be that when God speaketh He should communicate, not one thing but all things [...]'.[12] Emerson, who considered Plato to be the father of all modern thought, believed that the inner experience which we have just examined must be seen to be of a higher order than those belonging to our daily existence. Through what he called variously – indeed apparently indiscriminately – 'spirit' or 'mind' or 'soul', everyone could enter the world of other men or penetrate the essence of any thing. Such imaginative enterprises were not day-dreaming but excursions into a higher reality. For Emerson believed that the artist's actual work – which is of this world – is not so important as the miracle of creativity itself which comes from another realm. As Emerson puts it in an essay entitled 'History': 'Strasburg Cathedral is a material counterpart of the soul of [its architect] Erwin of Steinbach. The true poem is the poet's mind; the true ship is the ship-builder.'[13] (One cannot help wondering if the influence of Emerson's priorities – placing a higher value on intellectual and spiritual effort than on completed work – helps to explain why Musil failed to finish *The Man without Qualities*.) Though Musil's version of 'Geist' is more sober, self-critical and problematic, it has a strong family resemblance to Emerson's. For Musil, 'Geist' has a dual role in which Emerson's idealism merges incongruously with Nietzsche's scorn for the Ideal. It is an absolute – the timeless and unchanging standard by which all things which pass in this world of urgent relativities are measured. Yet it is also, infuriatingly, the law according to which there are no immutable laws!

Ellen Key, another ecstatic essayist, celebrated all those thinkers who have promoted individualism, including Emerson, Mill, Carlyle, Kierkegaard and Nietzsche; but, for her, the most important thinker was that ardent believer in the omniscience of the divine, Spinoza. So joyous and uncomplicated was her optimism about humanity that she was able, almost with the same breath in which she praised the genius of great men, to aver that socialism, with its stress on equality, would bring an upsurge in all human activity, cultural as well as economic. The field in which all her plans would be realised was a future where the whole of mankind would have the chance to develop with the self-assurance of Renaissance princes but where, evidently, growth of insight and enhanced spiritual awareness would guarantee the social harmony which was certainly not a feature of Renaissance life. Later, as we have seen, Musil was to present some of Ellen Key's ideas in an ironical light through the medium of Diotima, the 'Salondame', of *The Man without Qualities*. But in early manhood he was evidently overwhelmed – at least on first reading – by her essay 'The Unfolding of the Soul through the Art of Living'.[14]

A diet of such effusions may seem unhealthy for a developing intellect, but it must be seen against the background of Musil's inexperience of contemporary cultural activity and as a temporary escape from the scientific attitude of mind which he had been taught at school and which he was developing in his engineering studies. The importance of this latter influence should not be overlooked. Perhaps the clearest account of this aspect of Musil's view of things is given by Johannes von Allesch. Musil met von Allesch when studying philosophy and psychology in Berlin after giving up his research post in Stuttgart; they were to be friends for life. Von Allesch explained that, at military college, Musil came into contact with an 'attitude of mind which [. . .] is marked by a striving for naturalness, clarity, ease of assimilation and a corresponding simplification, indeed by a certain naiveté' and that this mental approach was 'always to hand [. . . as] a potential means for solving the tasks that confronted one'.[15] Elsewhere von Allesch suggests that this attitude can be described as positivistic, defining this as a 'reduction of reality in the direction of statistical disembodiment'.[16] Musil, when presented with a complex set of phenomena, would separate them – with a Cartesian sense of logical method – into their constituent parts and further reduce them by mathematical analysis. This tendency was confirmed when he later studied in Berlin, working under the psychologist, Carl Stumpf, for whom he wrote a dissertation on Ernst Mach, the physicist and philosopher.[17] Much later, Wolfdietrich Rasch noticed precisely the attitude which von Allesch identified when he had a number of conversations with Musil in Berlin in 1932. He observed that the way in which Musil tackled a given question reflected: 'the path of his intellectual development from engineer through thinker schooled in epistemology to novelist. He started with logical explanation of concepts of the kind he may have learnt from Mach and Stumpf and carried this process of rational perception through to its limits.'[18]

Mach had been appointed to the Chair of the History and Theory of the Inductive Sciences in Vienna in 1895. Besides exerting a profound influence on other philosophers – the Vienna Circle and contemporary British philosophy through Whitehead, Russell and Wittgenstein, owe a great deal to Mach – he had helped to shape general intellectual debate in Austria; some Marxists, lawyers and even literary figures acknowledged his influence. Perhaps it was Mach who set Hofmannsthal – who attended some of his lectures – on the train of thought that led to the writing of 'Ein Brief', in which Hofmannsthal pointed to the void that had opened up between words and the outside world to which they had earlier seemed so firmly attached.[19] Mach had noted that men hang words on to phenomena that seem to recur, they give names to 'things' which they say they recognise repeatedly. But Mach doubted that such identity existed anywhere apart from in men's minds, he suspected that each 'thing' that we see is in reality different from that 'same thing' that we think we saw earlier. The notion of recurrence and identity is only a convenience, a mental hook on which to hang sense data; it is the mind economising on mental effort, a saving of thought-energy. To the Greek, the atom was literally 'that-which-cannot-be-divided'; the modern physicist explores the parts which together form 'that-which-cannot-be-divided'! The etymology of this word, which continues in use even though the notion which it expresses has been found to be false, points up the pitfalls of language for anyone who is concerned that words should bridge the gap between mind and world. The words used by scientists to describe their findings cause considerable problems; how much more complex and embedded in illusion are concepts like 'individuality' and the 'I'. It is a small step from uncritical use of such words to the belief that they refer to entities which, when all the characteristics which men can identify have been stripped away, remain as an 'essence', a 'thing-in-itself'. Such thinking, for Mach, was fantasy. To study Mach was to be schooled in thoroughgoing scientific scepticism.[20]

Perhaps considerations such as these disposed Musil to be wary of psychoanalysis despite his fascination with questions of human motivation. Though he recognised that the psychoanalytic movement had brought some social benefits, notably a greater openness in sexual matters[21] – and, as a writer, he was far from squeamish about such things – the methods of this movement, the tendency of psychoanalysts to speculate on the basis of minimal evidence and to leap to conclusions about the realm of the unconscious to which they had no direct access, seemed to Musil to depart from proper scientific practice.

Although, in his scientific work, Musil was guided by positivism he was nonetheless very interested in the work of a philosopher who insisted that scientific method could only be justified intellectually by locating it in the tradition of idealism which led from Plato, via Descartes and Kant, to his own phenomenological method. The thinker in question was Edmund Husserl.[22] His influence on Musil is understandable when one considers that he was a member of the academic 'family' to which Musil's teachers belonged. Husserl at one time worked under Carl Stumpf, under whom, as we saw above, Musil wrote his doctorate in Berlin: Husserl had been taught by Franz Brentano, as was the distinguished Graz philosopher, Alexius Meinong, who, in 1908, offered to take Musil on as a member of his academic staff.

Husserl was determined, as Leszek Kolakowski put it, 'to discover the unshakable, the absolutely unquestionable foundation of knowledge; [...] to refute arguments of sceptics, of relativists; [...] to reach a perfectly hard ground in cognition'.[23] Mach taught Musil to question concepts, theories and ideas that others offered him, to examine the evidence of his own mind and senses, and then be prepared to doubt even that first-hand evidence as something shaped not by an innate faculty of truthfulness but by biological mechanisms for saving effort which increased the prospects for individual survival; Husserl pointed another way, offering a method for purifying the act of observation to the point where it would become an unmediated perception of the essence of things. Even the hallowed findings of exact science, the data recorded by perfectly calibrated instruments, could not be substituted, according to Husserl, for direct human experience which was the ultimate criterion of truth.

In an outstanding study of Robert Musil, Annie Reniers-Servrankx discusses the theme of observation through a telescope in Musil's work. The experience alienates the observer from the field he or she observes, yet, at the same time clarifies the image, bracketing it out from the familiar context which tends to blur its edges and put it out of sharp focus: 'for the first time', she writes, '[the observer] sees what he sees, instead of what he knows'.[24] The eye, no longer led by the concepts and ideas which the brain embeds in what it perceives, receives the actual image with a new immediacy, a new sense that it is there. Such moments in Musil's work, which seem to confirm the influence of Husserl, are tokens of his continued search for a truth which has somehow slipped past the veto of Mach's uncompromising relativism.

We are left, then, with a map of Musil's mental landscape as a young man where faint contours seem to flow into each other: we find a student of the unconscious resisting Freud and his school; an agnostic fascinated by powers beyond the reach of the intellect but accessible, under certain circumstances, to other human faculties; a highly-trained and highly-competent scientist who examined mystical literature with deep interest; an admirer of Nietzsche's irrationalist thinking who was a tireless advocate of 'Geist'. Some of those who write on Musil try to redraft his mental map with bold contours outlining clearly one attitude but providing only the faint trace of others. This misrepresents the situation. The map is unclear; the many different contours are indeed blurred, and in defiance of the laws of cartography (and, indeed, of logic!) they merge into each other – but they are all there.

# 3
## MUSIL BEFORE 'THE MAN WITHOUT QUALITIES' – THEMATIC AND STYLISTIC FEATURES OF THE CREATIVE WORKS AND ESSAYS, 1906–1924

All Musil's works including *The Man without Qualities* had strongly autobiographical elements. He wanted not to invent other worlds but to describe, criticise and so renew, the one around him. So he drew directly from life, preferring to rely on personal experience. When he reached beyond the frame of his own experience he proceeded cautiously, with careful consideration of all the evidence he could assemble, making unusual efforts to feel his way into the mind and senses of his subject.

Given that Musil's subject matter was derived from his own life it may seem surprising that he published so few creative works before *The Man without Qualities*, the first volume of which appeared when he was fifty years of age. Disposition and circumstance were responsible for this. He worked slowly, meticulously, self-critically: he tried to achieve both accurate representation of actual experience and stylistic perfection. He took time to learn his craft. He was no Hofmannsthal; he did not burst onto the Austrian literary scene as a precocious seventeen-year-old. Indeed, the earliest literary efforts are of interest only for their sense of isolation and neurotic self-preoccupation. In Musil's adolescent 'Nachtbuch' ('nightbook') of 'monsieur le vivisecteur'[1] we read:

I love the night because she wears no veil, during the day nerves are tugged this way and that until they are blinded, but in the night certain carnivores with certain throttling grips take hold of one's throat, as the life of the nerves recovers from the narcosis of the day and unfolds inwards, in an area where a new sense of oneself grows, as if, in a dark room with a candle in one's hand, one suddenly comes up against a mirror which for days has received not a single ray of light and which, greedily sucking this up, holds out to one only one's own face.                                (Tb1, 2)

Here the content is as pretentious as the form is awkward. This passage serves only as a measure of how far Musil progresses later. From this passage to the utter solitude of the following passage –

also from an early diary entry – is only a short step: 'Around me there is organic isolation, I rest as if under a covering of ice, 100 metres thick' (Tb1, 1). The feeling that Musil is cut off from all around him, the lack of any human warmth in this inner land-scape, the sense of being out-of-touch with anything which might provide proportion or direction, a non-specific yet overwhelming fear, all come together in this entry. But, as far as we know, Musil gave no finished literary expression to this existential dilemma, in contrast to another young contemporary: Kafka, in 'Ein Landarzt' ('A Country Doctor'), skilfully shapes the intense experience of isolation into a disturbing narrative whose central character, after a visit to a patient with a complaint which no medicine can cure, is pulled for ever by demon horses across trackless wastes of snow.[2]

Musil's earliest work grew, as we saw above, from preoccupation with self. At the turn of the century, Paul Valéry made the figure of Narcissus, staring at his reflection in a still pool, the image of twentieth-century mankind imprisoned in self-conscious thought – a pose available to all men and women of literary sensibility at the time.[3] But no creative writer can have scrutinised his own thoughts and feelings more closely, more single-mindedly, than Musil. Unlike the Classical figure, Musil was not held by the spec-tacle of his own beauty – though there is no doubt that elements of egotism and self-love are present in a young man of whom much was expected and who expected much of himself. Musil stared at, and into, the image of himself because here humanity, its potential and failings, were most accessible to him. There is no way to find out whether the events at the centre of his first novel *Young Törless* – the nocturnal beatings and sexual abuse of one of the pupils, with Törleß as a reluctant participant – were based on the author's direct experience, but other details were so clearly derived from Musil's spell at boarding school that he had to ask at least one contemporary to maintain a discreet silence.[4] Some years after writing *Young Törless* he extended his horizon to other minds, partly through the relationship with Martha, whose consciousness and memory he scrutinised with the intensity of a psychic 'voyeur'. But in his first novel Musil examined only his own past. The perspective was focussed so rigorously on the mind of the adolescent hero – only one or two asides by the narrator interrupt the spell – that, despite the convention of the third-person, past-tense narrative, the outer world is 'contaminated' by the feelings of the central consciousness in which sexuality stirs uneasily. We see this as Törleß's eyes become fixed on the hands of his friend, Beineberg:

it was in [the hands], which in fact were Beineberg's most beautiful feature, that the greatest revulsion was focussed. They had something lewd about them. That was probably the right comparison. And there was also something lewd in the impression of disjointed movements which the body gave. It was in the hands that it seemed, to some extent, to focus and seemed to radiate out from them like the anticipation of a touch which sent a loathsome shiver over Törleß's skin. He was himself amazed and a little shocked by this notion of his. For it was the second time already this day that something sexual had forced itself, unexpectedly and without proper context, into his thoughts. (GWᵢᵢ, 21)

Here Musil presents the dynamic tension of attraction and repulsion held in a precarious equilibrium within Törleß – the energy of sexuality in him is so powerful and so volatile that the reader senses it might explode at any moment, finding release along the most immediate, rather than the most desirable, channel. This is precisely what does happen. Basini, a rather effeminate fellow-pupil, will become the focus for Törleß's sexual energy and longing for the deeper human contact which is denied by the conventions of this military establishment.

The self-preoccupation of the consciousness at the centre places restrictions on the range of the narrative: after reading the novel, the reader would not be able to give even a vague description of the academy, its setting, buildings, staff, pupils or daily routine. All these things are present only at the periphery of this youth's vision. Yet even within this restricting frame, Musil expresses a great deal: the hopes, concerns and phobias that coexist and contradict each other in Törleß's mind; his adolescent sense of a secret inwardness, a unique quality of individuality which must be protected from the gaze of the outside world; fear that this uniqueness may turn out to be gross deformity, that, within, he may be disastrously different, a moral and spiritual monster (originally, Törleß's interest in Basini is stimulated by the unique opportunity that mental torture offers him for looking into his victim's innermost thoughts); the claustrophobia of finding the external world bursting with evidence of the activity of humans who were there before him.

This last sense, in particular, informs the opening paragraphs where Törleß's eyes follow the railway track as it recedes, to disappear in the horizon: 'A small station on the line leading to Russia. [...] On and on in a straight line ran four parallel iron tracks' (GWᵢᵢ, 7). These endless rails stand for nineteenth-century mankind's conquest of terrestrial space in the industrial revolution. They seem to depress Törleß with the sense that even the farthest horizon has been explored. Wherever he looks, he finds time coerced into timetables and parcelled into manageable periods by clocks, he finds figures in authority, walls that divide, and dull, dead routine. Even the return to the academy from the station becomes a forced march into psychic imprisonment:

this was how he felt it: as if it had to be so: *as a stone compulsion which captured and compressed* his whole life *into this movement – step by step – along this one line*, on this narrow strip which was drawn through the dust.
[...]
[...] [with] every *step that took him nearer to the restriction of the College something knotted itself more tightly within him.*
Now the bell was sounding its signal in his ears. For there was nothing that he feared as much as this bell, with its *irrevocable determining* of the end of the day – *like a brutal knife-cut.*
[...]
*Now you can experience absolutely nothing more*, for twelve hours you can experience nothing more, for twelve hours you are dead ...
(GWII, 16) (my emphases)

Given the central consciousness, all things in the text are not only objects but are vested with symbolical potential; they stand in a tense relationship with the psyche's phobias and problems. The stifling attic where Basini is beaten and sexually abused by Törleß's friend takes on, in the imagination of the reader, the shape of the psyche itself; a crow, glimpsed from a window of the school against a snowscape where all familiar detail has been smothered, embodies the desire of the adolescent to take flight across a world free of the evidence of human involvement, yet also expresses fear of that freedom; the blue sky, stretching onwards, outwards into the eternal, brings into focus – here the analogy is Törleß's own – the concept of the infinite from a maths lesson.[5] Every decision, every idea, conjures up its antithesis: to go one way means not to go another way, to be free is to lose the security of bondage, to be influenced by one person is to ignore another.

All these oppressions stimulate Törleß's fine but bewildered intellect. In the military atmosphere he develops not into an aesthete but into a positivist – albeit a positivist who is constantly defeated by the problems his confident philosophy is supposed to solve. An aristocratic youth arrives, Törleß befriends him, but then disagreement breaks out between them over the issue of religion; Törleß attacks belief all the more vigorously because he senses a response within himself; he roots out his own response, routs his friend's arguments, destroys their friendship; the other boy leaves. Törleß approaches moral questions with ruthless efficiency: Basini has been caught thieving, he has broken the code. The code prescribes ostracism for such conduct, ergo Basini must be denounced and dismissed. When, in a letter, his parents counsel leniency, Törleß cross-checks his moral calculations and can find no error – his parents' advice and therewith their moral logic must be at fault. He has grown up with the notion that character is something substantial, a personal possession of all human beings, a kind of scaffolding, perhaps, which provides a framework for decision-making and action – he can find no evidence of such reinforcement within his own consciousness. Just as the external world, as represented by his parents, fails him so, it seems, he fails himself. The claustrophobia of perplexity tightens around him.

It is from this perspective that we are invited to judge Törleß's treatment of Basini, the thief. The occasion when Törleß is first present at a session where Basini is beaten by Törleß's friends, Reiting and Beineberg, might have been devised as a test-case for character: how will the hero respond? That he does not do 'the decent thing' and spring to Basini's defence is without doubt an indictment of Törleß, and no argument can defend Törleß's shameful inaction as he listens to the sound of blows falling in the semi-darkness close to where he crouches. (It provides us, incidentally, with an early warning of the condition of the 'Bürgertum' in Austria and Germany in the thirties which was to do nothing when faced with confident brutality; Beineberg dresses up his sadism as self-schooling in pitilessness – this is the 'sentimental education' of the stormtrooper.)[6] But this narrative helps us to understand how it is that Törleß could become so morally disorientated, so completely cut off from all good example and sound advice. We share Törleß's confusion when his spiritually marooned consciousness fails to throw up any compelling reason, any categorical imperative, to assist Basini. Törleß turns inward but fails to find even the outline of a personal character, let alone the image of an ideal self. He is, so to speak, the 'man without qualities' as an adolescent. But there is, here, at least the negative proof of the latent worth of Törleß's invisible moral constitution: he can live with neither the shame of his mistreatment of Basini nor later with the secret of their homosexual relationship – he develops a state of feverish hypertension and runs away from school.

The novel brings an unusual intellectual sharpness to bear on things which seem essentially unavailable to intellectual perception and, at the same time, it charts the limits of such a way of seeing. Törleß, for the first time, feels sexual desire, having always associated sex with filth, animals and the hovels in which peasants live. He notes with dismay and revulsion that the local whore in her sordid room reminds him of his own mother, who lives in his memory as an elegant, loving, asexual presence – but, only a few weeks later, he inhales his mother's perfume with an explicitly sensual appreciation. Musil's solution is to have his narrator make frequent 'readings' of his hero's state of mind – in the way that a scientist plots plant-growth by means of a series of still photographs taken over a period of time. The reader is repeatedly reminded of this invisible process because the narrator seems to be an older Törleß (more comfortable within his personality yet perhaps otherwise not so different from the adolescent), watching over the shoulder of the younger self and quietly observing the stages on the path towards maturity. A modified version of this modest but subtly instructive narrative perspective will be used in parts of *The Man without Qualities*.

At the time he was writing *Young Törless*, Musil had a mistress – a working-class girl, Herma Dietz; their relationship lasted five years, ending with her death in 1907. His diaries record what appears more an obsession than a love-affair. They reveal the extent to which the Narcissism of the Törleß phase still held sway; he was still in the prison of solipsism. Later Musil used his diary entries as raw material for an account of the relationship in the story, *Tonka*. Tonka, a maidservant, is the focus of the young protagonist's attention and jealousy. He does not know whether she has been faithful to him – indeed, the doctors whom he consults assure him that he can be neither the father of her unborn child nor the source of a venereal infection she has caught. He is in a turmoil of uncertainty: the evidence of infidelity which has been confirmed by medical authority is counterbalanced by his sense of the utter genuineness of Tonka, who in her barely articulate way, assures him she is true. The hero has the impression that, through Tonka, life at large is conveying some incoherent message to him, side-stepping all laws which reason has defined. The narrative thus explores a case in which the certainties of science seem inappropriate where human relationships are concerned.

Perhaps Herma's death made the dilemma which Musil then faced into a permanent mode of perception – we find here an instance of the juxtaposing in Musil's work of militant scepticism and an underlying trust in things as they are. His mind shifts continually from active reasoning to passive contemplation, now doubting, now affirming the validity of mysticism. These contrasting states of mind pulse through successive Musil heroes; they are found in Homo, the protagonist in *Grigia*, a geologist with a mining expedition to a remote valley who is less anxious to find precious metal than to penetrate the superstitions and mysteries of the life of the impoverished local peasantry; in Thomas, the central figure in the drama, *Die Schwärmer* (*The Enthusiasts*), who has tried to keep faith with a youthful dream of a life in which precision will not be sacrificed to, but rather permeated by, passion; and in Ulrich, the hero of *The Man without Qualities*, whose deep interest in the writings of the mystics is never free of mental reservations. But the record in *Tonka* of Musil's relationship with Herma Dietz also reveals how far Musil has matured as a human being, for there is evidence here of a moral toughness that was absent in the account of Musil's earlier literary persona, Törleß. The protagonist in *Tonka* refuses to desert his mistress even though this means estrangement from his family, the rejection of the judgement of medical men who have been brought up in the same sceptical scientific tradition as he has, and the acceptance of a life of poverty and humiliation. It also means a parting from Narcissism; in the literary representation of the transformation in Musil himself, the hero is shocked by Tonka's death into full awareness of another person:

The world lay around him [. . .] He stood in the light and she lay beneath the earth [. . .]: then memory shouted out within him: Tonka! Tonka! He felt her from the earth to his head and her whole life. Everything that he had never known stood before him in this moment, the scales of blindness seemed to have fallen from his eyes. (GWII, 306)

With release from the remorselessly subjective mode of experience which was depicted in *Young Törless*, Musil's view of the world is transformed.

Not long after Herma's death, Musil fell deeply in love with Martha Marcovaldi, a striking woman in her early thirties, with dark hair and Southern complexion; she returned his passion. The depth of their love can be gauged by the selflessness with which Martha gave up her own career as a painter, devoting herself completely to Musil's well-being and to the success of his writing, and by the feelings which imbue Musil's portraits of Martha in different works – for example, as Claudine in *Die Vollendung der Liebe* (*The Perfecting of a Love*), as Regine in *The Enthusiasts* and, in blond metamorphosis, as Agathe in *The Man without Qualities*.

In a scene depicted on the first page of *The Perfecting of a Love*, Musil attempts to arrest in prose a few moments of their shared delight. The narrative perspective here is different from that which we identified in *Young Törless*. The subjectivism has given way to a delicate balancing of inner and outer worlds. Time (its slow but steady passing measured now in a glance, now in a gesture) and space (captured in the surfaces of a teapot, the geometry of the arrangement of objects) are strongly present here as two dimensions of existence which the couple would like to transcend through the agency of a third. This, the power of love, is strongly felt but imperfectly understood. This 'still life in words' focusses the reader's attention precisely on love in its real setting, on the complex interrelations of feelings and the external world.

'And I have no desire at all to travel without you . . .' His wife said that as she poured the tea, looking across while she did so to where he sat in an armchair with a bright flower pattern in a corner of the room, smoking a cigarette. [. . .] Like a pair of dark eye-lids calmly lowered, [the Venetian blinds] concealed the brightness of this room in which the tea now fell into the cups from a matt silver teapot, striking them with a low ringing sound and then seeming to stand still in the jet like a twisted transparent column of light straw-brown topaz. In the slightly concave surfaces of the teapot lay shades of green and grey colour, and blue and yellow; they lay quite still, as if they had collected there and could not move any further. But the woman's arm jutted away from the teapot and the look she gave her husband joined the arm to form a stiff, rigid angle.          (GWII, 156)

The intensity of mutual love seems for a few moments to arrest the play of light and the passage of time – a spell broken only when the woman moves her arm.

In this story, the woman, Claudine, has to take leave of her husband and visit her daughter in another town; at a hotel she is seduced by another guest – an event which perhaps corresponds to Martha's infidelity with a former lover after meeting Musil.[7] By the time Martha met Musil she had already been married twice and had had many affairs. Their love had to survive what one critic called 'the perversity of their sexual and emotional pasts'.[8] In the opening scene which we have examined above, the man and woman are discussing someone who has committed sexual crimes against girls and young women. The cultured setting and the subject of conversation are only superficially incongruous; the author is now accepting a wider responsibility than he was able to shoulder in *Young Törless*. Musil not only thinks for, he thinks as, other people: having rejected what he considers to be the redundant categories of middle-class morality (though he observed the outward code of 'bürgerlich' behaviour with exemplary rigour!), he examines what it is to live beyond these categories. Since the deviant expresses a human potential present in us all, what is it, Musil asks, that diverts that potential into the wrong channels? Musil is anxious to know why the mainstream of western civilised life has lost the intensity of earlier cultures. Only in social outcasts is evidence of that primal human energy to be found: the tranquil ecstasy of the mystic, the self-abandoning sensuality of the nymphomaniac, the madness of the murderer are all experiences that are forbidden to those in possession of their civilised senses. The choice facing mankind seems, to Musil, to be that between morality and intensity, between a life which uses only part of mankind's potential and one which distorts it. Musil suspects that, in the future, it will be necessary to alter the boundaries of what is at present seen as moral behaviour, so that civilisation is open to the potential which now is associated with powerful taboos; in his researches into this problem, Musil breaks the taboos.

Taking advantage of a special dispensation for the creative artist – whose task he sees as providing an impetus for change within a civilisation that has lost its way – Musil projects himself into the deviant. This action involves more than mere unaided creative imagination – ·it requires patient collecting of evidence, long preparation and contemplative testing of alternative modes of experience. These culminate with the author reliving the required mood, recording it in narratives which represent – in exhaustive, uncensored and often shocking detail – the interpenetration of outer and inner world, the flow of psychic processes through the river-bed of external objects. The following passage, which is typical in its disturbing frankness, records the scene after Claudine has sensed a would-be seducer outside the door of her hotel room:

She had already undressed. On the chair before the bed her skirts lay where she had just slipped them off. The air of this room, rented today to one person, tomorrow to another, touched and intermingled with the fragrance from within her. She looked around the room. She noticed a brass lock hanging down at an angle from a chest of drawers, her gaze rested on a small shabby carpet before her bed, worn out by many feet. She suddenly thought of the smell which was exuded and absorbed by the skin of these feet, absorbed into the minds of strangers, familiar, protecting like the smell of the parental home. It was a strangely ambivalent flickering notion, now alien and nauseating, now irresistible, as if the self-love of all these people were streaming into her and nothing remained of herself but a watching and observing. And still that person stood before her door, making his presence known only with faint involuntary noises.

Then a desire seized her to throw herself down on this carpet, to kiss the loathsome traces of these feet, using them to arouse herself like a snuffling bitch. But it was no longer sensuality now, only something which howled like a wind or screamed like a child. (GWII, 188–9)

Musil, apparently having conducted his experiments into the state of mind of a woman at such a moment – here we assume the close collaboration of Martha – casts this state in language interspersing the fictional representation with images. These are his equivalent to naturalistic detail, a series of what one critic has termed 'psycho-analogies'.[9] They transmit emotions and ideas from the mind of the person on whom the character in question is based to the mind of the reader across the inhibiting medium of the public world which separates them. In the following passage I have italicised most of the images in question:

Suddenly she knelt down on the floor, before her eyes the stiff flowers in the carpet sent out bigger, uncomprehending tendrils, she saw her full womanly thighs crouching over them in an ugly way like something quite without meaning and yet tensed with an incomprehensible seriousness, her hands stared at each other on the floor *like animals with five limbs*, she suddenly remembered the lamp outside, the circles it cast wandering across the ceiling in ghastly silence, the walls, the bare walls, the emptiness and, again, the person standing there, sometimes gripped by emotion, *creaking like a tree in its bark*, his blood rushing in his head *like bushy foliage*, while she lay stretching out her limbs here, separated only by a door, and somehow, in spite of that, felt the full sweetness of her mature body, with that persisting remnant of mind ['Seele'] which still stands motionless beside the disintegrating distortedness of mortal injuries, detaching itself from them into heavy unbroken perceiving, *as if beside a fallen animal*.

Then she heard the person cautiously leave. And suddenly understood, still torn away from herself, that this was infidelity; even stronger than lying. (GWII, 189) (my emphases).

This scene of self-abandon appears utterly out-of-place when set against the opening description of serene and civilised love; this is so because we have omitted the many pages of Musil's slow and deliberate transitional passages in which he tries to show the reader that this act of secret infidelity is continuous with, is part of the emotional logic of, a lasting relationship.

How can this be so? In the opening scene, examined above, a consciousness in the classical mould is at work: form wrestles with formlessness, the categories of perception with incomprehension, the author fashions a thing of beauty in words – an objective statement of his drive to understand and create. Yet, within the narrative, another mood emerges running counter to the urge to identify and describe in plastic detail: it dissolves distinctions, merges the beautiful with the ugly, fuses evil into the same totality as the good.

Even in the opening scene the spirit of all these mergers is present: this is, as we recognised earlier, love itself. Love, so runs the 'argument' in this narrative, does not belong in the classical mode; it is not exclusive. It is not, for example, the 'property' of the loving couple, blessing the objects which are privileged to fall within the aura of their feelings for each other. It is inclusive, embracing all things without discrimination, their contours fading as it touches them. The author seeks to persuade the reader here that Claudine is swept along by love – there is no active comprehending on her part – to exorcise at symbolic level her desire for exclusiveness, the privacy of her love. So, in the course of the narrative, the illusory 'good' of the opening scene is balanced out by her surrender to 'evil' when she is seduced by a guest at a hotel. Perhaps parodying the classical urge towards symmetry, the narrative sets the 'beauty' of shared bliss against the 'ugliness' of self-abasement. From this perspective, the carnal act which follows shortly upon the passage we have studied is, precisely, a 'Vollendung der Liebe' ('a perfecting of love'), at once grotesque and revealing.

Musil is not presenting his central character here as in any way exemplary. In his view, there are no precedents, no human models for others to follow. What he offers here is a lesson in un-learning – escape from the tyranny of routine behaviour and standard expectations.

Although the experiments of *Vereinigungen* (*Acts of Union*) were not a publishing success, they were the proving ground for ideas and literary techniques which were thereafter always available to Musil. The narrative of *The Man without Qualities* is frequently enriched by passages of this kind in which Musil examines aspects of psychic experience which perhaps no other author has rendered so accurately – this technique is a central aspect of what Musil called the 'geistige [. . .] Bewältigung der Welt' (GWɪɪ, 942) ('mind taking charge of the world').

In addition to the exploration of sexuality and love in *Acts of Union*, which we have briefly examined, Musil provides fragmentary studies of other ecstatic states in other works: in *Die Portuguiesin* (*The Woman from Portugal*) we watch the way that, as illness threatens the life of the medieval knight who is its central character, his weakened consciousness begins to discern the unity that underlies creation; in *Grigia* we find an analogous sense that the objects in the natural world which surround the hero, Homo, are subtle images expressing some kind of hidden design and purpose – as Homo surrenders to death when immured in a cave by the jealous husband of his peasant mistress, the reader feels that this ordeal is only a stage to perfect union with the wife whom he has left behind but loves beyond measure.

The most important of the works before *The Man without Qualities* is the drama *Die Schwärmer* (*The Enthusiasts*). It embraces the aspects of Musil's work which we have discussed above: the focussing on individual consciousness, the treating of life at large with the rigour of scientific enquiry, the meticulous rendering in language of extraordinary mental states, the enlisting even of sensuality and insanity in a search for moral renewal, the experimenting with imagery designed to provide a bridge between the fictional world and the reader and, finally, further attempts to mediate the realm of love.

For a work of such serious intent, and one which has been seen as providing a bridge to *The Man without Qualities*, *The Enthusiasts* has an unlikely plot. Nietzsche placed his vision of a 'New Man' high on a mountain, fitting him out with the robes of a Biblical prophet. Musil's 'New Man' and 'New Woman' are in modern costume on the set of what sometimes looks a little like a bedroom farce. *Also sprach Zarathustra* (*Thus spake Zarathustra*) can appear to the uninitiated like operatic exaggeration on Nietzsche's part; in *The Enthusiasts*, Musil goes to the other extreme, since the message may be obscured by the incongruous backdrop. Musil makes few concessions to help his audience to understand what concerns him. Perhaps he should have used a device such as a prologue to announce his intentions. This might have included a number of points such as the following which are vital to understanding the play.

The 'Enthusiasts' are the four central characters, Thomas, Anselm, Regine and Maria – they are between 28 and 34 years of age. As adolescents, some fifteen years ago, they all lived in the house which now forms the setting for a reunion; then they shared a

common desire – they vowed not to submit unthinkingly to the
pressures of their environment, nor to make the habitual compro-
mises of social life and become intellectually, emotionally and
spiritually interwoven with the lives of their contemporaries. In
maturity, not all the 'Enthusiasts' have remained true to this vision.
Two of them, Anselm and Maria, have struck a compromise with
modern civilisation. On stage we see the remnants of an existential
experiment which, given the odds against success, is virtually
bound to fail, indeed has possibly failed already. However, since
what is at issue is a new way of living without precedent or parallel,
no criteria exist to judge whether it has, indeed, failed (the proof of
this pudding being in the eating not the watching). No doubt, any
'bürgerlich' audience will condemn the characters portrayed for
their emotional excesses but these excesses are, in fact, tokens of
their experimental fervour which Musil hopes members of the
audience will be persuaded to emulate. Finally, the audience might
give consideration to the idea that the suffering of the two main
characters, Thomas and Regine, may be a mark of authorial
approval – an initiation of the 'New Man' and the 'New Woman'.

The plot is, in essence, quite simple: for some years Thomas, an
academic, has been happily married to Maria while Regine has
been unhappily married to Thomas's colleague, Josef. Anselm has
visited Regine and persuaded her to elope with him; the play starts
after Anselm and Regine have arrived at the house of Thomas and
Maria – the imminent arrival of Josef is anticipated with apprehension; the action turns on a series of encounters between the
characters in which the laws of modern 'elective affinities' – forces
of human attraction and repulsion – remorselessly subvert the
original pairings of Thomas and Maria, Anselm and Regine;
Anselm eventually leaves, pursued by the infatuated Maria,
Thomas and Regine are left to experience something akin to the
sibling-love which Ulrich and Agathe will feel in *The Man without
Qualities*.

It is characteristic of Musil's priorities that, in charting the paths
of star-crossed lovers, he is more interested in the stars – the
*Weltanschauung* which guides their lives – than portrayal of the
people themselves. Here, for example, is Thomas, giving a thumb-
nail sketch of the 'man of possibility' whom Musil will later develop
into Ulrich, the hero of *The Man without Qualities*:

There are people who will always only know what could be, whereas the
others, like detectives, know what is. Who conceal something that flows
where the others are firm. An intuition of how things could be different. A

directionless feeling without inclination or disinclination among the elevations and usages of the world. A homesickness, but without a home.

(GWII, 330)

The dialogue is aphoristic, thick with reflections, expressionistically explosive. Thomas, Anselm and Regine, particularly, are not only participants in the outward action, but blunt commentators on hidden psychic details. Anselm, for instance, with a powerful analogy from the insect world, expresses his sense that, in tearing himself away from the man whose influence has shaped his life at a vital stage, he has made himself a psychic cripple: 'And then comes a time when I deny myself. When I must tear myself away – like a grasshopper which leaves its trapped leg in the hand of a stronger one' (GWII, 328). In her speeches, Regine plunges beneath the level of convention and brings to the surface fragments of subconscious insight. In animated argument with Anselm, for example, she seeks to foster in him the desire to confound all rational people; in Regine's analogy, the notion of Darwinian struggle is extended to the realm of psychic conflict – if one becomes passive one is shaped by the external world, and the 'Enthusiast'-mode is swallowed up by conventionality: 'Haven't you lain in wait a whole life long and thrust at them like a pike to tear out a piece of their living flesh before they can catch you?' (GWII, 347).

In a dialogue which has many such moments of extraordinary verbal brilliance and innovation, the contours of each character and their complex interrelations emerge clearly as the play unfolds. Thomas is constantly aware of himself and the others, a tense, restless being who is both sensitive and emotionally tough – like his fictional descendant, Ulrich, he maps out from each moment the many paths of possible developments leading out to various points on an ever-widening horizon. The world as it is recedes almost into insignificance when contrasted with the range of what might be. Maria is a big, warm, beautiful woman, undistinguished intellectually but sensuous and stable, a refuge and source of strength for her husband. He draws a word-portrait of their marriage from his eccentric and alienating perspective, explaining what it means to live for so many hours each day in tandem with this other body, this other self:

When you have been married for a long time and always walk on four legs and always draw double breaths and think each thought out twice and the time between the main things is doubly full with minor things: then, sometimes, it's natural to ache like an arrow for a space where the air is quite thin. And you jump up in the night, frightened by your own even breathing which has just been going on without you [...] And there another like you lies, wrapped in flesh. Only then is that love.

(GWII, 321)

Here again Thomas' intellectual approach alienates him from the world he inhabits, the familiar is reduced to individual phenomena by precise perception. However, no irony is intended (indeed, throughout all the works that we are considering here there is barely a hint of irony – this mode will make its appearance only in *The Man without Qualities*); Thomas is celebrating his love for Maria in his own inimitable fashion. But, in the course of the years spent with Thomas, Maria has been exhausted by the arc-light of his constant awareness of their mutual love – she wants a less demanding relationship, she needs more conventional expressions of devotion, even at the risk that they may not be sincere. She is a renegade 'Enthusiast', succumbing to the temptations of the stereotype, making her peace with her environment, sinking with an inward sigh of relief into the comfortable role of 'bürgerlich' wife. So she, and the happiness of her husband, are at risk when Anselm arrives.

Anselm, while acknowledging Thomas' intellectual superiority, has talents of his own – he can smuggle his way into another's mind or feelings. The gift of empathy which Musil uses legitimately in the service of literary creation is put to self-indulgent use by Anselm, the 'Lebenskünstler'. Anselm, drawing on his intuitions of what each woman wants, is an experienced seducer. Needing constant reassurance, he quickly tires of his recent conquest, Regine, and turns to Maria for fresh consolations, sensing her need to be flattered, even deceived, after so many years of mind-stretching, heart-rending forthrightness from Thomas. Josef is more function than individual; he is the 'Bürger' in person – a 'wronged husband' who provides the conventional model against which the spontaneous behaviour, the undiluted anguish, of the other wronged husband, Thomas, will be judged. Regine seems to have retained in adulthood the emotional unpredictability of a hyperactive child – the Second Act is punctuated by the sound of her hysterical sobbing off-stage; in her, the span between thought and word, between thought and deed, is shorter even than in Thomas. Since she is not hampered by scruples, temptation goes hand in hand with promiscuity, and the suffering this brings has the inevitability of the rise and fall of the tides. Her life is a spectacle of transitional passages of intense boredom, linking moments of ecstasy and despair. The style of her life owes much to Thomas – he has had a powerful influence on her. In the final scene of the play, Musil presents, through Thomas and Regine who have been deserted respectively by wife and lover, a breviary of 'Enthusiast'-thinking:

REGINE: Help me, Thomas, tell me what to do if you can.
THOMAS: How am I to help you? One must simply have the strength to love [the] contradictions [of life].
[...] REGINE: I can't stay as I am! And, as for changing, how then! Like Maria?!
THOMAS: One simply wanders about. All those pit themselves against you who go their determined way while you are on the undetermined journey of the spirit ['Geist'], begging your way through the world. and yet, somehow or other, you are one of them. Don't say much when they look severely at you; quiet; one creeps away behind one's skin [...]
REGINE (smiling): Thomas, Thomas, you are an unfeeling man of rationality.
THOMAS: No, no, Regine, if I'm anyone at all, then I, of all people, am a dreamer. And you're a dreamer. Such people seem to be without feeling. They wander, watching what the people do who feel at home in the world. And have within them something that others do not sense. At each moment a sinking through everything into the void. Without going under. The state of creation.                                                      (GWII, 406–7)

In this exchange the audience is expected to construe from a few fragments – 'journey of the spirit, begging [...] through the world', 'dreamers' as 'people [...] without feeling', 'state of creation' – essential tenets of an 'Enthusiast'-*Weltanschauung*. This involves a life where principles give way to an immediate response to each new situation whereby all precedent is forgotten. That audiences tend to be puzzled rather than inspired by such ideas is understandable in view of the abbreviated form in which they are presented. (It would be of little help to most members of the audience to observe that these ideas closely resemble the 'Utopie der induktiven Gesinnung' ('Utopia of the Inductive Attitude') which preoccupies Ulrich and Agathe for interminable pages of the *The Man without Qualities*!) It is questionable whether a play was the appropriate vehicle for an exposition of an alternative mode of living.

The most suitable medium for what Musil had to say was surely the narrative of a long novel in which his public could appreciate at their leisure the richness of his language, could read and reread his prose to grasp his complex analyses of human motivation, could see more clearly the subtle interrelations between a psyche and its context, between a culture and the mental habits which sustain it. In the early twenties, as we have seen, Musil had started work on *The Man without Qualities*. The essays which he was writing in the same period were to be of great importance in the project, both because sections of the work would need the essay technique which he was perfecting, and because they gave him the opportunity to formulate his vigorous intellectual concern with the problems of society at large. Among other themes, he dealt at length with the question of creativity – the 'state of creation' which figures so enigmatically in Thomas' speech at the close of *The Enthusiasts*.

The essays are intense, they deal at a very demanding level with difficult subject-matter (including the relationship between contemporary culture and science, the crisis in the theatre, mystical experience, and the nature of modern man's awareness of himself and the world) and they show Musil's concern with style. Musil is here learning to write in the way that will become so distinctive in *The Man without Qualities* – with depth and clarity, with a determination to grasp the essentials of each subject he tackles, undeterred by the intellectual effort which this entails, and a sharpness of vision, surfacing in analogy or image, which sometimes takes the reader's breath away. The essays are not contemplative but dynamic.

This has to do with Musil's ideas of the task of the creative writer, the 'Dichter' (a term which, though usually translated as 'poet', in fact spans drama and narrative fiction as well as poetry). Musil argues that the present age is one of crisis. Christian belief and trust in Reason, which shaped Western mankind by providing a basis for a universal moral education and spiritual models after which individuals are to shape their lives, have been undermined by the growth of scientific knowledge which is morally and spiritually inert. Into this breach, according to Musil, the 'Dichter' has to step. Musil scorns those who claim to be 'Dichter' but who are content with satisfying the public demand for not-too-serious entertainment. The true 'Dichter', he argues, is committed to a far more serious and demanding undertaking: to make mankind aware of the damage which the inner structure of society has sustained (of which most people remain unaware) and to explore positive ways ahead. Just as the early Christian evangelist offered more than the letter of his creed, and the Enlightenment 'philosophe' more than an encyclopaedia of Reason, so the 'Dichter' has to be more than a mere writer – he has to communicate passion. He has to find some of the energy and sense of purpose that had been felt in earlier ages, while still using literary means appropriate to this age of objectivity and scepticism.

The true 'Dichter', according to Musil, deals in ideas; by 'ideas' Musil understands something more than the subject-matter of knowledge – he means insight suspended in its own special emotional element. Like the evangelist or 'philosophe', the 'Dichter' has to provide a context, and an atmosphere of conviction within which his or her ideas can grow. Thought with little feeling has little life; thought with no feeling has no life at all. The 'Dichter' has to appeal powerfully to the emotions of the reader for otherwise his or her ideas will not take root. The task of the 'Dichter' is all the more daunting, from Musil's point of view, because in contemporary society thought is withering away for want of sufficient sustaining feeling.

Musil explains this phenomenon in the following terms: in the course of history ideas spring up, flourish and form ideological systems. But as ideas pass from generation to generation they lose their original strength; even when an ideology is consolidated – as, for example, when the spirit of Christianity merges into the Established Church, or the principles of the Enlightenment take shape in a written constitution – this marks a stage in its decline. As Musil puts it: 'To put an idea into practice means, in that same act, to destroy a part of it' (GWII, 1055).[10] In contemporary civilisation the often violent competition between ideologies is not a sign of vigour; despite the vehemence of their proponents the ideologies tend to die as the core of belief or conviction at their heart cools down.[11]

What happens is that mankind allows itself to be shaped by external factors. This is not to imply that Musil takes up the arguments of the materialists; rather, he suggests, contemporary men and women are tyrannised by the accumulated evidence of past human effort. In the cultural 'scrap-yard' of the nineteenth and twentieth centuries, creativity is lost. What the Greek, for example, shaped in the heat of passion – whether building, statue or play – functions as a lifeless model which inhibits the creative freedom of living architects, sculptors and dramatists. A clear example of this is the notion of 'Bildung' as propounded by the humanistic grammar school. Boys, who follow their masters and look to the example of Greece and Rome, obediently turn their backs on the present and future. Such an attitude is wildly inappropriate given the contemporary challenge of technology and the problems of mass urban civilisation. It is, in fact, impossible to ignore contemporary experiences since they force themselves inexorably into every modern consciousness, whether the individual recognises this or not. Individuals cannot choose the forces which influence them; these are, in part, functions of the world which surrounds them: 'Man exists only in forms which are supplied to him from outside. "His rough edges are worn smooth by the world" is far too gentle an image: the formulation ought to be that he presses himself into its mould. It is the social organisation which in the very first instance provides the individual with the form of the expression and it is only through the expression that the human being takes shape at all' (GWII, 1370).[12]

This insight codetermines Musil's assessment of the role of the 'Dichter': as the evangelist or 'philosophe' did in their time, he or she must interpret the world to contemporaries and give advice on how to respond to it. This task involves at least an attempt at synthesis of the main areas of human activity and human understanding; Musil's 'Dichter' is not content with self-analysis. Since the contemporary world is overwhelmed by 'the wealth of contents which can no longer be mastered, the swollen store of factual knowledge' (GWII, 1045), the 'Dichter' has to become a polymath, exploring the main avenues along which science and scholarship have travelled.[13] Perhaps more important than acquiring the knowledge itself is understanding the way it is acquired – the 'Dichter' must grasp, for example, the nature of empiricism 'for which the world is an unending task with progressive partial solutions' (GWII, 1127)[14] and see how it produces that attitude in which the observer/scientist is detached from the field of study and is left a lonely consciousness outside the perceived field. But such an exploration of what Musil called the realm of the 'ratioid' ('ratioid') is only a part of the task which the 'Dichter' should perform. The 'Dichter' is not only Apollo, lighting the world with the critical sun of intelligence, but Dionysos, caught up in unadulterated, un-self-conscious feeling. There is not only the field of the 'ratioid', but also that of the 'nicht-ratioid' ('non-ratioid'), which tends to be neglected by contemporary culture with its suspicion of passion. Musil sets the 'nicht-ratioid' against the 'ratioid': 'Instead of the rigid concept comes the pulsing representation, instead of equations come analogies, instead of truth probability, the essential structure is no longer systematic but creative!' (GWII, 1050).[15]

Further exploration of the field of the non-ratioid reveals an area of experience of which many detailed accounts survive from earlier cultures in which it was highly valued. But it has virtually disappeared in the contemporary world, Musil argues, or at least tends to be neglected as an insignificant aberration, unworthy of serious investigation. Musil expresses its relation to the realm of common experience as follows:

The world in which we live and usually take active part, this world of authorised modes of understanding and states of mind ['Seele'] is only a pale substitute for another one to which the true relationship has been lost. Occasionally one feels that all those [familiar things – PP] were non-essential, for hours or days these melt away in the blaze of another kind of relating to world and fellow-men. One is a blade of straw and a breath, the world is the trembling sphere. Every minute, all things emerge anew; to look upon them as fixed data is perceived to be an inner death.

(GWII, 1054)[16]

He named this 'der andere Zustand'[17] ('the other state'). Though in the sceptical contemporary world it was only proper that such experiences be approached with scepticism, Musil was convinced of the authenticity of many accounts and was able to corroborate some of them by close observation of experiences of his own, notably those connected with love. 'Der andere Zustand', which was to be of importance to *The Man without Qualities*, Musil described as an enhanced subjectivity, an overflowing of the energy of selfhood into the world outside the self: 'the border between I and non-I [is] less distinct [. . .] than usual [. . .] Where, otherwise, the I masters the world, in the "other state" the world streams into the I or mingles with it' (GWII, 1393).[18] In this state, some people – most noticeably those 'Ethiker', teachers of ethics whose works formed the mystical tradition[19] – experienced an ecstatic union with the world. In 'der andere Zustand' is to be found, perhaps, the origin of that passion which, when communicated to others through the medium of ideas, imparts to them a persuasive force which may seem to have the quality of the 'déjà vu'. 'Erkennen', writes Musil, 'ist Wiedererinnern' (GWII, 1051)[20] ('To have insight is to remember again').

The 'Dichter' propagates 'Geist'. 'Geist' is not practical understanding, mankind's problem-solving intellect, nor is it Reason, that Enlightenment sense of the coherence of the mind of man and the creative intelligence manifest in the structure of the universe. It is rather a medium through which mankind is made aware that its spiritual home is not only of this world: 'Geist' reminds us that the realm of potential human experience spans more than what commonly passes for 'reality'. It reaches into areas that are often dismissed as mystical or illusory.

Musil's views on the nature of creative writing do not change significantly after this time. In notes, written in 1935, for a preface to *Nachlaß zu Lebzeiten* (*Posthumous Writings in my Lifetime*), his edition of short prose works, he restates his views about the intellectual effort which creative writing should entail, arguing again that the author must reach down into so deep a substratum of feeling that it draws on the same experiences as religion:

Creative writing [. . .] is giving meaning. It is an interpreting of life. For it, reality is raw material [. . .] Meaningful insight into things is different from sober comprehending. It is not only a structure of understanding but, in the first instance, a structure of feeling. To give things meaning is, at any rate, also to give them inner life. It is, without question [. . .] related to religious experience; it is a religious undertaking without dogma, an empirical religiosity. (GWII, 970–1)

In the works of the years 1906–24, we see Musil adding to his insights into himself and into the world and to the range of creative tools to express his findings. He learns how to write convincing dialogue, he develops a powerful essayistic technique and refines his psychic imagery to levels of extraordinary subtlety. These elements, together with telling social satire, philosophical commentary, and mystical reflection, will all be blended in unique multi-layered narrative prose. The puzzled and amoral observer of *Young Törless* is scarcely recognisable in the critical but open-minded narrator of *The Man without Qualities*.

# Part 2
# 'THE MAN WITHOUT QUALITIES'

# 4

# INTRODUCTION

## The novel in the context of Musil's life

The earliest material that can be identified as a definite source for
*The Man without Qualities* was written around 1903; this consisted
of passages on two friends of Musil's, Gustav Donath and Alice
Charlemont.[1] Gustav and Alice were to become the characters
Walter and Clarisse who play a major role in *The Man without
Qualities*.[2] Clarisse in particular figured prominently in manuscript
material, above all in connection with her plans to free the
murderer, Moosbrugger. But Musil made little headway with this
material and, in the first two decades of this century, he was
working on the other literary projects which we have already
examined. But in the twenties he began serious work on the task of
fusing all the themes that obsessed him into one major – one might
even say encyclopaedic – novel.

First, around 1920,[3] the project bore the title *Der Spion* (*The
Spy*); this very quickly became *Der Erlöser* (*The Redeemer* – a
notion connected with Clarisse's plan to bear the hero a child who
would 'redeem the world') and by the mid-twenties this in turn had
been re-christened *Die Zwillingsschwester* (*The Twin Sister* –
referring to the hero's sister, Agathe). These were not so much
separate projects as a continuum of creative activity which merged
each set of drafts into the next and eventually, by early 1927, had
transformed itself into *The Man without Qualities*.[4] (Adolf Frisé
gives 6 February 1927 as the date when the title *Der Mann ohne
Eigenschaften* (*The Man without Qualities*) was first mentioned by
Musil; this was in a broadcast on Berlin radio.)[5] Part I and Part II of
the novel were published in 1930; in 1933 a second volume
appeared, but this contained not Part III and Part IV in their
entirety, as Musil had originally intended, but only the first
thirty-eight chapters of Part III. The response from critics and
public alike to the two published volumes of *The Man without*

49

*Qualities* was most encouraging – but times were changing, and not in Musil's favour. Musil had settled in Vienna after World War I and, apart from a period spent in Berlin from 1931–3 (he went there to try to gain the detachment from the setting of *The Man without Qualities* which he hoped would help him to complete the work), he remained there until 1938. With the proscription of his works in Germany and Austria, Musil's main source of income dried up and his financial situation became precarious. He left Vienna to live in exile in Switzerland on funds raised or donated by admirers, and on charity. He died, virtually destitute, in 1942. *The Man without Qualities* was still far from being finished – in fact it had progressed by only a couple of dozen chapters beyond the point which Musil had reached in 1933.

This failure is all the more poignant when viewed in terms of the projects which Musil planned to complete once the rest of *The Man without Qualities* had been published – among other things he wanted to write a satirical novel, which might well have been a kind of modern *Gulliver's Travels*,[6] and a collection of aphorisms.[7] It is evident that Musil would have liked to be judged by a far larger corpus of writing than he in fact produced. The reasons for his failure to finish *The Man without Qualities*, let alone to make a start on other works, have to do both with the nature of the undertaking and with the circumstances of his life.

The novel attempted a synthesis of the qualities of Musil's earlier writing. It explored the experiences of one man – single-minded to the point of solipsism yet constantly struggling to distinguish some sign from beyond the self – that had been pioneered in *Young Törless*. It exploited the psychological sophistication and the new imagery expressing nuances of consciousness which Musil developed in *Acts of Union*. Love again (as in *The Enthusiasts* and *Three Women*) was treated as a bridge between mundane and mystical experience. Moreover it revealed the ways in which the experiences of the individual were shaped by habitual patterns of thinking and feeling in contemporary society, thus continuing themes which Musil had explored in his essays in the second and third decades of this century. Musil displayed other qualities which had not been found in his earlier creative work. He recorded, for example, how some famous contemporaries thought and felt, presenting a kind of 'private life of the master thinkers' including Walther Ràthenau, Ludwig Klages, Franz Werfel and others.[8] Added to this was a brilliant satirical wit and an astonishing breadth of learning.

Musil might have finished the project if extra-literary factors had not added to its inherent difficulty. To a large extent, *The Man without Qualities* is a record of facets of Musil's own life starting from the time of his early manhood; but the most productive period was the decade stretching from the early twenties to the time when Volume Two was published. It is no coincidence that this was the time when Musil was, both intellectually and creatively, in his prime. But he was exhausted by the enormous effort to publish Volume One which contained Part I and Part II of the novel, and then made what may have been the mistake of bringing out Volume Two before he had finished the whole novel.[9] He decided on this compromise because he could not complete the work as quickly as he and his publisher wanted.[10] He later regretted his decision and would have liked the opportunity to revise some of the material in Volume Two[11] but the 'fait accompli' of publication made this impossible. Ill-health, failing powers of organisation, a loss of some of his earlier intellectual stamina, financial worries, the political upheaval of the *Anschluß*, voluntary exile in Switzerland and the problems associated with the transport of bulky manuscripts and reference materials slowed down the progress of the planned continuation of the interim Volume Two to snail's pace. Although Musil left some five thousand pages of manuscript material, a proportion of which he undoubtedly would have included – after yet more revision – in the continuation of Volume Two,[12] at the time of his death in 1942 some nine years after the publication of Volume Two, only a further fourteen chapters had reached anything approaching the state of a final draft.[13]

## The scale of the project

Musil had only written one novel before embarking on *The Man without Qualities* and this, *Young Törless*, was short and concerned only a fairly brief period in the life of a pupil at a boarding school in Moravia. By contrast, *The Man without Qualities* was an immense undertaking.

The novel constantly threatened to overwhelm its author. Musil did not only have to be a creative writer but, given the ever-expanding scope of the work, he also had to be his own archivist, and his own secretary – the former trying to keep his 'plot' and 'character' files in order and the latter concerned with sensible organisation and prospective date of publication.[14] As the years passed the sheer volume of material, organised according to a complex indexing system (as befitted a former librarian), seems to have presented a problem since he occasionally had difficulty finding the notes he wanted for a particular section and his memory sometimes let him down. Added to this was a striving for perfection that bordered on the obsessive. He wrote, rewrote and re-rewrote. When his proofs came back from the publishers he would set to work again; only the actual publication of the text set a limit to his repeated amendments. In Musil's literary papers, which do not include the extensive material which he left behind in his Vienna flat in 1938 and which was destroyed during World War II, we find whole sets of chapter drafts which exist in several different versions.

It is not possible here to reconstruct all the stages of composition of the novel but one should begin by noting the three chief sources of material. First, Musil draws on his own experiences from earliest childhood – in all phases of the novel the hero is invariably Musil's literary persona. Second, these experiences are supplemented by close observation, indeed by intense re-living of the experiences of the people of his immediate environment. A third important component comes from close reading of books, articles and newspapers which provide Musil with material which he imbues with the vicarious energy of his interest.

This wealth of material is then arranged around three fictional themes, spanning a period of about twelve months which ends with the outbreak of World War I: first we have the experiences of Ulrich von. . . , a Viennese intellectual and gentleman of leisure in his early thirties, whose search for a meaning to modern life involves him in strange experiments including attempts to penetrate the mind of a murderer, Moosbrugger; second, there is the profound relationship which develops when this man meets his sister, Agathe, whom he has hardly seen since childhood; third, the novel presents a social satire on life in the last days of the Austro-Hungarian Empire, based on plans to celebrate seventy years of rule by Franz Joseph in 1918, which goes under the general heading of the 'Parallelaktion' ('Parallel Campaign').

From consideration of the above themes it will already be apparent that *The Man without Qualities* is not one novel but at least three.[15] This in itself places great demands on the creative skills of the author. Of course, there are many points at which the three major fictional themes naturally intersect: the hero is central to the experiment in finding an ersatz-*Weltanschauung*; he is a partner in the brother–sister romance; he is also for the most part the central critical intelligence recording the activities of the 'Parallelaktion'. So it is with other characters, too. Musil has them move through several spheres within his narrative: Arnheim (based on the industrialist and man of letters, Walther Rathenau), who is Ulrich's antithesis in the search for a code of life, is a central figure in the 'Parallelaktion', and his 'affair' with Ulrich's cousin provides a contrast with the relationship between Ulrich and his sister; Clarisse is infected with Ulrich's compulsive interest in the murderer, Moosbrugger (a figure who, for Ulrich, seemed at one stage to hold a key to a more intense kind of existence), she is responsible, through her concern for Moosbrugger, for reestablishing Ulrich's links with the 'Parallelaktion' at a time when he would otherwise have allowed them to lapse, and, through her waxing and waning passions for Ulrich, she constantly threatens to come between Ulrich and Agathe; Agathe, herself, is involved with all three main strands of the plot – besides being one of the partners in an extraordinary love experiment she prompts Ulrich to intensify his reflections on the contemporary world and also, in her own right, has a minor role to play in the 'Parallelaktion'.

Had Musil concerned himself only with the few characters examined above his narrative would already have been complicated enough. However, there are many other characters whose course he has to chart through the twelve months or so of the duration of the plot, all of whom have to be introduced, and then reintroduced at appropriate points so that their existence, and the horizon of actions, ideas and problems which the reader associates with them, are brought repeatedly to the reader's attention.

If Musil, at an early stage in the composition of *The Man without Qualities*, had been able to settle on a masterplan which would have regulated all the action, the meetings, the relationships, the developments, the ideas, in the novel, all might have been well. But to have done so would have been to isolate the work from what was happening in Europe around him. Musil constantly responds in the novel to what is going on about him as he writes. This central evolutionary process within the work dictates changes of direction not only on matters of detail but of central plot substance.[16] Such changes, like stones thrown into a pond, affect not only the immediate narrative context; their ripples spread out through the whole text – but Musil is rarely able to make the necessary adjustments through the whole novel before some new change claims his attention.

Another element complicates the construction of *The Man without Qualities*: the fiction demands that the narrative progress through one year of the hero's life, but Musil finds it essential to include in the novel the emotions and the thoughts that he has accumulated as he has grown older in the extended period of the novel's composition. When we consider that this period lasted, at a conservative estimate, for a full two decades, in the course of which Musil was reduced from comparative wealth to poverty and from health and vitality to feebleness and failing intellectual powers, it is scarcely surprising that the reader begins to feel on occasions that the hero, to judge by what he thinks and says in later sections of the novel, is much older than he ought to be according to the span of time that has passed in the novel itself.[17]

For all Musil's drafts, marathon stints of intense reflection, indices of characters and ideas, years of sustained writing to which dozens of notebooks and thousands of pages of manuscript bear witness, the novel did not follow a fixed plan – it simply grew (and grew and grew!). Musil felt that this work progressed only by dint of dogged determination, that he had to earn his insights and inspirations by hours spent at his desk; the creative process involved not only thought but stamina, it was visceral as well as rational.[18]

### The novel drafts to 1927

Virtually all the themes of *The Man without Qualities* were charted by 1927. Moreover, Musil in his drafts of the plot, had by 1927 got well beyond the stage at which the published narrative broke off in the middle of Part III in 1933 (indeed, even the material which Musil was preparing for publication in the last years of his life had still not progressed as far as the point reached by those 1927 drafts). The following brief survey is intended to provide an overview of the various elements from which the plot is composed:

*a(i)* The hero, called in drafts of the mid- to late twenties Achilles, Alexander Unrod or Unold, or Anders, becomes, of course, Ulrich.[19] The hero is both philanderer and moralist, an urbane idler and a troubled intellectual concerned about himself and about the state of society in general. He decides to take what he calls an 'Urlaub [vom] Leben' (47) ('leave from life'), in other words, he attempts to live for a while as if he were not actively involved in life – to use an image appropriate to this sporting hero, he resolves to be a 'gentleman' not a 'player' in the 'game' of life. It is an experiment which does not last very long. He undergoes a prolonged spiritual identity crisis in the course of the work. For a time he is obsessed with the murderer, Moosbrugger. (This obsession is more than merely philanthropic; the hero seems to see in Moosbrugger, at those times when the murderer slips into insanity, a kind of primordial intensity of experience which the hero wants to recapture for humanity in general. We are reminded of the Expressionists' concern with ecstatic modes of experience.)[20] The hero wants to make a gesture of protest about the spiritual sickness of contemporary society; this prompts different kinds of actions, including – in early versions of the work – an attempt to free the murderer from prison. (In later versions the hero gradually loses interest in the murderer, and the focus of protest shifts to the hero's sister.)

*a(ii)* The hero has lost touch with his sister since their childhood; however, when they meet as adults a close relationship develops between them. They both refuse to accept the social taboo which restricts the relationship of siblings, they fall in love and live together. (Although, in unpublished sections of the novel, Agathe and Ulrich commit incest it is unclear from published sections and from the material which Musil was working on late in life whether he had decided to retain this aspect of the relationship.) It is evidently Musil's intention to seek to capture through this aspect of the work a level of intensity in human experience which has largely been lost in civilised life. Thus it can be seen to counterbalance the Moosbrugger material. According to the earlier versions of the novel, when this private social experiment has failed, the hero exploits his sister's beauty in the course of a spying mission on the eastern borders of Austro-Hungarian territory.[21] Musil planned to introduce a decisive change in the hero's attitude to life in Part IV, but it is not clear from the *Nachlaß*, Musil's literary estate, what this change was to be.[22] As the work matures, and as Musil composes draft after draft, so the hero mellows and his actions become more and more circumspect and less shocking: the attempt to free Moosbrugger is dropped, so is the spying mission, and some commentators insist that the incest motif disappears, too. Ernst Kaiser and Eithne Wilkins, for example, argue that the idea of incest between brother and sister is progressively repressed by Musil as he works on the continuation of the novel in the late thirties and early forties.[23]

*b)* Besides Agathe, his sister, the hero is on terms of intimacy with a number of other women, who provide links with some of the sub-plots in the novel. As we saw above, perhaps the oldest theme of the novel was the triangle of hero, his boyhood friend, Walter, and Walter's extraordinary wife, Clarisse; this central theme survives into the published *The Man without Qualities*.[24] Clarisse, who has received Nietzsche's works as a wedding-present from the hero, causes him to regret his choice of gift when she takes it into her head to carry out Nietzsche's programme for the renewal of mankind through the actions of the 'Superman'. She is a plague both on Walter and on Ulrich: she tries to goad her husband, a painter who rarely finds the time or the energy to paint, to the pitch of genius by rationing the exercise of his conjugal rights; on at least one occasion, she tries to seduce the hero in the hope that by him she will conceive 'the redeemer of the world'.[25] For a while she is obsessed with Meingast, an itinerant sage (based on the philosopher, Ludwig Klages); then, in unpublished sections, she transfers her attention briefly back to the hero again, until, after her passionate pursuit of a Greek who reveals himself to be homosexual, she slides into complete insanity.

*c)* Another sub-plot introduces a large number of characters, including 'Diotima', the hero's cousin. (She seems to be a 'collage' of Musil's impressions of several women with literary interests.)[26] In 1913, Diotima has a literary salon in Vienna at which she plays host to the members of the 'Parallelaktion', whose plans to celebrate the Seventieth Anniversary of the Kaiser's accession to the throne take on the dimensions of an eccentric moral and political crusade. Musil designs the 'Parallelaktion' as a setting for his ironical observations on the political and social institutions, and the ruling classes, of the Austro-Hungarian Empire. It will be examined in a separate section below.

*d)* Ulrich and Arnheim vie with each other for preeminence at the 'Parallelaktion'; in this contest, the latter's worldly success and intellectual showmanship compete with the former's quiet self-confidence and intense, if usually private, reflective power.

*e)* Two other characters connected with the 'Parallelaktion' whom the hero meets on frequent occasions should be mentioned: these are Graf Leinsdorf, a leading Austrian aristocrat who is blinkered by the prejudices of his class, and General Stumm von Bordwehr, surprisingly effective despite his constant self-deprecations and comically rotund and unmartial appearance, who constantly turns to the hero for information, advice and reassurance and is mercilessly ragged by him for his pains.

*f)* The hero's liaison with the nymphomaniac wife of a prominent lawyer (his pet name for her is 'Bonadea'), provides some light relief in the plot of the novel. There is a more serious side to this sub-plot because the hero – never able to resist the opportunity for further research, however impromptu, into the interconnections between thoughts, actions and feelings – is able to observe the transformations of consciousness that take place in Bonadea when she is possessed by sexual desire. More generally she serves as a case study of the attitudes adopted by an average Viennese lady in the period immediately before World War I.

*g)* Gerda Fischel, whose father, Leo, is a Jewish bank official, has fallen in love with Ulrich; her fiancé, Hans Sepp, is a German nationalist, an anti-Semite, and, incidentally, intensely jealous of Ulrich. In his description of Gerda and her parents Musil takes the opportunity to portray the ravages of class-consciousness, the strain of keeping up appearances on a restricted budget, the bitter connubial in-fighting that derives from sexual problems. In brief, this is Musil's vision of a fairly typical Viennese bourgeois family.

*h)* Although in the novel Musil does not pay much attention to the lower classes, he does examine the relationship between Arnheim's awkward and unhappy Moorish valet, Soliman, and Diotima's delightful Galician-Jewish maidservant, Rachel; Rachel, in one draft, was to look after Moosbrugger after his escape from prison.[27]

*i)* Agathe has relationships with several men besides her brother. She leaves her second husband, Hagauer, a schoolmaster and educational theorist, and comes to live with Ulrich; while sharing her brother's home, she takes up with another educationalist, Lindner. With her brother looking on in a state of intellectual paralysis, Agathe falsifies her father's will to ensure that Hagauer will gain no financial advantage through the money which is due to her (and over which, in Austrian law, he would have control). In earlier drafts of the novel, brother and sister flee the country for fear of legal action by Hagauer in connection with the falsifying of the will,[28] embarking on a journey to the south, a 'journey to paradise', as it is called, marked by incest and a search for mystical union. After the failure of this search the pair take up the spying mission.[29]

What Musil would have made of a significant part of this material we cannot tell; both in the drafts and in the sections of *The Man without Qualities* which were published in his lifetime Musil left a number of questions unanswered. The most important of these are as follows. What are the consequences of Agathe's meddling with her father's will? Do Ulrich and Agathe commit incest and how is their relationship to develop? What happens to Clarisse, her husband and the philosopher who is living with them? What decisions will be reached at the 'Parallelaktion'? Will the hero come to any conclusions about himself and about some goal which he should pursue? How will the novel end? For all their quarrels over the *Nachlaß* of *The Man without Qualities*, scholars agree on one point: no definitive final version of the novel can be established however hard one combs through all that Musil wrote.[30] None of the above questions will ever be answered. Even when a historical-critical edition of *The Man without Qualities* is available – and it will certainly not be available in the foreseeable future – these questions will remain open. However, it is possible, by careful examination of the text of *The Man without Qualities*, to gain insight into the ways Musil set about structuring his material.

# 5

# A CRITICAL APPROACH TO THE STRUCTURE OF 'THE MAN WITHOUT QUALITIES'

## Introductory remarks

As indicated above, I do not believe that Musil structured the novel as a whole according to a master-plan – there were no 'architect's drawings' for *The Man without Qualities* which Musil carried through single-mindedly. It does, however, seem likely that Musil intended the completed novel to be roughly symmetrical.[1] If it had been completed it might have looked as follows:

Part I – 'Eine Art Einleitung' ('A Kind of Introduction') (completed, with nineteen chapters)
Part II – 'Seinesgleichen geschieht' ('The Same Kind of Things Happen Again') (completed, with one hundred and four chapters)
Part III – 'Ins Tausendjährige Reich' ('Die Verbrecher') ('Into the Millenium (The Criminals)') (thirty-eight chapters completed, perhaps some sixty or so more envisaged)
Part IV – 'Eine Art Ende' ('A Kind of Ending') (possible title – no chapters written and only a few pages of notes extant, including Ulrich's so-called 'final statement'.[2] Musil may have intended Part IV to be roughly as long as Part I.)

Under these headings we can see a shape emerging: Part I provides an introduction to Ulrich and 'Kakanien' (this being Musil's ironical term for Austria-Hungary – the words 'kaiserlich' and 'königlich' referring to the Constitution of the Empire are here compressed into their initial letters, 'k' and 'k', to form a play on words, linking Austria-Hungary to the child's word for excrement), the world he inhabits. Part II explores the 'Parallelaktion', Ulrich's plan for an 'Urlaub vom Leben' ('leave from life'), his preoccupation with Moosbrugger, the hero's circle of friends, and reaches a climax when the hero undergoes a significant change in attitude at the point when he is about to leave Vienna to go to his father's funeral and meet his sister. Part III is, of course, incomplete (and, accordingly, a review of what Musil wrote and published must

58

merge into speculation about which draft material would have survived, with inevitable modifications and rewriting, in a final version). It presents the gradual dissolution of the 'Parallelaktion' into in-fighting between factions. It demotes the Moosbrugger sub-plot as the hero loses interest in him. It appears to continue the experiment in enhanced living between Ulrich and Agathe (probably to the point where this fails). It probably sees the Clarisse-theme through to its conclusion with her madness. Finally – and again this must be speculative – it presents some further decisive change in the hero's outlook and way of life (this being the 'Wendung des Schlusses', the 'turning-point at the end', which Musil mentions).[3] Part IV was then possibly to have presented a kind of balance sheet, reviewing Ulrich's development and the state of Austria-Hungary as World War I starts.

Beyond this we know of Musil's constant rewriting of material from his character-files and theme-files into provisional chapter groupings and thence into final draft form. Again, however, such an approach indicates not a pre-determined structure to which Musil was trying to shape his raw material but rather constant adaptation and experimentation within certain tentatively established parameters. *The Man without Qualities* is largely the product of an intuitive process within the frame of the rough plan which I have outlined above rather than the exact carrying out of some grand design, which has been lost. For all his technological training, when it came to creative writing Musil trusted to intuition. However, even intuition can be analysed, and I shall now consider some of the evidence of the way Musil shapes the novel into coherent form.

In the following sections I shall consider different aspects of the structuring process as used by Musil: the wide range of narrative levels through which Musil has individual ideas move; the different ways in which the themes of *The Man without Qualities* help the narrative to cohere; the role of the observer in the novel; the relevance for *The Man without Qualities* of what Richard von Mises, a philosopher-mathematician and friend of Musil's, called a literary 'Gedankenexperiment' ('thought-experiment'); finally a few details of Musil's use of language in the novel. In the present account of aspects of *The Man without Qualities* I shall stress, whenever appropriate, the ways in which such aspects complement each other in the complex process that is involved in any close reading of this narrative. The intellectual stimulation and aesthetic pleasure which we derive from the text

come less from the diversity of such aspects than from their
interrelations.

### Ideas

Critics have examined the complex intellectual content of *The Man
without Qualities* from many different perspectives, but few of
them have considered the very close link between a given idea and
the place in the narrative where it appears.[4] It may be joined with a
certain belief, or expectation, or feeling; it may merge into the
peripheral detail of some situation.[5] Associations of this kind give
the ideas which are worked into the narrative of *The Man without
Qualities* their peculiar energy. When these ideas are considered in
isolation their forcefulness and originality evaporate. Take, for
example, an idea 'travelling incognito' in Part II, Chapter 93.

Here a meeting is in progress at the salon of one of Vienna's most
distinguished hostesses, Diotima. General Stumm von Bordwehr, a
cheerful and, to all appearances, innocuous member of the
Imperial Armed Forces is present. However, he feels a little out of
his depth in this company and his intellectual discomfiture is
suggested by the awkward posture he has adopted: 'The General's
bright blue coat had rucked up as he sat, forming wrinkles over his
belly like a troubled brow' (422). One might be tempted to see this
amusing detail as the narrator's attempt to suggest quite simply that
the figure which this military gentleman cuts is something less than
dashing. For the attentive reader it is more than that: it is a
reminder of what has happened earlier in the text. Stumm, though
a novice in things of the mind, plans to take the world of ideas by
storm. He has planned this campaign with exemplary military
thoroughness, drawing up diagrams of the lines of engagement of
ideas at times of important historical confrontation. In this way he
intends to discover which idea has defeated all the rest and reigns
supreme. But in his representations of ideological struggle, he has
noticed something profoundly disturbing: many ideas 'desert the
flag' and reappear in the enemy's ranks![6]

Stumm, the soldier, expects ideas to submit to military discipline
but finds them as fickle as the men who profess them; Ulrich offers
his former company commander only cold comfort: ' "Dear
General, [. . .] you take thinking too seriously" ' (376). Stumm is
further confused by Ulrich's words; Stumm's creased uniform,
suggestive of a furrowed forehead, symbolises the perplexity of the
soldier at the treachery of the intellectual realm.

This image of intellectual embarrassment also calls to mind another of Stumm's deficiencies: it is difficult for such a portly and jovial man to command respect. He has orders to infiltrate the 'Parallelaktion' but this is very difficult in view of Diotima's antipathy towards the military. Stumm must somehow convince Diotima of his value to her. As if to whet the edge of his endeavour, Stumm has become infatuated with Diotima; but, as the image which we have examined above suggests, he does not have the intellectual and physical attributes to provoke a similar response in her. He is forced to seek support elsewhere.

Thus the simple image which gently pokes fun at Stumm's appearance reveals, in its wider context, the mutual interpenetration of the realm of ideas and the physical world. A similar message is expressed in Part II, Chapter 82, where, within the compass of a single chapter, the interrelations of feeling, thought, action and word are presented with great clarity: Ulrich has gone to talk to Clarisse, the wife of his childhood friend, Walter. She has written a letter proposing that the 'Parallelaktion' should organise a 'Nietzsche Year'; in the eyes of the organisers of the 'Parallelaktion' this is simply the proposal of an eccentric that does not deserve consideration. But in the presence of the woman who has originated the idea Ulrich experiences something of its charge of passion; his mind, compulsively theorising, grapples with the relationship between any given notion, a bare idea, and the phenomena which are inseparably involved with it, the tremor of excitement that is mental and physical at once. Clarisse's exceptional nervous energy constantly bubbles to the surface in word, posture, action, gesture; one senses an extraordinary spontaneity in her nature, an almost unmediated translating of thought into deed. Even in the present situation, where she represses something that she was about to say, Ulrich has a very strong sense that a psychic event has found its corporeal correlative: ' "No" answered Clarisse [...] Her thin lips were about to say something, but remained silent, and the flame shot out in silence from her eyes [...] Now she smiled, but this smile curled up on her lips like a residue of ash after the event in her eyes had gone out' (353). Ulrich's awareness is fine-tuned to every physical expression that articulates what passes through Clarisse's mind: 'Her thin body spoke and thought softly, too; virtually everything that she wanted to say she first experienced with her whole body and felt a constant need to be doing something with it' (354).[7] They continue to discuss Clarisse's desire to put Nietzsche's ideas into practice; though

Ulrich does not say this in so many words, he has quite clearly derived the insight which he now expounds from his present feeling that in Clarisse the energy of mind and body come from a common source: ' "You would like to live according to your idea [. . .] and would like to know how this is possible. But an idea is the most paradoxical thing in the world. Flesh is bound up with ideas like a fetish. It becomes magical when an idea's there" ' (354). Then we come to the very heart of Ulrich's statement which is also the focus of the whole chapter: ' "an idea: that's you; in a particular state" ' (354). One feels that, in this situation, this is precisely the right expression. No other formula would fit this unique constellation of place, mood and moment. Such a statement might be taken from its context and used, for example, to illustrate Musil's conception of the way the mind works. But this would involve detailed commentary, for the statement draws not only on the rest of Ulrich's speech but also, as we have seen, on the observations worked into the narrative in other parts of the chapter. As he rounds off his argument, Ulrich makes precisely the point that an idea loses its persuasive appeal in the same measure as the special conditions under which it came into being fade into oblivion; only when it has thus been drained of its energy does it become part of a man's store of familiar notions; he tells Clarisse: ' "after a while [a single idea] becomes similar to all other ideas that you have already had, it conforms to their disposition, becomes a part of your views and your character, your principles or your moods, it has lost its wings and taken on a solidity bereft of mystery" ' (354). Just as, in an individual person, any idea, however fleeting it may appear to be, has the potential to be transformed into a constituent of the permanent character so, in *The Man without Qualities*, some notions which seem to arise spontaneously in a given passage recur – though often in modified form – in other parts of the novel. This part-explicit, part-subterranean articulation of ideas constitutes the thematic texture of *The Man without Qualities*.

**Themes**

It is only to a limited extent that the shape of *The Man without Qualities* is determined by the plot. There is no strong narrative line in Part I, only a meandering introduction to Ulrich and the world he inhabits. In Part II several narrative threads are taken up: Ulrich's notion of a year's 'Urlaub vom Leben', the first meetings of the 'Parallelaktion' with their mixture of idealism and intrigue, the love affair between Arnheim and Diotima, and Moosbrugger's dealings with the law. None of these sub-plots is in any way dramatic; indeed each is a concatenation of non-events. Ulrich's 'Urlaub vom Leben' involves, as the term implies, withdrawal from experience; even the most casual reader will see that the 'Parallelaktion', a peace movement scheduled to reach its climax at a time when the Great War would be raging, is doomed to failure; Arnheim and Diotima who find no suitable way to express their love for each other are seen to drift apart; and, as the reader is reminded as he shares a few of the hours of Moosbrugger's imprisonment, the processes of the law are sure but also infernally slow. Nor do the first thirty-eight chapters of Part III satisfy the reader's desire to see some decisive development in the plot of the novel. Instead of tying off one or more of the threads of the narrative, the author here introduces another: the relationship between Ulrich and his sister, Agathe. Musil, as we have seen, was to spend the last years of his life trying without success to bring this slow-moving section of the work to some kind of conclusion. Yet, despite the proliferation of somehow insubstantial narrative lines, the novel has a coherence whose origin we shall trace both here and in subsequent sections of this study.

While Ulrich was still at school he wrote an essay in which he speculated that the world came into being in a completely arbitrary fashion; when God looked upon His creation, Ulrich argued, He said to Himself: 'it might just as well be different' (19). Existence, as it presents itself to people as sophisticated as the hero, somehow does not quite live up to expectations; what is, is not what ought to be. Because this is so, nothing is sacrosanct. Early in the text the reader is given the strong impression that the universe is an arrangement of things which, though they appear definite and permanent, are nothing of the sort. In passages early in the novel, each critical insight by narrator or hero tends to confirm, and is in turn confirmed by, this notion. In thus putting all things into question – by presenting God's relationship with the world as it exists in a particular epoch as one of only provisional toleration – Musil expresses something of his protest against the contemporary condition of mankind. The nerves which carry this and other critical messages through the body of *The Man without Qualities* are the themes of the novel.[8]

The first appearance of such themes may seem quite casual: they may occupy perhaps a chapter, perhaps merely a few paragraphs. But once they have been established in the reader's memory, a sentence, a phrase, perhaps even a single word, is sufficient to bring them to mind once more. A prominent example is the term, 'Eigenschaften' ('qualities'). In the early part of the work, particularly, 'Eigenschaften' or one of its derivatives, 'ohne Eigenschaften' ('without qualities') or 'Eigenschaftslosigkeit' ('lack of qualities') is frequently repeated. For example, in the third chapter of *The Man without Qualities* we are directed to examine Ulrich's father from the perspective of the 'Eigenschaftslosigkeit' ('lack of qualities') of the son; the chapter is entitled: 'Auch ein Mann ohne Eigenschaften hat einen Vater mit Eigenschaften' ('Even a man without qualities has a father with qualities'). What, briefly, does Musil mean by the term 'Mann ohne Eigenschaften'?

We must remember that, living before the outbreak of World War I, Ulrich is surrounded by the evidence of the vigour of nineteenth-century assumptions. For the majority of Ulrich's contemporaries, 'character' is a collage of their views on racial origin, of half-baked notions about hereditary make-up and environmental influence, and of firm, if erroneous, opinions about moral substance. 'Character', in other words, is like a family ghost – no instrument can measure it, yet it is indisputably real to all who share the secret of its existence. Just as fellow-scientists have begun to question the laws of Newtonian physics so Ulrich questions the 'laws of character' which those around him hold. This is one facet of Ulrich's dialectic of dissatisfaction with the world as he finds it. The dialectic involves putting in question his own 'character' as well as that of other people – this leads him to the disturbing discovery 'that he is equally close to and equally far from all qualities and that they are all, whether they are his own or not, strangely a matter of indifference to him' (151).

There seems to be no fixed element that he could call his own; he has, literally, no 'Eigen-schaft' ('own-ness'). He believes that the right way to view character is to accept a new theory of relativity – that all selves are constituted in unique but transitory conjunctions of time, space and substance. They are relative to the disposition of the moment. The correct perspective is to look at circumstances as a guide to human feelings and behaviour. In the following quotation, two images of Ulrich's self are juxtaposed without contradiction since they represent separate moments, separate identities in the historical sequence that makes up his being:

According to his feeling he was tall, his shoulders were broad, his chest cavity bulged like a spreading sail on a mast, and the joints of his body were clothed in muscles like slim limbs of steel whenever he was moved to anger, quarrelled or Bonadea nestled up to him; on the other hand, he was slight, delicate, dark and soft as a jelly-fish floating in the water whenever he read a book that moved him or was touched by a breath of that great love without a home, whose Being-in-the-World he had never been able to grasp. (159)

What appears, in the out-dated assessment of contemporaries, as the unsplittable atom of the self, is revealed to Ulrich, the impartial observer, as floating particles of sensation and emotion that coalesce in the brain at one moment, then disperse the next. 'Eigenschaften' ('qualities'), if they exist at all, are of only seeming solidity. This is an insight which even Walter – who does his best to be as substantial a being as Ulrich is vague – is compelled to confirm. Having given Ulrich his title 'Mann ohne Eigenschaften' ('man without qualities'), Walter explains to Clarisse what it means: ' "Nothing. It is precisely nothing! [...] The cast of men which the present has thrown up!" ' (64).

If 'ohne Eigenschaften' ('without qualities') is a generic feature of contemporaries in much the same way as 'sapiens' attaches to 'homo', why call Ulrich a 'Mann ohne Eigenschaften' at all? This is a matter of appearance rather than substance. Walter, like that other more prominent intellectual, Arnheim, believes that, in the absence of 'Eigenschaften', it is necessary to invent them. Walter projects an image of himself as an artist, rich in sensuous experience, whose creative will is severely tested in a trial of strength against the bureaucratic job he has been forced to take. That Clarisse and Ulrich see through this pose is a source of constant anger and anguish for him. Walter wants to camouflage his lack of substance in an impressive display if not of productivity, at least of artistic frustration. In other words, he wants to live out the nineteenth-century mode of externality for a few more decades. This pose demands that he turn his back on the present. Walter's existence – in this he resembles Arnheim – is a series of elaborate deceptions of himself and others.

Self-deception is a form of self-defence. To deny in practice the absence of character which one accepts in theory is to renounce a burden which all contemporaries should share. To accept, on the other hand, the consequences of the dissolution of character is to live in a moral and spiritual vacuum: 'the dissolving of the anthropocentric attitude which for so long had considered mankind to be the centre of the universe [had probably] finally reached the "I" ' (150). To accept fully what has happened is to embark on the search for a new moral system. This is the decision which Ulrich has taken at the start of the novel. He earns his title by accepting the burden of responsibility for the spiritual dilemma of mankind.

When readers take up the novel for the first time they have only a vague – and quite possibly incorrect – notion of what 'Mann ohne Eigenschaften' means. As they read the novel and examine the word 'Eigenschaften' as it is used in a variety of situations they assimilate its terms of reference; at the point in the narrative when, according to the chronology of the plot, Walter invents the name 'Mann ohne Eigenschaften', readers are able to examine Walter's version critically in the light of its usage earlier in the text.[9] Thus the theme of 'Eigenschaftslosigkeit' ('lack of qualities') helps to mould the readers' attitudes to the characters in the novel. Neither this nor any other theme is explained by an authoritative statement to be found at some point in the text; to discover what a 'Mann ohne Eigenschaften' is one must read the novel, there is no short cut. The sum of the thematic variations is the total statement of *The Man without Qualities*, the work as Musil published it.

I want now to show briefly how another theme – that of love – undergoes several metamorphoses, even within a relatively short section of text.

## The theme of love

When Diotima first meets Arnheim she feels strongly attracted to him. We might expect a measure of sympathy from the narrator for this lady who has led a sheltered life and who has loved no man but her husband. But the narrator is sceptical of her motives and implies that an inward calculation has preceded, perhaps even precipitated her falling in love.[10] The narrator seems to suggest a kind of dialogue within her subconscious: her latent passion catalogues Arnheim's virtues – his fame, his fabulous riches, his intelligence – faltering only when contemporary anti-Semitic prejudice whispers in her ear, then reasserting itself with the thought of how wonderfully he talks.[11] The narrator implies that, though this is love, Diotima casts her eye over Arnheim almost as a stockbroker might examine a company balance sheet – namely with a view to investment. The narrator mentions Diotima's 'small capital sum of her capacity for love' (104); her husband, the narrator wryly observes, 'did not offer it the right investment potential' (104). In Diotima, Arnheim, the businessman, has found his female counterpart. (Later, as we shall see below, the image will reappear, this time with deeper irony, to explain Arnheim's reluctance to risk too much in a deeper involvement with Diotima.) The narrator thus stresses the calculations which Diotima makes even in matters of the heart: Diotima leaves to servants the body-chemistry of mutual attraction; she refines all the plebeian ore of her feelings for Arnheim into pure affinity of souls. In other words, the narrator shows us that, for Diotima, falling in love is a process distorted by her self-image; even this precious experience is subordinated to ambition.

The narrator now turns again to Ulrich who is with Bonadea, waiting for her to dress. His mind leaps back to the time in early manhood when he had fallen ecstatically in love. The contrast with his present situation is complete. Then he had felt no 'desire for possession' (123) and indeed his love unfolded fully only when he had left the beloved, a major's wife, and journeyed to a remote island many miles away. There he experienced love as a state of mystical oneness with creation:

He had found himself at the heart of the world; from where he was to the distant loved one was just as far as to the next tree; inwardness linked beings without space, changing all their relationships, just as two beings pass through each other in a dream without merging. But otherwise this state had nothing to do with dreaming. It was clear and brimming with clear thoughts; but nothing about it was moving towards cause, purpose and physical desire but everything was extending in a constant succession of circles, as when an endless jet of water falls into a basin.          (125)

The narrator's description of Diotima's passion for Arnheim had a strong element of satire; this account of Ulrich's first experience of love could scarcely be more lyrical – there is no trace of satire or irony, rather a sense of deep commitment on the narrator's part – here love is pure, intense, caught in its pristine state before it is channelled into the mould of character.

Thus, within the space of a few chapters, we are offered Musil's 'metamorphoses of love': love as a calculation which the narrator treats with satirical scorn, love as sensuality, to which the narrator seems indifferent, and love as ecstatic loss of self, for which the narrator seems to have a profound sympathy. Thus when Arnheim and Diotima meet for the first time in private the narrator has presented a number of different vantage points from which the progress of their affair may be examined.

When the first gathering of the 'Parallelaktion' ends, Arnheim waits until the other guests have left so that he can be alone with Diotima. Neither has experienced a moment like this before. But the mood is disturbed, from Diotima's perspective, by the stirring of an 'alien' emotion: she cannot ignore that this meeting is spiced with vague sexual imaginings: '[Diotima's] chastity [was] confused by a quite unaccustomed notion; her emptied house, in the absence of her husband, seemed to her like a pair of trousers which Arnheim had put on' (183). But Diotima knows how to keep uncouth feeling in its place. She simply dresses it up as something else, readmitting it to her salon disguised as 'the marvellous dream of a love where body and soul are completely one' (183)! Thus the narrator demonstrates the extent of Diotima's emotional dishonesty.

There is no suggestion that Arnheim senses the sexual ambiguity of the present situation. Here, in the present situation, an air of awkward innocence hangs about him: 'in this moment there was something which made this man, who dealt on an equal footing with American money-barons and who was received by emperors and kings, [...] stare at Diotima in a trance' (183). People such as Diotima and Arnheim identify this sensation as 'Seele' ('soul'). At this point the narrator's impatience with Arnheim breaks through; he substitutes for 'Seele' an image of grotesque extravagance; we are to imagine a woodworm boring its way through timber. The worm, the narrator explains, '[can] twist as it will, indeed can turn back on itself, [...] but it always [leaves] empty space behind' (184). This is the narrator's 'revenge', so to speak, for the emotional hypocrisy of Diotima and Arnheim, his deflation of their inflationary image of themselves and each other.

In a later scene marking the zenith of their love, Diotima, overcome by emotion, beseeches Arnheim to be silent. She cannot, however, resist the urge to explain why they should be silent and Arnheim responds symbolically to her call and fills in even this moment with yet more words.[12] In the chapter which follows, despite all his protestations of love and his offer of marriage, Arnheim makes the 'sensible' decision not to become any more deeply involved with Diotima. It is made explicit that Diotima's 'investment' in their affair has been squandered and that 'Seele' – as interpreted by this pair – was indeed a sham: ' "A man who is conscious of his responsibility" Arnheim said with conviction "is after all only allowed, when he makes a gift of his soul ['Seele'], to sacrifice the interest and never the capital!" ' (511). The businessman behaves, in other words, in a way that Diotima might, with greater circumspection, have predicted – and, indeed, he acts according to the kind of inward calculations which guide Diotima's actions too. When Arnheim subsequently offers Ulrich his friendship he does so because he feels 'Ulrich would probably be a man who would not only sacrifice the interest but the whole capital of his soul ['Seele'] if circumstances required this of him!' (541). In describing Ulrich, Arnheim uses the same terms as he had done in accounting for his own actions and with this observation Arnheim confirms themes that have been established in the novel and makes explicit the comparison between Ulrich and himself.

However, the special force which Arnheim has given to the term 'Seele' in talking of Ulrich identifies their dissimilarity of temperament. The underlying authenticity of the love which Arnheim and Diotima feel is not denied in the text. Arnheim undoubtedly draws from the same wellspring of feeling as Ulrich[13] and we have no cause to doubt that Diotima does too. Musil shows that love, whoever it affects, is always pure in origin. What, the text compels us to ask, has turned a mystical vision which the narrator traced out in words of such passion into the grotesque image of the woodworm through which the narrator expresses his implacable scorn? What transforms the ecstasy of love into the emptiness and frustration of the 'Seele'-parody in the relationship of Arnheim and Diotima? This is a question which, at this stage, Musil leaves open in the reader's mind.

### The observer in 'The Man without Qualities'

The opening chapter of *The Man without Qualities* has attracted a great deal of critical attention.[14] The introductory paragraph provides an abstruse analysis of obscure meteorological data and statistics, then ends with a more down-to-earth statement: 'In words which, even though a little old-fashioned, describe the facts very well indeed: it was a beautiful August day in the year 1913' (9). Then the narrative continues in its earlier mode of abstraction:

Cars shot out of deep narrow streets into the shallowness of bright squares. Pedestrian darkness formed cloudy strings. Where stronger lines of speed drove right across their loose-knit haste they broadened out to trickle on more quickly thereafter and regain, after a few oscillations, their regular pulse. Hundreds of notes were woven into each other in a wire-rope of noise out of which individual sharp points protruded and along which ran cutting edges which then smoothed out again and from which clear note-splinters broke away and flew off. (9)

Readers will gather that they are in a city, but otherwise they feel disorientated in this fog of weightless impressions. Then once again the narrator seems to relent: he confides to his reader 'that he is in the Imperial Capital and Seat of His Majesty, Vienna' (9). It is only by special dispensation, so it seems, that the reader is allowed to know the time of the year and where he or she is. One wonders why Musil chose to open his novel in this curious way.

The title of the first chapter, 'Woraus bemerkenswerter Weise nichts hervorgeht' ('Which, strangely enough, leads nowhere'), implies that the reader is not expected to follow any ordinary narrative thread here; this chapter, as we have seen, is a non-introduction to *The Man without Qualities*. It is significant that Ulrich makes his first appearance only in the second chapter; here, standing at a window in his house with a stop-watch in his hand, he is engaged in an eccentric 'time-and-motion' study. He is attempting to analyse traffic-flow and pedestrian-movement. The reader realises that the abstractions of the opening chapter become meaningful as soon as their context is given. They are revealed as the record of the kind of observations and reflections that have passed through Ulrich's consciousness over the past few moments. Ulrich, we are told, 'had spent the last ten minutes, with watch in hand, counting the cars, carriages, trams, and the faces of the pedestrians obliterated by the distance, all of which filled the net of his gaze with a vortex of haste' (12). In the first chapter the reader was confused by the feeling that the data recorded in the narrative had no shape or order. Here those data are seen to be impressions focussed in the eye of an observer, Ulrich. The narrator sees Ulrich's retina – in German 'Netzhaut' – as, literally, a net[15] in which Ulrich collects the material for his study. Just as the narrator watches and records this operation with a scrupulous attention to the working of eye and brain, so Ulrich attempts to see and understand the detail of the world with an unusual accuracy. The meshes of his perception are uncommonly fine. Where Ulrich sees bright shapes and hears vibrant sounds predicated on unseen and perhaps unknowable laws, an average city-dweller going about his daily business might be expected to receive only a blanket impression of the familiarity of his environment.

This scene follows the pattern of Ulrich's intellectual disposition. It moves from a period of rapt attention to a moment when Ulrich becomes aware of what he is doing and senses the hiatus between the things he observes and himself as observer, and finally notes the way in which an instinct for ironical self-criticism asserts itself: 'After he had spent a few moments making mental calculations [Ulrich] put his watch in his pocket with a laugh, realising that he had been doing something nonsensical' (12). Ulrich is incorrigibly self-conscious; indeed, he is a man in a mask.

One day as he leaves home, Ulrich is suddenly aware of the way in which his habit of intense reflection has helped to shape the person he has become: 'the striving for truth [had] filled his inner self with movements shaped by the intellect ['Geist'] [. . .] and given him an expression which was, strictly speaking, false and theatrical' (129). Self-awareness is self-alienation. Ulrich's whole physical being, the set of his features and the sensation of muscles which move his body in a particular way, are suddenly present in his consciousness. He feels that his physical self does not properly belong to him; it is somehow 'out there', on the street with the traffic and the other pedestrians. The outward shape of personality is formed of images which he cultivated earlier in his life and which now project themselves quite unconsciously – these public selves as 'gentleman', 'intellectual', 'sportsman', can they be said to form parts of his authentic self?

Self-alienation is a source of inner confusion but it can also be turned to advantage. Ulrich has a touch of Nietzschean opportunism about him; as if to bear out Nietzsche's words, 'Everything that is deep loves a mask'[16] he delights in dissembling. The narrator of *The Man without Qualities* constantly points to the disjunction between what other characters feel Ulrich is like and what Ulrich himself feels he is like. The unmasking of the hero, the continual movement from the polite but sceptical man seen from outside to the man glimpsed within, who is by turns passionate or despairing, is one of the aspects of the irony of *The Man without Qualities*. How different the irony in this novel is from irony in its Socratic form! For Socrates the ironic mask is a kind of teaching aid. Socrates, we feel, knows what he is getting at, he understands what it is that he feigns not to know. In Ulrich the mask has become part of himself – he does not know what it is that he is concealing from the world. Musil may have been thinking of Ulrich when he wrote in one of his manuscript notes: '*Socratic* is: to feign ignorance. *Modern*: to be ignorant!' (Tb II, 736).

Something of the mood of the ironic dialogue between inner and outer self in Ulrich is found, we may remember, in the critical attitude of the narrator to the world he surveys. There is a degree of solidarity – albeit only implicitly expressed – between the attitude of the narrator and his hero; the hierarchy of perception in the text of *The Man without Qualities* is reinforced by this shared ironic vision. But though this aspect of irony in the work thus appears to spring from a common source, its flow is neither constant nor even. Maurice Blanchot suggests that Musil's irony is 'la lumière froide qui invisiblement change de moment en moment l'éclairage du livre'.[17] This analogy is well chosen since it evokes those changes in attitude, the modulations of irony, which pass so smoothly that the reader adapts as unconsciously to them as an eye compensates for different intensities of light.[18]

Let us briefly turn our attention away from the hero to consider the point of view which underpins his position – the ironic perspective of the narrator. The narrator delights in puncturing inflated self-approval. The light of his intellect illuminates eccentricities which are invisible to individual characters in the warm, fire-side glow of self-approval. We shall see this clearly in our study of the 'Parallelaktion' but we shall follow it now through a short section of the novel.

Nothing, when examined with ironic intensity, is quite what it appears to be in other kinds of illumination. Part I, Chapter 11, is concerned with Ulrich's attempts, at an earlier stage in his life, to make mathematics his career. This choice stems from a somewhat uncritical enthusiasm, at a more innocent phase in his intellectual development, for the potential of science and technology to alter the whole environment of human existence and also, and possibly more importantly, to overturn traditional attitudes. The narrator looks back at this phase with anything but indulgence. The hero is placed in the context of other hot-heads of his generation:

most people in their youth [...] have found it ridiculous that the older generation clung to the existing order and thought with their heart, with a piece of meat, rather than with their brain. These younger people have always remarked that the moral stupidity of the older generation is just as much a lack of a capacity to make new connections as intellectual stupidity in its usual form, and the morality which is natural to them is one of achievement, of heroism and change. (41)

A more worldly wisdom weighs down the narrator's observations – he seems to be implying that these young revolutionaries of the mind have failed to include in their calculations the inertia of convention which will reduce them all to breathless impotence:

In spite of this, as soon as they reached the years of realisation, they knew nothing more about it and wanted to know even less. This is why many of those who have made a career of mathematics or science look upon it as an abuse, if one makes a decision to take up a particular science for the reasons which Ulrich chose. (41)

The chapter ends with a modest concession by the narrator to the hero's achievement: 'In spite of this, according to expert judgement he had achieved more than a little in this profession' (41).

But the matter does not rest there – the pride of the successful young 'Wissenschaftler' is taken down a peg at the beginning of the next chapter when Ulrich's existential efforts are set alongside those of a far more simple soul, Bonadea. This opens wryly with the words: 'It turned out that Bonadea, too, was striving for great ideas' (41). This juxtaposition is more worldly wisdom from the narrator at Ulrich's expense; Musil thus achieves not merely a transition from one character to another, but from the mode of the essay to that of the novel proper, and from the things of the mind to what, in view of Bonadea's particular predisposition, might discreetly be called the things of the body.

Though very little time has passed since their first meeting Ulrich has already had ample opportunity to assess her leanings. He has already given her her soubriquet: 'He had christened her Bonadea, the good goddess, [. . .] after a goddess of chastity who possessed a temple in ancient Rome which became, by a strange inversion, the centre of all kinds of debauchery' (41). Bonadea is unaware of any secondary connotations to her new name – she takes an innocent pleasure in its surface meaning. But the reader is invited to share Ulrich's secret satisfaction at its appropriateness as her double life is revealed:

She was the wife of a respected man and the tender mother of two handsome boys. Her favourite term was 'really decent'; she used it to refer to people, servants, shops and feelings when she wanted to pay them a compliment. She was capable of pronouncing the words 'the true, the good and the beautiful' as naturally and as frequently as another says 'Thursday'. Her need for ideas was satisfied at its most profound level by the image of a calm, ideal way of life in a circle formed by husband and children, while deep below lurks the dark realm, 'lead me not into temptation', its shivers subduing the radiance of happiness to a soft, lamp-lit glow. She had only one failing: the mere sight of a man aroused her to a quite extraordinary degree. She was by no means wanton; she was sensual, as different people have different afflictions, like suffering from sweating palms or from excessive blushing; this was seemingly in-born and she could never resist it. (42)

So, with constant fine adjustments to the ironic focus, the narrator moves the reader's attention from subtly sceptical reflections on Ulrich's earlier ambitions – with their reminder that the hero, too, is not immune to criticism – to the self-deception practised by a relatively minor character.

This narrator-observer – whose attitude is at once close to, yet not quite identical with, that of the hero in his more self-critical moments – seems to have chosen Ernst Mach rather than Socrates as mentor. Perhaps it was inevitable that Musil, having spent several years investigating Mach's ideas when writing his doctorate, should acknowledge, if only indirectly, the philosopher's influence on his outlook. Though Musil's dissertation sprang from a desire to take issue with Mach, it was also a tribute to his importance. Mach was one of the men who taught Musil to examine the detail of the physical universe with painstaking accuracy and to take account of the operations of eye and brain as they arrange this detail in a particular order.

In the preface to Mach's work *Die Analyse der Empfindungen*[19] there is a rather curious picture: a figure, apparently headless, is resting on a couch in what is quite clearly a study, with shelves, books and a window; in the foreground is a torso with a left arm resting on the hip, the legs and feet tapering in the foreshortened perspective of a drawing into the middle-ground where, apparently unattached, one sees a right hand holding a pen, and the sleeves of shirt and jacket. It is only when the baffled reader realises what the 'border' at the top, right-hand side and bottom of the picture represents that the picture can be seen to belong legitimately in a scientific text rather than a surrealist exhibition. This border is formed respectively by the left eyebrow, the left-hand side of a nose and the left-hand flourish of a large and carefully trained moustache; these are all seen through the left eye of their owner, Mach, who having covered over his right eye has noted down with naturalistic accuracy what he perceives through the other. The fragments of our original impressions are quickly fitted together when, in the text of his work, Mach explains the relationship between the details in the picture and its border; we grasp that the figure in the picture has no head because a man looking at himself as he reclined on a couch would not see his whole head but only a blurred outline of features that stand at the outermost extremity of the eye's range of vision, namely nose, eyebrow, and, if he has one, moustache. Here, then, Mach subjects the normally subconscious functioning of human perception to an intense scrutiny.

Just as a puzzled reader, after feeling utterly perplexed by Mach's drawing, suddenly realises that it is an attempt to represent what a man sees as he looks out at the world through his own eyes, so Musil's reader, initially confused by the opening paragraphs of

*The Man without Qualities*, feels a sense of relief when Ulrich, the scientist with his stop-watch standing at the window of his Viennese home, comes into view. It is true that Chapter I is not finally explained by Ulrich's appearance. Ulrich makes no attempt to fit these observations and sensations into some vision of reality; indeed the reader will come to realise that Ulrich has no settled theory, no ideology and no comprehensive plan or project. However, though Ulrich does not offer a frame of meaning, here, as elsewhere, he provides a point of reference.

Consideration of Mach's ideas helps to explain why so few of the characters in *The Man without Qualities* live comfortably within the shell of their identity. For what many consider to be the sacred and substantial elements of selfhood appear from Mach's entirely non-complacent perspective as something far more arbitrary and precarious; Mach speaks of 'the complex of memories, moods, feelings, attached to a particular body [...], that are described as the "I"'.[20] Moreover the 'I', this bundle of elements, is, he argues, no more than '*relatively* constant' (my emphasis). These words imply a deep human crisis; the traditional virtues and the traditional notion of character can scarcely be reconciled with this scientist's version of an underlying inconstancy which disturbs the very atoms of one's personal existence. Most of the characters in *The Man without Qualities* are touched by the uncertainty which seems to come from some sixth sense that such a crisis is upon them. But they protect themselves from the implications of this predicament by ignoring it. Just as Diotima blithely transforms earthly desire into the soaring flight of sublime passion, others reshape experience to suit their own self-image. Their interrelated attitudes and expectations – their shared illusions – are given the generic title, 'Wirklichkeit' ('reality'), a term which in Musil's usage has several levels of meaning, as we shall see later. The juxtaposition in *The Man without Qualities* of Ulrich's critical perception and the less critical habits of mind of other characters throws these illusions into ironic relief.

## 'The Man without Qualities' – 'Gedankenexperiment'?

Von Mises, a philosopher-mathematician and friend of Musil, suggests an approach to the novel as a genre that is particularly helpful in our analysis of *The Man without Qualities*. Von Mises describes novels as intricate 'Gedankenexperimente' ('thought-experiments').[21] In any novel, he asserts, each reader retraces the mental path taken by the author, the author's creativity being of an active kind, the reader's passive.

Von Mises' definition of the novel as *'Gedankenexperiment'* (my emphasis) does not allow for the way in which a literary work is felt to have a life, or at least represent a kind of life, which is independent of its author. It overlooks an author's sensitivity and openness to experience. But it does remind readers that the whole creative process is internal: it is an experiment that is conducted within the author's mind. Imagine the novelist sitting in his study going over in his head the narrative of his novel: an accurate account of this activity ought to read approximately as follows: 'If there were a man "x" and if event "$e_1$" were to happen for the following reasons "$r_1$", "$r_2$" and "$r_3$", then the result might be event "$e_2$" and if . . . ' and so on. The 'ifs' remind us that novels are based on speculation, not fact. Thus von Mises argues – and similar views have been advanced by Jean-Paul Sartre and Roland Barthes – that a literary work represents printed evidence of a special kind of conjectural mental activity.

This all fits *The Man without Qualities* so well that one suspects that it may have been drafted with that work in mind. The primary focus of this novel is in the subject, the inner world; the reader is given frequent glimpses of the author at work. Even in the titles of the four Parts of the novel Musil points self-critically to his efforts as author: Part I is 'Eine Art Einleitung' ('A Kind of Introduction'), the projected Part IV, 'Eine Art Ende' ('A Kind of Ending'); the title of Part II is 'Seinesgleichen geschieht' ('The Same Kind of Things Happen Again'), whereby Musil combines the notion that contemporary civilisation is caught in a joyless routine of more or less meaningless activity with a reminder that the novel is a reconstruction in words of certain aspects of an epoch which finished with the outbreak of World War I; even Part III advertises the problems which Musil has faced in the process of composition – the subtitle in brackets, 'Die Verbrecher' ('The Criminals'), is a superseded alternative to the one finally chosen: 'Ins Tausendjährige Reich' ('Into the Millennium'). Individual chapter headings also make the reader pause and remember that the novel is an artefact; the most striking of these is Part II, Chapter 28, entitled 'A chapter which can be skipped by everyone who has no high opinion of an involvement with ideas', which introduces a passage where Musil goes through the motions of interrupting the narrative to explain to us how a man's mind works when he is trying to solve a problem. Few chapter headings are simple milestones in the plot; most relate to the author's intellectual preoccupations. They continually remind the reader of the probing intelligence at the heart of the work which repeatedly compares some detail of actual reality with potential alternatives – this is the message contained in the heading of Part I, Chapter 4, 'If there is such a thing as a sense of reality, then there must also be a sense of possibility.' Even those sections of the novel which deal directly with the historical reality of Austria-Hungary and which are quoted with delight by historians have a distinctive ironical tone which reminds the reader of the presence of a bemused and highly critical observer. The following extract is from Part II, Chapter 98:

The inhabitants of this imperial and royal, royal-imperial twin monarchy found themselves confronted by a difficult task; they were obliged to feel themselves to be imperial and royal Austro-Hungarian patriots, but at the same time to be also royal Hungarian or royal-imperial Austrian patriots. It was understandable, in view of such difficulties, that their preferred slogan was 'Forward with the strength of unity!' To be precise, viribus unitis. But the Austrians needed far greater strength for this than the Hungarians. For the Hungarians were, first and last, nothing but Hungarians [...]; the Austrians, on the other hand, were originally and ab initio nothing and were supposed from the viewpoint of their leaders to feel themselves to be [...] Austro-Hungarians [...] Even Austria did not exist. The two parts Hungary and Austria fitted together in the same way as a red, white and green jacket does with yellow and black trousers; the jacket was a garment on its own, the trousers were what was left of a yellow and black suit which did not exist any more and which had been separated in the year 1867. (450–1)

Albrecht Schöne has demonstrated how the use of the subjunctive in *The Man without Qualities* is another way in which the critical narrator reminds the reader of his existence as a conjecturing agent.[22]

Von Mises' image 'Gedanken*experiment*' (my emphasis) suggests a correspondence between the activities of novelist and scientist. But, it may be objected, the scientist deals in exploration of the physical world, the novelist in imaginary events. Experiments involve the collection of empirical data, the making and testing of hypotheses, rigorous self-criticism on the part of the experimenter. By contrast, the novelist self-indulgently spins a tale which no one would attempt to falsify or disprove since it makes no claim to being objectively testable. However, as von Mises indicates, the two activities are not so different from each other as they might appear at first sight. The scientist has an idea of what he may find when he examines his data. Without his professional intuition, formulated in terms of a hypothesis, he would not know where to start. Once he has chosen the direction of his investigations, his route can be altered by the signs which his trained eye reads along the way. The novelist, in establishing his narrative links between events, is not exercising imagination alone. He tests the fictional connections he makes against his collected observations on life.

The reader who repeats the novelist's experiment will expect the evidence presented to ring true, although he will not expect all he reads to fit into the mould of his experience. Neither the scientist nor the novelist presents an innocent view of the world; their findings are ordered according to the traditions of science or the traditions of novel-writing. A novel, like a scientific treatise, puts the raw material of experience into a context and gives it meaning.

It may be objected that most novels do not read like accounts of experiments in understanding human experience. This has to do with the way that novelists tend to record their 'Gedankenexperimente'. If the novelist were to give a full account of what happens inside his brain when he writes a novel, his work would, as we have seen, be a sequence of conditional clauses. But instead of saying: 'If there were a man "x" and event "e1" were to happen ...', novelists tend to assert: 'There was a man "x" and event "e" happened ...' In other words, they turn conditional into indicative, speculation into statement, and their fictional narrative reads, more often than not, like a report of something that actually happened. Because the conditions without which the narrative would not make sense are suppressed, readers, critics and novelists, as well, tend to forget them.

This does not mean that they are not experiments. Novelists like Balzac present themselves as omniscient with insight into the inner secrets of the characters: the narrative of their works does not present the kind of reality which they see, hear, touch and smell in daily life, but a distillation of the essence of that reality. Such writing flouts the laws which govern a proper 'Gedankenexperiment'. The self-critical author, by contrast, accepts the actual conditions under which his experiment is conducted and shows that he has no Olympian seat before the spectacle of life – he is in the thick of things with human beings, suspended between two unknowns – the depths of inwardness and the endless expanse of possibilities in the external world.

Again, it seems almost as if von Mises derived his comments on the experimental nature of fiction from a study of Musil's novel.

Musil's narrator makes no pretence at omniscience. His forays into the external world are followed without fail by a return to some bolt-hole in the subject where he pauses to reflect and recoup his forces. Most frequently this subject is his hero, as we see in a short but powerful extract from the early part of Part III where Ulrich contemplates his father's corpse. The record of external detail is reduced almost to note form:

He lay on his plinth as he had stipulated; in evening-dress, the shroud reaching half-way up his chest, with the starched shirt emerging above it. Hands folded without a crucifix, medals on display. Small hard eye-sockets, sunken cheeks and lips. Sewn into the gruesome eyeless skin of the dead which is still part of their being yet already alien; the travelling-bag of life.                                                                        (677)

The reader could scarcely ask for a more economical, objective and unemotional record than this. The transition to the subject follows: a son responds to the sight of his dead father. But the move from the external to the internal, from visible detail to private and part-'invisible' emotional echo does not involve any perceptible loss of authenticity. The words used to express the hero's response reach as surely inwards as those which fixed external detail: 'Ulrich felt an involuntary shock at the root of being where there is no feeling and no thought; but nowhere else' (677). Here, as so often in Musil's work, one senses that the fiction is backed up by direct experience, recorded with the scruples of the scientist.

Ulrich is, of course, a scientist, too, and delights in complex play on the interrelations of the actual and the hypothetical, on fact and mental image. In one scene, Ulrich invites Diotima to love him as if they were characters in a novel. What in another novel might be simple self-indulgence on the part of the author is here linked to an undertaking which the hero takes very seriously: the notion of living experimentally, of treating what happens to him as if it were taking place in a laboratory, with himself as a kind of moral guinea-pig. (We shall explore the experiment, Ulrich's 'Urlaub vom Leben', in a later section.) This undertaking allows the author, as we shall see, to have some fun at his hero's expense, because the fictional world is no more predictable than the real one.[23]

But Musil takes the account of the interplay of fact and fiction into another dimension: people, he argues, habitually fictionalise their lives. Where understanding or observation fails, they use their imagination; in moments of irrational inspiration they raise their hypotheses about feelings, motivations, character

– whether their own or other people's – to the status of established fact. Like most novelists, they leave out the conditionals and raise speculation about reality to the level of reality itself. 'Gedan-kenexperimente' – albeit ones conducted with little concern for objectivity–are not the prerogative of novelists, they are a way of life in the real world! Musil owes this insight to countless observations on the culture which surrounds him.[24] The 'Parallelaktion' provides at least anecdotal evidence for this law of contemporary existence; each individual folly in this bedlam of life-systems gone wrong is carefully assessed, categorised and documented by a consciousness which accumulates knowledge as a contribution to the understanding of the aberrations that make up contemporary civilisation.

The narrator, however, trains his attention most intensely on the mind of the hero. The techniques of observation of mental phenomena which Musil developed and refined in *Acts of Union* are used throughout *The Man without Qualities*; in the following example, Ulrich's intelligence is observed at work, functioning as a tool of scientific enquiry. The simile italicised in the text below serves, in the absence of any more suitably scientific notation, as a psychic bridge between the text and the reader:

Unfortunately, in belles lettres there is nothing quite so difficult to represent as a person thinking. Once, when a great discoverer was asked how he had managed to think up so many new things, he answered: by thinking about them all the time. [...] [The] solution of a mental task [happens] in much the same way *as a dog, with a stick in its mouth, tries to get through a narrow door; it turns its head to left and right until the stick slips through*, and we do something very similar, the sole difference being that our attempts are not quite indiscriminate since we know roughly from experience how it's to be done.　　　　(111–12) (my emphasis)

This narrative precision is directed not only to thoughts but to feelings, as well. We see this, for example, at a critical point in the narrative when a decisive change of mood and attitude in the hero is recorded. Identification and description of feelings are not an exact science but here, by dint of reflection and the selection of appropriate imagery, Musil succeeds in formulating with unusual skill the change which Ulrich senses within himself:

It was a releasing, as if a piece of knotted string had been untied; and since neither walls nor objects really changed, since no god entered the room of this unbeliever, and Ulrich himself by no means compromised the clarity of his judgement [...], it could only be the relationship between his environment and himself that was subject to this change; with respect to this relationship, it could be neither the objective part nor the senses and understanding which are its sober counterpart that changed – what seemed to be changing was a deep feeling as wide as ground water on which these buttresses of factual thinking and perceiving otherwise rested.    (664)

This emotional change, which takes place at the end of Part II, prepares the ground for a different kind of 'Gedankenexperiment' in Part III. Here Musil takes Ulrich and his sister – two beings who are as near perfect as he can make them without overtaxing the reader's credibility – isolates them from almost all external influences (Ulrich's home becomes an island of domestic tranquillity on which they take refuge, shunning the round of social calls expected of them), then observes how their relationship develops when protected from many of the distorting influences of the contemporary world. This is Musil's attempt to identify in individuals the wellspring of authentic moral behaviour.

In another respect, however, Musil does not fulfil the expectations one might place on a scientist-turned-novelist – that of providing a straightforward and unambiguous account of his experiments. His use of certain terms is deliberately inconsistent; he plays language games with his reader. He takes ironical pleasure in stretching language beyond all common limits to show that words can change according to the context in which they are used or according to the person who is using them. This is true of some of the words which are central to an understanding of *The Man without Qualities*.

## Language and the structure of 'The Man without Qualities'

In order to appreciate the subtlety of the narrative, the reader must develop an awareness of Musil's language games. Take, for example, a sentence (from Part II, Chapter 62 of *The Man without Qualities*) in which a term occurs which we find very frequently in Musil's writing, both in *The Man without Qualities* and elsewhere, namely 'Moral' ('morality'): 'Morality, in its normal sense, was, as far as Ulrich was concerned, no more than a force field in an advanced state of decomposition which must not be confused with that field [in its original form – PP] on pain of loss of ethical force' (251). Here Musil is pointing deliberately to a feature of his writing which is usually left to the reader to fathom: that some words do service both as linguistic signs in daily use in contemporary Austrian society and as terms which Musil has invested with his own meaning. 'Moral' refers both to 'morality' as the tired and flawed code of behaviour and public posturing in Austria-Hungary and as an authentic desire to do what is right – whatever that may be – which is present in all human beings but which tends to be overlaid by more pressing though less worthy considerations. In this latter sense 'Moral' merges into the field of meaning which Musil attaches to 'Ethik' ('ethics') – a term used with great consistency throughout *The Man without Qualities* and indeed throughout all his writings to refer to direct individual mystical experience from which ultimately, in Musil's view, all moral acts and all moral systems originate.[25]

Musil plays a similar language game with 'Seele'; here the span of meaning is even wider. At one end of the spectrum is the scientific idea of 'Seele' as the sum of man's conscious and unconscious faculties: Musil, at one point in his diaries, reflects on the wonderful array of skills which are required to strike a billiard ball at the correct angle and at the right speed to propel another ball into a pocket. All an observer sees is the player sauntering up to the table, cigarette in mouth, taking casual and effortless aim and potting the ball; but it is evident that somewhere within him something has been responsible for the co-ordination of subtle movements and intricate calculations. Musil asks: 'Does *my mind* ['Seele'] play billiards?' (Tb II, 1168) (my emphasis). There is nothing religious about this reflection – Musil is merely reminding himself that the total powers of the mind extend well beyond the frame which we tend to associate with its operations. This totality, unconscious as well as conscious, is 'Seele' in this scientific sense.[26] We find it used in this sense in the graphic description of inmates in the lunatic asylum in Part III, Chapter 33:

In their beds in the next room there hung or sat a row of horror. Without exception, distorted bodies, dirty, stunted or paralysed. With degenerate sets of teeth. Wobbling heads. Heads that were too big, too small, completely misshapen. Jaws hanging loosely down from which ran saliva, or mouths moving like animals chewing, in which there was neither food nor word. Lead bars a metre thick seemed to lie between *these minds* ['Seelen'] and the world.                                     (984) (my emphasis)

When, on the other hand, we read in *The Man without Qualities* the statement 'Morality replaces the soul with logic' (506) it is clear that Musil is using the term 'Seele', in a more familiar, and non-scientific sense; 'Seele' is evidently here not 'mind' or 'psyche' but 'soul', and its meaning overlaps with religious usage. As far as I can judge, in the above statement there is not a trace of irony. Musil is arguing that after the age of religious belief has come an agnostic age which sets great store by appearances and rationality; one of the effects of this change is that a concern for the kinds of experiences which can be described in the broadest sense as religious has been replaced by a utilitarian emphasis on actions that are based on principles and are directed towards rational ends.

However, sometimes the term 'Seele' does have an ironic barb, particularly when Musil uses it to refer to attitudes of mind which he considers affected and spurious. Such characters as Diotima and Arnheim, as we have seen, make a cult of what they call 'Seele', expressing in this term, which they use *ad nauseam*, their feeling that their relationship is qualitatively different from other people's. They see themselves as belonging to a spiritual élite. So, for a chapter which deals both with Diotima and Arnheim's relationship in general, and with Arnheim's private spiritual malaise in particular, Musil chooses the heading 'Ideals and morals are the best means of filling the great hole called *soul* ['Seele']' (185) (my emphasis). Here it is immediately apparent that Musil is poking fun at Arnheim and to a lesser extent at Diotima; at a deeper level of irony within this heading, of course, the author seems to be mocking 'Seele' itself, which, of course, is one of his own most passionate concerns. This we saw above in a brief examination of a passage from an essay which provided evidence that Musil takes the range of experiences that 'Seele' embraces very seriously indeed.[27] Arnheim's mood matches Ulrich's feelings when in love with the major's wife, an episode which we also discussed briefly above.[28] In *The Man without Qualities* and indeed in other writings, Musil refers to the mystical feeling described in the above quotation as 'der andere Zustand' ('the other state'). Perhaps the primary preoccupation of Musil's declining years in exile in Switzerland was his striving to capture in words this most elusive of moods. Such obstinacy in the face of a formidable task was typical. Musil repeatedly made words do service to describe things they do not normally describe and to perform functions they do not normally perform. He saw words as tools for understanding that too often, in unskilled hands, botched a job. He used them in a familiar context but then raised an ironic eyebrow to alienate his reader from this usage; or he used them outside the familiar context to convey a message of his own.

To read Musil closely is to become aware of the many kinds of language in which his 'Gedankenexperimente' are recorded and the range of meaning of many of the terms he uses. The reader learns that such terms change their frame of reference, within specific limits, according to the context where they are found. 'Wirklichkeit' ('reality'), 'Wahrheit' ('truth'), 'Gefühl' ('feeling'), 'Geist' ('intellect', 'spirit', 'force of mind') and many others are so many chameleons which, within certain parameters, select their colouring according to their environment. This is also true – as we shall see below – of images. Here again the reader learns to detect the private Musilian laws which govern the field of reference of particular images. Any glossary of Musil terminology in *The Man without Qualities* would have to take account of such changes; but since Musil has made the linguistic range of these 'colour changes' so consistent it is as well for the reader to develop his or her own spontaneous awareness of, and responses to, given terms in the many and varied contexts in which they occur.

Our survey of some of the ways in which Musil structures the narrative prepares the way for an attempt to come to terms with what I see as the main concern of the novel – the attempt by one man in central Europe towards the beginning of the twentieth century to construct for himself a meaningful existence. This was a time when the competition of creeds had given civilisation the bracing but anarchic constitution of a free market in ideas, and when each individual was accordingly presented with the freedom, and the agony, of choice. Few people agonised as thoroughly as the hero of *The Man without Qualities*.

But such an attempt needs a context. Before examining this attempt itself, it is necessary to study, in some detail, two important concerns which help to provide this context in the novel – 'Wirklichkeit' ('reality') and the 'Parallelaktion'. Musil's preoccupation with 'Wirklichkeit' is the theoretical framework of the world which his hero encounters, while the 'Parallelaktion' helps to fill this framework with practical experience.

# 6

# AN INVESTIGATION OF 'WIRKLICHKEIT' AND THE 'PARALLELAKTION'

## 'Wirklichkeit'

The most revealing feature of 'Wirklichkeit' (reality'), from Musil's point of view, is the point where the objective and the subjective touch. Musil concentrates on the ways in which individuals see and interpret the outside world. In the narrative of *The Man without Qualities* many points of view are recorded, and all are human and partial; Musil does not try to see as if through immortal eyes. Musil's 'Wirklichkeit' is a co-operative venture which involves the full cast of characters he presents, each contributing his or her individual mental operations to the joint enterprise of a representation of Viennese 'Wirklichkeit'. The work moves from the viewpoint of one character to another, or ascends or descends within a character's mind from one level of consciousness to another. These movements are all so clearly articulated that it seems that Musil deliberately left traces of his 'Gedankenexperiment' in the finished text, just as in some paintings the marks of the artist's brush are clearly visible.[1] By thus revealing to his readers something of the novelist's craft Musil intended to encourage them to think critically about the kind of evidence which anyone considers when speculating about how another thinks and feels.[2]

Thus it might seem from this perspective that Musil's version of Viennese 'Wirklichkeit' in *The Man without Qualities* was merely Diotima's 'Wirklichkeit', plus Arnheim's 'Wirklichkeit', plus Leinsdorf's 'Wirklichkeit' and so on through the full 'cast' of characters in the text. But this is to overlook two other aspects of 'Wirklichkeit' which are essential to Musil's exploration of the theme: first, elements of the interpretation of the contemporary world common to most of the characters portrayed – above all their shared illusions about modern life (as exemplified, above all, in those who take part in the 'Parallelaktion'); second, beneath the subjective perspective, beyond the illusions, there is a basic stuff of experience, a 'Wirklichkeit in itself', so to speak, which all humans can and do encounter in the course of their lives, however hard they try to avoid it. Thus, although 'Wirklichkeit' in *The Man without Qualities* often has a negative charge, it may also be used positively to refer to the objective context in which all human life is lived out.

### 'Wirklichkeit' articulated in Musil's 'Gedankenexperiment'

Much of the *The Man without Qualities* is couched in the third person, past tense narrative mode. Musil reminds the reader in his first chapter that the familiar, when looked at closely, may appear as something extremely curious. The narrator is describing two witnesses of an accident:

Let us suppose [this condition is to be fulfilled, of course, by the reader – PP] they were called Arnheim and Ermelinda Tuzzi, [then, in the next few words, the narrator denies his own fictional premise – PP] which is not the case, however, since Frau Tuzzi in August was staying in the company of her husband at Bad Aussee and Dr Arnheim was still in Constantinople [the narrator plays an impossible narrative game: 'What I propose to tell you is not true but fictional; my fictional speculation that the lady and gentleman are Arnheim and Frau Tuzzi is, unfortunately, false because the logic of my fiction has ordained – this very moment as I sit at my desk with my tongue in my cheek! – that Arnheim and Frau Tuzzi are somewhere else' – PP], then one is confronted by the riddle of who they are [the narrator's voice can again be heard: 'If you accept, as you must if you are going to continue reading, the condition expressed after the words 'Let us suppose', then you will be caught up in a non-sequitur. Whichever way my sentence is construed, its syntax is wrong; this portion of narrative deliberately confutes the logic of my fiction!' – PP].(10)

Behind the game there is a serious intention. Musil is actually reminding the reader of the conditions of this 'Gedankenexperiment' without which the novel would be an incoherent sequence of words.

When written out these appear cumbersome and self-evident but they are essential to the narrative. They might be expressed as follows: (a) 'Although time and space are unalterable facts of human existence and cannot be tampered with, the reader in an act of imagination (which is not subject to the laws of time and space) is to turn back the clock and remove himself to Imperial Vienna just before the First World War'; (b) 'The characters whose actions and thoughts I propose to consider never actually existed – at least not quite in the way they are presented in my narrative – but, had they existed, it is conceivable that they might have been at a meeting discussing such things as the following: ...'. A work in which such conditions were actually written down before each statement would be intolerably boring; it would, also, not seem to be a novel precisely because, for a novel to create the atmosphere readers expect of it, these expatiations on its conditions must to a large extent be hidden. The ability to read novels is one of those skills like learning to read or to type which, though acquired gradually and with effort, become 'second-nature' after a while and rarely rise to the level of consciousness. However, even when Musil does not express these conditions directly, he evidently wants his reader to be aware of them. In the first chapter of *The Man without Qualities* he thrusts them on the reader's attention, simply by altering them, as we have seen, in mid-sentence.

Why does Musil remind us of some of the mental operations which the reader must perform to follow even the simplest fictional narrative? In my view he is presenting an analogy which, though original in Musil's time, has become a commonplace of literary commentary since McLuhan[3] – that the reader reading a novel is performing a function which is similar to the way in which he or she interprets the objective world. We encountered this idea in connection with Ulrich's reflections on Bonadea and her 'System[...] des Glücks'(552) ('system of happiness')[4]. 'Wirklichkeit', whether in the world at large or in a novel, involves acts of the imagination. Just as a literary work requires the intermeshing of narrative and the reader's imagination, so 'Wirklichkeit' in its wider context is an inconceivably complex 'Gedankenexperiment' conducted by mankind as a whole.

This emerges from consideration of the account of the first meeting of the 'Parallelaktion'. I have arranged a number of extracts from the relevant chapter in the order of their appearance in the text. The first orientates the reader:

Shortly afterwards, at Diotima's house, the first major session of the patriotic campaign was held. (162)

Here we encounter standard, third person, past tense narrative of the kind which Musil has poked fun at in his opening chapter: 'Beware!', he seems to be saying, 'Here you are entering a world that is fictional!'

Among the characters at the meeting is the hero. He is bored. Another condition is here added to those already accumulated:

He began – God only knows why [the narrator assures us that he is not omniscient – PP], perhaps to while away the time or to avoid simply standing there all on his own – to think of the carriage-ride to this meeting. (175)

We have been present at a meeting but are now required to absent ourselves from it temporarily – the extra sub-condition between the parenthetic dashes implies that the absence will be temporary – and go back via the memory of one of the characters to something that happened to him a little earlier. The spatial and temporal shifts required of the reader are already quite complex and there are more to follow. Ulrich recalls the words of the old aristocrat in whose carriage he had driven to the meeting:

'That one's Pepi, and that one's Hans' Graf Leinsdorf explained on the journey [as he proudly points to the two horses pulling the carriage – PP].
(175)

This intriguing scrap of evidence of how another man's mind works has imprinted itself on Ulrich's memory. Leinsdorf's words are recalled because there is something about them which puzzles Ulrich – they are foreign to his way of thinking. One imagines Ulrich following Leinsdorf's glance, trying to see the horses through the older man's eyes and perhaps speculating in more general terms about the kind of relationship with the world that Leinsdorf's words imply. Is the old gentleman weak in the head as he fills his world with the objects he has named or is he doing something quite normal? But Ulrich passes quickly on to a train of thought which is distinctively his own and stands in sharp contrast to the careless way in which Leinsdorf has fitted the horses into his personal vision of the world. Ulrich wonders how such magnificent animals might actually experience their environment:

It was difficult to comprehend what was going on in the animals; it was a fine morning and they were running. Perhaps feeding and running are the only great horse-passions, if one takes into account that Pepi and Hans had been gelded and knew love not as tangible desire but only as a bloom and glow that occasionally covered their view of the world with clouds giving off a faint radiance. (175)

Ulrich is here making an effort to see things as the horses see them (and the effort continues after this for some twenty-five lines of text); we know, of course, that it is a man who is making this attempt, and we are reminded in the text that this vision is anthropomorphic, but it does seem that Ulrich, after experiencing

Leinsdorf's naive vision, tries to bring the world back into sharper focus.

In the course of this scene the reader has been 'present' at a meeting, he has 'left' the meeting guided by Ulrich's memory, he has pondered the significance of Leinsdorf's innocent words, made strange when framed by Ulrich's intense curiosity, and now finally he is wondering what it is like to be a horse! Having persuaded the reader to become absorbed in this last activity, the narrator prepares a gentle shock for him:

And suddenly Graf Leinsdorf had sat up in the cushions and asked Ulrich:
[...]                                                                    (176)

Leinsdorf's question breaks in on Ulrich's equine reverie, and, with the interruption, the reader realises that he has become as deeply involved in Ulrich's daydream as he was in the meeting where this private act of memory is performed. The daydream has the same quality of immediacy as the meeting. But even at this moment of vivid surprise the narrator keeps a syntactical grip on the complex mental operations he performs. His use of the pluperfect tense indicates that this interruption, having taken place before the meeting described at the outset of this scene, is another act of memory.

The return to the 'reality' of the meeting – a triumph of mental agility in its own right – is effected quite unobtrusively. One moment Leinsdorf is in the carriage with Ulrich:

[Leinsdorf] let [...] himself fall back again into the cushions [...]    (176)

The next moment he is back with Ulrich at the 'Parallelaktion' meeting:

Ulrich, in fact, felt a stirring of affection for this naive old aristocrat, who was still conversing with Diotima and Arnheim [...]                    (176)

From the moment when Ulrich left the meeting in imagination to the point when he returns to it, little more than two paragraphs have elapsed, but the reader has been asked to follow five shifts of consciousness;[5] or, to express this in von Mises' terms, the reading of this section of narrative has added five extra sets of conditions which the reader must observe to follow through this 'Gedankenexperiment' to its conclusion.

What does Ulrich make of a reality which is formed, in part, from the often inferior 'Gedankenexperimente' of contemporaries?

## 'Wirklichkeit' – the case against

### Past is present, present past

In Part II, Chapter 41, Ulrich gazes up at a church and wonders at the way the hard contours of the stone impress the massive evidence of belief on his unbeliever's consciousness. Ulrich sees the church not only as a symbol of the way that religious dogma dictates to the faithful the way they ought to feel; it stands for the tyranny of past over present, the way that traditional modes of thinking and behaving leave their mark on modern life.

Ulrich spent only a few seconds standing in front of this church but these reached deep within him and pressed on his heart with the great primeval resistance against this world which has hardened into millions of tons of stone, against this petrified moonscape of feeling which one has been set down in without willing it.                                                     (130)

One notices the air of pessimism about the word 'willenlos' ('without willing it') in the above passage – a view strengthened in the subsequent sentences where Ulrich reflects that a man's private emotions are rather like a metal plate which the world stamps with its myriad images.

Some men are more susceptible than others to the unrelenting pressure of the past. Ulrich, having returned home after his father's death, is amazed at the undertaker's attitude to life. When Ulrich asks him to explain the origin of the various specialised terms and phrases which are intended to help the bereaved in their selection of the appropriate arrangements for the funeral, the undertaker is unable to do so even though he uses these terms every day of his working life: 'He stood before Ulrich like a reflex arc of the human brain, connecting stimulus and action without any accompanying awareness' (692). As far as Ulrich can judge, the man not only makes the funerals he supervises a slavish imitation of traditional practice but also conducts his daily life according to the same principle.

'Wirklichkeit', for the undertaker, is the source of a single and absolute imperative: 'Conform!' In this atmosphere of death Ulrich is filled with such horror of tradition that he sweeps it aside with words that read like an abjuring of the past and its hold on the present: 'Not only is Father dead, but the ceremonies which surround him are dead, too. His will and testament are dead. The people who appear here are dead [...] all of this belongs to the limestone of life, not to its sea!' (696).

## *'Seinesgleichen geschieht'*

Clarisse finds Ulrich's intellectual detachment infuriating and challenges him about it. When he leaves her house and boards a tram to
return home his mind is troubled by what she has said, because he
senses that there is some truth to it. His intellectual activity seems a
a poor thing when measured against the lives of others – for
example, the evident bourgeois satisfaction of the woman sitting
next to him with an opera glass in her lap; but a mood of defiance
takes hold of him and he is filled with the conviction that, if he has
renounced activity, then people such as those sitting close to him
have surrendered their freedom: 'This serving-as-raw-material-for-
history was something that annoyed Ulrich' (360). These men and
women are pawns in the hands of a higher power. In Ulrich's
imagination the tram becomes a symbol of the way the pressures of
the moment have numbed their will, propelling them forward in a
direction and into a future which are not of their choosing:

> The shining, swinging box in which he rode, seemed to him like a machine
> in which a few hundred kilograms of people were shaken this way and that
> to make future of them [...] [He] was incensed by this unresisting
> acceptance of changes and conditions, the helpless contemporaneity, the
> subservient absence of any plan, the simple jogging-along with the
> centuries which was really unworthy of human beings.               (360)

Ulrich asserts his freedom by getting off at the next stop and
continuing his journey on foot.

The chapter from which this scene is taken is entitled 'Seinesgleichen geschieht oder warum erfindet man nicht Geschichte?'[6] ('The
same kind of things happen again, or why doesn't one invent
history?') 'Seinesgleichen geschieht' – which, as we have seen, is
the title of Part II of *The Man without Qualities* – is important for an
understanding of the work as a whole, and of Musil's view of
'Wirklichkeit' in particular. 'Seinesgleichen' is described as 'that
which has already been pre-shaped by generations, the ready-made
language, not only of the tongue but also of perceptions and
feelings' (129).[7] As he glances at the woman in the tram Ulrich is
conscious of a ritual being performed. Though she may feel that her
existence is unique, Ulrich considers that she is merely living life at
second hand. In Part II, Chapter 116, where Ulrich reviews his life
so far and promises himself that things will change from this
moment onwards, the link between 'das Seinesgleichen' and 'Wirklichkeit' is firmly established. Here we read: 'Seinesgleichen

geschieht [the same kind of things happen again] because life – bursting with self-importance over its here and now, but in the last analysis a very uncertain, indeed positively unreal condition! – hurls itself into the couple of dozen cake-moulds which make up reality' (591). The precious stuff of life is transformed into second-hand experiences and stereotyped behaviour which form much of contemporary 'Wirklichkeit'. Some men and women are, in Musil's view, fully aware of this process. They feel alienated from the actions which convention assigns to them: self-consciousness inhibits spontaneous action. Musil often signals this by expressing an instance of 'das Seinesgleichen' or stereotyped 'Wirklichkeit' through the medium of a theatrical image. In Part II, Chapter 120, for instance, Ulrich is standing at the window at a meeting, watching the crowd beneath demonstrate against the 'Parallelaktion'. The people below mistake him for Leinsdorf and make threatening gestures towards him, but Ulrich realises that their anger is feigned. Ulrich sees their action as a theatrical performance:

The gaze of them all was directed from below at his face and sticks were brandished emphatically at him. A few steps further on where the road branched off and gave the impression of disappearing into the wings, most of them were already removing their grease-paint; there would have been no point to making further threats without an audience, and, in a way which seemed quite natural to them, the excitement disappeared from their faces at the same moment. (631)

Thus we have a curious mirror effect. The 'Parallelaktion' is a symbol of the poverty of contemporary 'Wirklichkeit', but here the protest against the 'Parallelaktion' is itself unmasked as meaningless gesturing.

Theatricality is detected in unlikely places. One night Ulrich bumps into a prostitute; he notices her 'night make-up' (651) and this term perhaps suggests a dramatic performance to him. He has heard more or less what she has said and is in no doubt about her meaning; but he has her repeat her words and runs through in his mind the kind of scene that will unfold if he falls in with what she wants; he imagines that she will put her arm through his 'with a tender confidence and a slight hesitation of the kind that only occurs when those who know each other well meet for the first time after parting through no fault of their own' (651). Here again we find elements of theatre: the 'greasepaint', the repetition of the lines, the rehearsing of the gestures. The narrator soon makes the analogy explicit. This scene, he says, is: 'the human comedy played by ham-actors' (652).

Sex without passion is not the preserve of prostitution. The relationship between Gerda and Ulrich also bears the stigma of 'Wirklichkeit'. When Gerda comes to see Ulrich at his home she knows that he will think that she is offering herself to him. She surrenders to the situation. Ulrich, for his part, has ceased to be attracted to Gerda but attempts to seduce her out of misplaced gallantry. The divorce of action and will is, on both sides, total; the reader is made to feel that this scene in the novel runs its course with virtually no personal involvement by the two people concerned. Eventually Gerda becomes hysterical but, even as she screams, her consciousness records the hiatus between deed and will: 'She was overcome by a sense of theatricality, but sat alone and forlorn in the dark auditorium and could do nothing to stop her fate being played out with screaming and fury, nor indeed to stop herself being involuntarily caught up in the play' (623). *The Man without Qualities* is, at one level, Musil's protest that such situations occur so often in the contemporary world.

### *'Systeme des Glücks'*

Ulrich's response to Clarisse's taunting is, as we have seen, one of surprising strength. His irritation seems excessive. Why is it that he feels such scorn for the simple existence of the people whom he sees on the tram? In fact his feeling is derived from an instinctive urge to restore his inner equilibrium. His annoyance is the outward manifestation of a concern for the delicate inner balance of his life. The principle of conduct which is glimpsed here is demonstrated more clearly in Bonadea, Ulrich's mistress.

Bonadea, who considers herself a completely modern woman, naturally dresses according to the very latest fashion. The narrator is not impressed by the work of Viennese couturiers – not once does he pause to describe Bonadea's latest extravagance; what *does* interest him deeply is the effect that fashion has on Bonadea as evidence of her total view of things: 'She had always dressed as a woman of elegance must and, every six months, she felt an awe at the latest fashion as if she were in the presence of eternity' (525).

Fashion is only one aspect of what the narrator calls 'Systeme des Glücks' (522) ('systems of happiness'). Such a system comprises 'convictions, prejudices, theories, hopes, the belief in something or other, thoughts [. . .]' (526). These enjoy a pseudo-objective existence in the external world, for the individual unconsciously projects them, and then 'discovers' their existence, apparently in outer reality: 'By advancing us the wherewithal which we lend to them, they all serve the purpose of presenting the world in a light whose rays emanate from us, and this is basically the task for which everyone has his special system' (526). The narrator uncovers the individual's internal 'accounting' showing that here debit is indistinguishable from credit and cause inseparable from effect – the circular argument reflecting the circular principle on which the 'System des Glücks' depends. Bonadea follows the fashions; Leinsdorf gives his horses childish names; Diotima and Arnheim go through the charade of 'Seele'. The reason for all these practices is fear of the unpredictability of life with its real dangers:

With considerable artistry of varying kinds we create an illusory illumination with the assistance of which we manage to live alongside the most monstrous things while remaining completely calm [...]. Such a way of behaving is considerably below the level of our understanding, but it is precisely this which proves that our feelings are heavily involved.

(526–7)[8]

Turning his back on his actual situation, the individual spins around himself a cocoon of habits, conceptions, ideas and beliefs, and – thus snugly protected from life – calls *this* 'Wirklichkeit' ('reality').

Ulrich, having discovered underlying strategies for psychic survival in the people around him will ultimately recognise that he, too, has a 'survival strategy'.

### 'Wirklichkeit' and science

Though one might expect science to appear in the novel as a kind of antidote to 'Wirklichkeit' in the form thus described, in fact it is something else to add to the catalogue of 'convictions, prejudices [...], thoughts [...]' (526); it is spun into the cocoon, and it, too, becomes part of 'Wirklichkeit': Leinsdorf devotes himself to patriotic good works feeling that this is his duty as an aristocrat; Ulrich's father serves the legal system and the social hierarchy he believes was ordained by God; Bonadea subjects herself to the dictatorship of fashion. Each, in his or her own way, has renounced selfhood and freedom. Ulrich sees through these systems and so they have no hold on him. But science is a subtler threat for it places in jeopardy the notion that men have any self or any freedom to renounce at all. Once mankind had a personal relationship with creation; now, science finds no evidence of any such relationship: 'the dissolution of the anthropocentric attitude which for so long

94

held mankind to be the centre of the universe, but which has now been in retreat for centuries, [has] finally reached the "I"' (150). Once at the heart of things, mankind is now just particles blown about by unfeeling cosmic forces, with scarcely a shred of identity, a scrap of initiative, to call its own. Ulrich explains to Diotima:

'The "I" is losing the importance which it has had up to now, as a sovereign issuing actions by decree; we get to know the laws of its development, the influence of its environment, its structural types, its disappearance at the moments of most intensive activity, in a word, the laws which govern its formation and its behaviour.' (474)

Curiously it is not only people like Diotima who seem unpertur-bed by such developments; scientists themselves have not drawn the necessary conclusions from their activity. Their work foments a revolution in thinking about mankind, but in their private lives they carry on as if nothing had happened. What is to be done about such a state of affairs? Ulrich's answer is simple – too simple. Reality, he says, must be abolished.


### Doing away with 'Wirklichkeit'

Ulrich, in conversation with Diotima, offers rather unhelpful advice on how to manage people: '"You've started something extremely dangerous, great cousin. People are perfectly happy if one leaves them unable to turn their ideas into reality!"' (289). Diotima, rather irritatedly, retorts: '"And what would you do then [...] if you ruled the world for a day??"' (289). Ulrich gives the strange reply: '"I would probably be forced to abolish reality!"' (289).[9]

Ulrich has taken Diotima for a walk in the country, she has got her feet wet, and now, as she stands 'led astray and fearful [...] on a clod of earth' (288), she has to suffer Ulrich's inconsiderate intellectualising. Ulrich overlooks her plight; what he has to say is more important to him than Diotima's elegant shoes and dress: '"We vastly overestimate immediacy, the sense of the present, that which is here now; I mean, just like your being here with me in this valley as if we had been put in a basket and the lid of the moment has fallen shut. We overestimate that"' (289). Stranded on her little island of earth surrounded by water, Diotima is hardly likely to pay attention to what Ulrich is saying; she has other more pressing, more 'real' things on her mind: the state of her clothes, her wet feet, her annoyance at Ulrich's lack of gallantry – in other words, precisely that concern and urgency which Ulrich now describes with such detachment and unconcern for her present state. Ulrich explains that each moment in a person's life makes such strident claims that what are otherwise dominant drives – beliefs, principles, aspirations, goals, resolutions – tend to be pushed to one side. 'Wirklichkeit', exerting its power through the moment, makes men and women passive; they merely react to situations, keep up appearances as best they can, letting strategy and conviction go by the board. But Ulrich's flippant disregard for Diotima is, at another level, a joke at his own expense – he demonstrates quite clearly here that 'Wirklichkeit' makes pressing demands that overrule intellectual considerations. It is a lesson, however, which he finds easier to preach than to practise himself.

### Narrator and hero

Though the narrator often seems to be, as it were, looking over Ulrich's shoulder, his point of view is not identical with the hero's. This holds true even if one believes that Musil is indistinguishable from the narrator of *The Man without Qualities* and that Ulrich and the narrator are one and the same person.[10] Ulrich is caught up in the world of the novel – his detachment is again and again deflated by being presented as an illusion; the narrator sees that world from a little further off and has the advantage of hindsight as well. Ulrich senses the forces that threaten society and tries to understand them; the narrator has actually seen what happens when they are unleashed – he has been through World War I.[11] The narrator's understanding of the world is not more profound than Ulrich's, but he appears to draw on a larger store of experience. I believe that more readers and commentators would recognise the importance of this distinction between narrator and hero had Musil expressed it as clearly as he intended. But sometimes his attempts to do this are unsuccessful.

This may have been a consequence of Musil's failure to keep in touch with his public. Had he been writing with a particular audience consistently in mind, with constant 'feedback' from readers of recent publications, he might have been more successful in judging what he had to make explicit and what he could leave readers to deduce.[12] Sometimes when he tries to make things clear the narrative remains obscure. His treatment of the theme of the hero's attitude to 'Wirklichkeit' is a case in point.

Very early in the text of the novel the narrator discusses what he calls 'Wirklichkeitssinn' ('sense of reality') and 'Möglichkeitssinn' ('sense of possibility').[13] He contends here that the contemporary situation requires the kind of person who, *while not losing sight of the world as it is*, views it as a springboard for positive future developments. Here we have a theory in search of some narrative substance; passages such as the chapter where these terms are discussed exasperate many critics who find the text often dry and philosophical. In this case another, more serious charge must be added to this, for in fact here the theory is mismatched to the action in the novel which it is evidently intended to explain. The previous chapter has dealt with Ulrich's father, the subsequent one will be concerned with Ulrich, and it is natural for the reader to assume that the terms in the present chapter, 'Wirklichkeitsmensch' ('man of reality') and 'Möglichkeitsmensch' ('man of possibility'), relate to father and son respectively.

Though Ulrich's father is indeed a 'Wirklichkeitsmensch', a considerable part of the narrative of *The Man without Qualities* is concerned with the various ways in which Ulrich fails to live up to the theory of living as a 'Möglichkeitsmensch'. These failures have to do, paradoxically, with Ulrich's attitude to 'Wirklichkeit'. The reader is quite right to feel that the work is unclear on this point. It is difficult to see Ulrich other than as the man of possibility. The 'Möglichkeitsmensch' is the kind of person 'for whom a real thing has no more meaning than a thing in the mind' (17) and 'who is the first to give the new possibilities their meaning and their purpose' (17) – this certainly sounds as if it must refer to Ulrich! But, if we read very closely, we realise that the 'Möglichkeitsmensch' sets bounds to his experimenting, he wants to make it work in practice as well as in his head, which means that he must pay attention to what can actually be achieved. So he focusses his thoughts on 'possible *reality*' (17) (my emphasis) for 'It is reality which awakens the possibilities, and nothing could be so absurd as to deny that' (17). Ulrich *does* deny this as we have seen; his desire to do away with reality is a recurrent motif in his conversations with Diotima.

Part I, Chapter 4, can be seen as Musil's rather unsuccessful attempt to equip his reader with the means to judge the quality of his hero's perception and the worth of his undertakings. The narrator suggests that Ulrich has to tread a middle way. If he is overwhelmed by a world which insists that he think and feel and live as it – a complex and collective 'it' – demands, he will fail; if he gives free rein to his imagination and devises solutions which, however intellectually distinguished they may be, have no actual bearing on lived experience he fails also. For the greater part of the novel as published by Musil, the hero makes mistakes that belong in the latter category. I believe that the novel would have gained if Musil had made the critical detachment of the narrator from the hero more tangible. It is only when the reader tunes his attention very closely to the narrator's irony that he senses the constant touches of amused irritation at the way that the hero, with the insouciance and inexperience of (relative) youth, fails to grasp the urgent messages that life is sending him.

### Ulrich's solipsistic position collapses

Throughout the period with which Part II of *The Man without Qualities* is concerned, Ulrich's desire to lead a quiet and private existence is continually frustrated. His official duties with the 'Parallelaktion' divert his attention from his intellectual experiment, the 'Urlaub vom Leben'; Bonadea comes to his house on threadbare excuses and seduces him; Clarisse pours scorn on him for his passivity and tries to drag him out of himself; Gerda Fischel and her boy-friend, Hans Sepp, a supporter of the Pan-German party, berate him for being a reactionary. But it takes Ulrich a very long time to realise that, though it may appear that external claims on his attention are making his life difficult, in fact it is his attitude to 'Wirklichkeit' which is at fault.

Some months have elapsed since the time when Ulrich was arrested. Interest in the 'Parallelaktion' has already dropped off so much that, long before a meeting is scheduled to finish, only the 'inner circle' is left in the salon. Arnheim, Diotima, Leinsdorf, Ulrich and General Stumm have been joined by Tuzzi who has just returned home. Even these few faithful members are so devoid of ideas that the narrator catches them 'off their guard' in a symbolic pose as they wait vacantly 'as if they were standing around a well looking in' (587) for an inspiration that never comes. This moment of inactivity betrays the meaninglessness of the whole undertaking.

As conversation starts up once more, Ulrich comes quite literally to his senses. His gaze and attention are fixed sharply on the people and objects around him; at the same time he is subjecting his former ideas to a complementary critical scrutiny: 'What was the meaning of his having said to Diotima that one ought to abolish reality?!' (590). In fact, this was simply wrong-headed and, in practical terms, he had actually lived according to different principles, as a man 'who looked upon life as a task demanding activity and a sense of mission' (592); despite his scorn for 'Wirklichkeit', his most pressing underlying concern has always been to test out his intellectual designs in actual reality.[14] To this inner awakening corresponds an opening of his senses to the immediate environment which Ulrich now sees and feels with rare intensity: 'Tuzzi spoke. As if his ear were hearing the first sounds of the morning, Ulrich heard him say [. . .]' (594). (What Tuzzi actually says is not important for our purpose; what matters is the careful attention that the narrator pays to Ulrich's new delight in the *act* of hearing.) Each person stands out, framed in Ulrich's intense interest. Abbreviated sentences, punctuation, indeed the arrangement of the print on the page heighten this effect: 'Ulrich looked at Diotima' (595) – this is a finished statement; 'Tuzzi smiled' (595), 'Arnheim sat unmoved' (595) – here one has the impression that Ulrich's eyes are moving slowly from one person to the next; they alight finally on Stumm von Bordwehr: 'The General was cleaning his horn-rimmed spectacles' (595) – this last sentence is one whole paragraph. It is as if the narrator were striving to give the effect that Ulrich is fixing each visual impression in his memory as vivid monuments to an insight which now seems to him so obvious that he can hardly understand how he has overlooked it before – namely that involvement in existence is a categorical imperative.

But the intensity of Ulrich's awareness of others increases his sense of being separate from them: 'it seemed to him that all decisive moments in his life had been accompanied by just such an impression of astonishment and loneliness' (596). Ulrich is borne to and fro by powerful emotions: the need to leave this community and the fear of the solitude that will then take hold of him. He feels 'as if something was trying to tear him away from the people with whom he was sitting, and although they were all quite indifferent to him, his will suddenly planted arms and feet firmly to resist it' (596). It is only when Ulrich's impulse to give his life a new direction becomes unbearably strong – Musil is preparing for the meeting with Agathe and the brother/sister experiment in living – that the hero becomes aware how deeply involved he is in the 'Parallelaktion'. Despite his non-committal attitude Ulrich has become, in part at least, precisely the 'Wirklichkeitsmensch' ('man of reality') whom he despises.

Involvement in the 'Parallelaktion' has, however, taught him something positive: that his half-serious suggestions for abolishing 'Wirklichkeit' were a disguise for his yearning for action. What, then, have we learnt of Musil's view of 'Wirklichkeit'? If we approach the notion through Ulrich's perspective as this emerges in Part I and Part II we will be left with a false impression: that Musil sees 'Wirklichkeit' as the stereotyped world of 'das Seinesgleichen' – 'Wirklichkeit' in these terms is contemporary civilisation seen from the jaundiced viewpoint of a discontented and, in the eyes of the world, relatively unsuccessful intellectual. But we must recognise another aspect. For 'Wirklichkeit' is not only the sham, but the substance beneath the sham as well – and this substance catches Ulrich unawares, first from the angle of objectivity – the great historical surge of energy that is active even in people and institutions that seem to have capitulated to 'das Seinesgleichen' – and second from the angle of subjectivity, his own inner self beyond the level of consciousness that protests against the intellectual pose and demands fulfilment. He finds time to explore this dimension of 'Wirklichkeit' only after he has thrown off the irksome duties connected with the 'Parallelaktion'.

As we have seen, Musil's view of 'Wirklichkeit' is very complex and is made up of many strands, only some of which we have been able to consider here. In the present study, the investigation of this theme has served two functions: first, to demonstrate that some of the themes with which Musil structures *The Man without Qualities* can be subtle, intricate and extensive (themes such as 'morality', 'Geist', 'der andere Zustand', 'genius' and many others could be shown to be equally complex); second, to serve as a measure of the process of maturing in the hero. The 'Parallelaktion' provides, as we have seen, the immediate setting for much of Ulrich's activity in Part I and Part II; it deserves investigation in its own right.

## The 'Parallelaktion'

In Musil's Kakanien, in 1913, plans are afoot to mark the seventieth anniversary in 1918 of Kaiser Franz Joseph's accession to the throne with a whole year of public celebrations. Since Germans have already made plans to celebrate, in the same year, the thirtieth anniversary of the rule of their Kaiser, the Austrian enterprise is given the name, the 'Parallelaktion'. Against his will and better judgement, Ulrich finds himself appointed secretary to the 'Parallelaktion' by its initiator, Graf Leinsdorf, and thus becomes a reluctant participant in its activities.

The 'Parallelaktion' is Musil's invention. It is designed as a fictional focus for aspects of Musil's study of human behaviour; Ulrich would like to remain aloof, but his consciousness is constantly assailed by inanities which rouse his intellectual curiosity. Examination of the 'Parallelaktion' reveals different aspects of its function as a literary device. First, it provides a frame within which upper-class society in Austria-Hungary immediately before World War I can be examined in some detail. (Historians have acknowledged the depth and succinctness of Musil's judgements on Kakanien, considering them to be valuable commentary on pre-World War I Austrian history.) Second, a hero who is constitutionally rather a hermit than a diplomat is forced, via the 'Parallelaktion', into repeated meetings with the kind of people whom he would avoid if left to himself, including Leinsdorf, Arnheim, Diotima and Stumm; his involuntary involvement in a rich social life provokes a wide range of confrontations and stimulates innumerable observations which enrich the novel. Third, not only does the device of the 'Parallelaktion' lead to much dramatic 'business' within the plot of the novel, but it also offers Musil the opportunity for complex interweaving of narrative strands and provocative juxtaposing of material. (A chapter which explores the inner world of Arnheim, for example, is followed by one which recreates the mood of Moosbrugger in his prison cell – the reader is left to puzzle over whether this arrangement is to be seen as a contrast or a comparison.)[15] Fourth, the 'Parallelaktion' has an inherent irony, the planned year of celebration is due to fall at a time when Franz Joseph will, in fact, be dead and the Empire he ruled will be on the point of dissolution. Accordingly, the reader is naturally disposed to question the thoughts, feelings and actions of the leading members of Kakanien society – to see these as possible factors in the impending disaster. Thus, the narrator's observations and commentaries seem to arise as spontaneous replies to questions which readers tend to ask themselves. With the subtle prompting of that consistently ironic enquiry, with the setting of intention against action, of fact against appearance, of will against way, and drawing on all the resources of the 'Parallelaktion' as a literary device, Musil guides us towards an awareness of some of the forces at work in European culture; he formulates his insights with the epigrammatic precision of one who, even in his dismay at human folly, makes paradox, antithesis and inconsistency serve a purpose which we shall attempt to identify in this section.

Musil took evident pleasure in engineering Ulrich's involvement in the 'Parallelaktion'. Ulrich himself has no intention of following his father's instructions and offering his services but his creator determines otherwise. The press has heard rumours about the

'Parallelaktion' before it has properly come into existence – a workers' newspaper condemns it, saying that 'this is merely a new sensation for the ruling class to set alongside the latest sex-murder' (156) – a formulation which incidentally plays on the juxtaposition of socially acceptable and insane behaviour which is a recurrent theme of the 'Parallelaktion'. A worker, the worse for drink, argues with two 'Bürger' about the merits of the 'Parallelaktion', a policeman appears, Ulrich unwisely offers a comment of his own and is arrested. When Ulrich reveals that his father is a nobleman the official taking his particulars no longer feels competent to handle the case and, eventually, Ulrich is interviewed by the Police Commissioner himself. He, it transpires, has recently been approached by Leinsdorf to trace Ulrich whose name does not appear in the official list of addresses; recognising that he has before him, not a criminal but a gentleman like himself, the Police Commissioner devises his own charming 'sentence' – Ulrich must report to Leinsdorf without delay! Ulrich, having exploited class solidarity to extricate himself, feels a social obligation to carry out the terms of the 'sentence' and goes to see Leinsdorf. At this meeting he is appointed secretary to the 'Parallelaktion'. Thus it appears that the 'Parallelaktion' is both the initial instigator and the ultimate beneficiary of this chain of coincidences. From this point onwards in Part II, much of Ulrich's time will be spent in making sceptical remarks about suggestions put forward to, and put forward by, the 'Parallelaktion' committee – but the manner in which he becomes a member of the 'Parallelaktion' indicates the extent to which he is unconsciously bound by the loyalties and habits of his social class, the 'Bürgertum', which has thrown in its lot with the aristocracy.

Leinsdorf represents some of the eccentricities of the Viennese aristocracy. He is not yet an old man, but his intellectual horizon is circumscribed by a desire to freeze the Empire in its present place, defying the force of history or, as he formulates it in the fluent language of paternalism which lulls to sleep only his own critical faculty, '"to offer [...] a helping hand from above"' (89). He persuades himself, against the background of constant ideological strife in his country, that all the Emperor's subjects, of whatever nationality or class, would be able to agree with his views if only they can be put across with sufficient persuasive force. He is assisted in this conviction by an inability to work out quite what his own position is. A favourite saying of his is: '"after all, we're all socialists at heart"' – we can imagine how such a sentiment must have shocked his fellow-lords in the Austrian Upper Chamber. But what he understands by socialism would scarcely have been recognised as such by any contemporary social democrat. In a private conversation with Ulrich he confides: "that true socialism wouldn't be, as people tend to think, the worst thing that could happen. [. . .] [A] social-democratic republic with a strong ruler as its head [would be] by no means an impossible structure for the State" (849)! It is easy to imagine why a man of such conspicuous lack of political awareness will alienate the supporters and the opponents of the Establishment alike, while all the while remaining convinced that he is promoting both patriotism and the cause of peace which he sets as the provisional goals of the 'Parallelaktion'.

He directs Ulrich to another key member of the 'Parallelaktion' who is committed to the same goals, namely Diotima. This 'Hydra of beauty' (95), as Ulrich calls her – thereby gently mocking her frequent allusions to Classical culture – has made a successful transition from relatively humble 'bürgerlich' origins to the fringes of Viennese high society. Her salon owes its success to the patronage of young aristocrats (who happen to find it a convenient rendez-vous for their love affairs)[16] and to her skill in holding forth from the store of intellectual and cultural trivia which she has accumulated, first as a model schoolgirl, later through her contact with the world of diplomacy as the wife of a senior Foreign Office official. Her brain functions 'like a small damp sponge which releases what it has stored within itself without putting it to any particular use' (98); she is an appropriate subject through which Ulrich can study the contemporary use and abuse of idealistic sentiment. The name 'Diotima' itself contains a satirical message. This twentieth-century Diotima might see herself as being blessed with the wisdom of the Diotima for whom Socrates expressed such deep admiration; she might derive further satisfaction from the thought that the poet Hölderlin – in whose work the Classical merges with the Romantic – gave the same name to the woman he adored. But, as the action unfolds, this Diotima will be revealed to be doubly unfit to bear such a noble name – she will be shown to be as lacking in common sense as she is unwise in her choice of lover.

On the very day on which Diotima meets Ulrich for the first time – and here the shaping hand of the author is clearly to be seen – she has met the other man who will play an important role in her life, the Prussian, Dr Paul Arnheim. She knows him as a person of diverse talents: an entrepreneur, a patron of the arts, a leading intellectual and writer. But she is too politically naive to consider that his presence in Vienna might not be pure coincidence and that his decision to prolong his stay might be due to anything other than desire to be close to her. One of Arnheim's firms manufactures artillery and armour-plate,[17] thus the 'Parallelaktion' has an appeal for him which is rather like that of a trade fair for a modern industrialist – it seems an excellent place to do business. He will quickly strike up a confidential relationship with a man who shares his interest in armament – the jovial representative of the 'Ministry of War' at the 'Parallelaktion', General Stumm von Bordwehr. Though Diotima's intuitions about Stumm are correct – for all his affability, Stumm always sends a shiver of some indefinable apprehension down her spine[18] – Diotima's growing love for Arnheim makes her deaf to Ulrich's warnings and blind to Arnheim's support for Stumm.

Diotima's first action on behalf of the 'Parallelaktion' is to insist that Arnheim be included in the deliberations of the central committee – thus, in an inspirational moment of Kakanien incompetence, a Prussian is set at the very heart of what is supposed to be a rallying-point for Austrian patriotism. Diotima brings this about in a mood of ecstatic enthusiasm 'in a kind of melting state [. . .] in which the "I" goes out into endless expanses and, conversely, the expanses of the worlds enter the "I", whereby one can no longer recognise what belongs to oneself and what is eternal' (110). In this passage Musil is unquestionably describing the state which elsewhere he calls 'der andere Zustand' (a sense of the mystical oneness of creation, which deeply fascinates him) – but here it is presented in virtual parody, for this state is brought about simply by the idea that Arnheim is indispensable to the 'Parallelaktion'! Prompted by his observations that people like Diotima habitually squander their most intense feelings on such worthless notions, Ulrich will reiterate his conviction that, for mankind to take hold of its own destiny, it must devote itself to systematic and impartial study of the realm of feeling. His advice to the 'Parallelaktion' – expressed to Leinsdorf at a meeting when all initiatives seem to have cancelled each other out – gives shape to this conviction:

'Your Grace, [. . .] there is only one task for the 'Parallelaktion': to make a start on a general spiritual ['geistig'] inventory! We must do roughly what would be necessary if Judgement Day were to fall in the year 1918, the old spirit ['Geist'] were finished and a higher one were to begin. In the name of His Majesty, found a World Secretariat of Precision and Soul ['Seele']; before this happens, all other problems are insoluble or are only pseudo-problems!' (596–7)

This 'inventory' of the products of 'Geist' does not have an important explicit role in *The Man without Qualities* – though the title of Part III, 'Ins Tausendjährige Reich' ('Into the Millennium') may be seen as a gesture toward it. There is little support for Ulrich's proposal among other members and it is scarcely ever mentioned again. But it should not be overlooked since it is the direct expression, in the action of the novel proper, of one of Musil's central preoccupations. Although he chose, as the setting for his work, Austria before 1914, his intention was not primarily to reconstruct what had happened at that time. As Musil expressed it: 'The real explanation of real events does not interest me' (GWII, 939). He wanted not growth in knowledge about the past but growth in wisdom and understanding for the present and the future. The facts were not important in themselves but 'always inter-changeable' (GWII, 939); in a fictional representation of the pre-World War I era, Musil could make the attitudes, the illusions, the self-delusions which had helped to shape the course of history more transparent, more accessible to his reader than if he had written a historical account. Musil was fascinated by the prospect of the gains that would accrue to mankind if the critical criteria that science applies to the study of objective data could also be used in the study of feelings. He has Ulrich refer briefly to his 'inventory'-proposal in Part III, Chapter 38:

'[. . .] Today we are faced with too many kinds of possible ways of feeling and living. But is this difficulty not similar to the one which the understanding masters when it confronts a host of facts and a history of theories? And for this we have found a method, incomplete yet rigorous, which I do not need to describe to you. I ask you now, would it not be possible to find something similar for feeling?'                                                 (1038)

The implication is that, in the novel, a preliminary experiment is in progress to establish what might be learnt through a concerted effort, a large-scale inventory, of such a kind. Throughout this part of the narrative, the often ill-considered passions of contemporaries – such as Diotima's desire to make Arnheim the secretary of the 'Parallelaktion' or Leinsdorf's yearnings for social harmony – are filtered through the ironical consciousness of a narrator whose point of view is, as we have seen, close to Ulrich's. As suggestions pour in to the organisers of the 'Parallelaktion' from all quarters of the Empire, Ulrich diagnoses within many of them a blind attachment to some imperfectly perceived truth, some spurious ideal, which acts as a spur to fanaticism. As he explains to Leo Fischel, a bank director who shares something of Ulrich's pragmatic and sceptical liberalism and who plays a peripheral part in the 'Parallelaktion': 'You must know from study of history that true belief, true morality and true philosophy have never existed; yet the wars and acts of baseness and malevolence which have been unleashed on their account have borne fruit in reshaping the world' (134).

However frivolous Ulrich's remark may seem, he is making a serious point: he contrasts intention and effort. People tend not to see where their passions lead because they are caught up completely in the aura of overwhelming importance with which their feelings endow their words and deeds. What is needed is a dispassionate observer who can register the discrepancy between intention and effect – an observer who is not guided by 'Gefühl' ('feeling') but by 'Geist'. But with most of those connected with the 'Parallelaktion' the heart rules the head.

At the first meeting of the Central Committee the mood is one of confident expectation. We enter the meeting via a key-hole. Here Rachel, Diotima's Galician maidservant, is taking a surreptitious look at the assembled company. Although she sees only fragments, Rachel's eye is guided towards the essential: it alights on the 'gold-sabre-tassel of General Stumm von Bordwehr whom the War Ministry had dispatched, even though it had not actually been invited' (167). The uninvited guest will unobtrusively manoeuvre himself and his Ministry into the very centre of proceedings. Stumm's appointment as an unofficial ambassador for the armed forces to the 'Parallelaktion' turns out to be a master-stroke by his superiors, who may fail in the face of the enemy but who are capable of devising skilful stratagems to defeat their fellow-countrymen. Stumm's personality is perfect camouflage for his mission: fun-loving, self-deprecating, irrepressibly considerate and charming, he never loses sight of his goal – to obtain new artillery of deadly accuracy and fire-power. It seems that only Ulrich and Tuzzi, Diotima's husband, see through him; but Stumm counters Ulrich's taunts with such good-humour, deference and modesty, that even the hero seems to be taken prisoner by his subtlety. At the first meeting, following an opening address from Leinsdorf and Diotima's suggestion that the sub-committees of the 'Parallelaktion' should be modelled on the ministries, Stumm shows his hand: 'Si vis pacem para bellum!' (180), he urges – in his view, the best expression for what Diotima calls the 'grand patriotic action' (171) is to reequip the army! Though Leinsdorf, fearing for his vision of

Austria as European peacemaker, quickly diverts attention away from the proposal it remains the only one of real substance that is put forward at any time.

Diotima's suggestion to structure the sub-committees of the 'Parallelaktion' according to the pattern of Austro-Hungarian ministries is accepted; however, the only major ministry which is not represented – the Ministry for War – will become the one with the most profound influence on 'Parallelaktion' proceedings. The excluded ministry quickly learns to subvert the working of an organisation of baffling inefficiency, which becomes little more than a scheme for meaningless job-creation. The various committees produce reports which are sent to Leinsdorf, who reads them assiduously on behalf of the Central Committee, and are then shelved indefinitely, pending a decision.[19] Items requiring more pressing attention are subject to an even more time-consuming bureaucratic ceremonial: they go first to the Court, thence to an appropriate ministry, on to the Central Committee of the 'Parallelaktion' and only then are they consigned to the limbo of a special working party.

An impressive amount of paper is passed to and fro; Ulrich develops a special filing system of his own with projects assigned to the category 'Forward to' or 'Back to' (depending on whether they relate to some past ideal or to a future utopia); Diotima searches frantically for the 'great idea' which will serve as a focus for all 'Parallelaktion' undertakings; Leinsdorf, with aristocratic scorn for all the intellectual activity around him, immerses himself, wherever possible, in the more earthbound suggestions of 'rifle clubs' and 'dairy co-operatives' which arrive in increasing numbers. But nothing of any real significance happens.

It is at about this point in the narrative that the scenes are described, which we examined briefly above,[20] in which Ulrich tries to explain to Clarisse why he is so inactive. We remember him, sitting on a tram pondering the chain of ideas which her aggressive questioning has prompted. As he looks around at the people sitting close to him, he reflects:

A hundred years ago they sat with similar expressions in a postchaise and in a hundred years' time God only knows what will be happening to them, but, as new people in new machines of the future, they'll be sitting there in just the same way – this was what he felt, and he was incensed by this unresisting acceptance of changes and conditions, the helpless contemporaneity, the subservient absence of any plan, the simple going-along-with-the-centuries, which was really unworthy of human beings.          (360)

What irritates Ulrich intensely here is the sense that the lives of those around him in the tram are shaped not by some overriding inner commitment or passion but rather by the outer structure of the world that surrounds them. Their lives are moulded by the peripheral, not the essential. Accordingly, they are in a passive frame of mind which encourages those people or movements in whom passion is strong, even if understanding is weak, to take them over. This observation is all the more ironically appropriate since the 'Parallelaktion' has taken over the directing of Ulrich's life.

However, there is an important distinction to be made between the life which Ulrich is leading and the life of those self-important individuals who surround him at the 'Parallelaktion'. They are impelled by what he calls 'the attitude of personal greed *vis-à-vis* experiences' (364), they concern themselves with 'where, when and to whom [something] happened' (364); he, on the other hand, considers primarily 'what happened' (364). We can see the differences of emphasis clearly in a subsequent chapter, 'General Stumm's attempt to bring order to civilian understanding' (370). Stumm has approached the problem of helping Diotima to find some 'great idea' for the 'Parallelaktion' with exemplary military efficiency, drawing on the resources of the Kriegsministerium (Ministry of War) to develop a 'battle-plan' covering the whole history of ideas! (Here the notion of a 'general inventory of the spirit' surfaces, in somewhat eccentric form, in Stumm's mind!) Stumm discovers that ideas have no loyalty; they pass indiscriminately from one faction to another and even cross the no man's land between ideologies and appear in the camp of the enemy.[21] This insight into intellectual affairs fills Stumm with consternation; as he expresses it in the vivid imagery of the soldier: '["It's just like] travelling second-class in Galicia and picking up crablice! It's the most filthy feeling of helplessness that I know"' (374). Stumm's discomfort comes from a completely instrumental concern with the ideas he is studying; they are only incidental to his real interests which are private and personal: he wants to further his career, he wants to dazzle his fellow-officers with a show of intellectuality, he wants to please Diotima, for whom he burns in unrequited Platonic passion. Ulrich sees things from a completely different perspective. He has no interest in personal advantage or in the success of the 'Parallelaktion'; Stumm tries to make ideas serve schemes for self-enhancement, Ulrich studies them for themselves. Stumm, in his pursuit of ideas is impelled by 'Gefühl' ('feeling'); Ulrich takes up the personally disinterested standpoint of 'Geist'.

In Diotima and Arnheim, the inflation of personality reaches even more grotesque proportions: their self-importance is such that the point where their love for each other reaches a summit of unbearable anticipation is described as the 'Silent meeting of two mountain-tops' (182) – the image which each projects towards the other, the sense of partaking in an occasion without precedent, the awareness of being representative figures in the vanguard of civilisation, all bind their love in powerful constraints. Although the love which each feels for the other is undoubtedly strong – the account of Arnheim's love-sickness, for example, is certainly not without sympathy[22] – it is quickly buried in effusions and generalities. The narrative contrasts what they want with what they get. The 'Parallelaktion' is a catalogue of such frustrations, juxtaposing feelings with thoughts, intentions with effects.

It is also, of course, a high-profile political phenomenon which, under pressure from the tensions and phobias of Kakanien public life, becomes a kind of working model of those forces. So, for example, when the 'nationalities' start to see the 'Parallelaktion' as a source of pan-German intrigue, Leinsdorf, with a stroke of stunning political ineptitude intended to bring about the reconciliation of all parties and factions, appoints a Pole to head the propaganda committee and thereby alienates the Germans as well! 'German youth', here represented by Gerda Fischel's boy-friend, Hans Sepp, start planning an anti-'Parallelaktion' demonstration.[23]

Thus, though a lot is happening all around the 'Parallelaktion', the enterprise itself is imitating Austria-Hungary at large and going nowhere fast. Leinsdorf makes repeated calls for action, but has no idea at all what form the action should take. Stumm apologetically reminds the members of the Central Committee of his suggestion about artillery and is supported by Arnheim and Tuzzi, but Diotima is horrified by such talk – it would mean rearming, she cries![24] This moment is the one we examined above when Ulrich comes to his senses and fixes his eyes on his environment in a new awareness of what is happening to him and around him. Now, too, at this point of unusual mental clarity – and therefore at a juncture to which Musil attaches enhanced significance – Ulrich puts forward his idea that the 'Parallelaktion' needs to turn its attention – on behalf of mankind at large – to a comprehensive review of the effects of human feeling on the course of human affairs – to take a dispassionate look at the influence on civilisation of passion in its countless forms. This, of course, was the proposal for an 'Erdensekretariat der Genauigkeit und Seele' ('World Secretariat of Precision and Soul') which we examined above.

Arnheim immediately attacks Ulrich's proposal as being typically impractical and intellectual. It is almost as if Arnheim has been given insight into Ulrich's most intimate intellectual concerns. He seems to have grasped intuitively the scheme that Ulrich is trying to work out through the 'Urlaub vom Leben'.[25] Ulrich is proposing to extend to humanity at large the attitude which he has adopted himself – and humanity as a whole cannot 'play at life' as Ulrich tries to do. Who, Arnheim wonders, will wake the dead when the hypothetical battles which he sees being waged in Ulrich's scheme have been fought?[26] Who – and this suggestion indicates yet again Musil's interworking of different narrative themes – would be willing to take responsibility for seeing what would happen if Moosbrugger (the murderer who is at the centre of so much of Ulrich's thinking) were freed? Ulrich does not answer these questions; instead he goes onto the offensive with an observation of his own designed to show that, however precarious his own attitude may be, the position of his rival is at least as untenable: '"I have been told that your participation in everything connected with the 'Campaign' that is in progress here – and [. . .] Frau Tuzzi [. . .] is to be seen only as a supplementary consideration! – is intended to help with the acquisition of large sectors of the Galician oil-fields?"' (642). Ulrich, with unabashed frankness, points to the way that Arnheim – in pursuit of material gain (and here Ulrich is relying on a strong rumour on the stock exchange which he has heard from Leo Fischel)[27] – has cruelly played with the feelings of the woman who loves him, has repressed genuine feelings of his own, and has flouted the trust of the other members of the 'Parallelaktion'. Perhaps Ulrich's openness is designed to make Arnheim aware of what kind of person he, Arnheim, is: for Arnheim has failed to recognise his own deviousness and, in an astonishing feat of Tartuffian self-deception, has maintained intact his own high opinion of himself! Illusions such as these are the 'building-blocks' of the 'Parallelaktion'. The structure, in itself, is meaningless, but it serves to instruct the reader. Each building-block is to be seen in relation to its neighbour, with the edifice as a whole, and with the total ironic intention of the author-architect. This is a 'folly', built by the 'Geist' of Kakanien.

Ulrich eventually decides to give up his post at the 'Parallelaktion', indeed to turn his back on contemporary civilisation as a whole. The outer stimulus for this decision will be the news of the death of his father which will take him away from Vienna for an extended period. But the 'Parallelaktion', it seems, is not willing to give Ulrich up without a struggle! Stumm is the first to discover that Ulrich has returned to Vienna, and he informs him of what has been going on in his absence. Piecing together some of the things Stumm has said, Ulrich works out the basis of the secret agreement between Arnheim and the Ministry of War: Arnheim's firm, if allowed to acquire interests in the Galician oil-fields, will supply the Austrian navy cheaply;[28] the Austrian armed forces thereby gain a close relationship with a supplier of armour-plating which will be all the more necessary given the strains emerging in a sensitive area in Galicia, on the border of the enemy, Russia. It might be expected that the Foreign Ministry would object to such close co-operation between a Prussian arms supplier and the Austrian forces, but the expert on whom they have relied to provide them with up-to-the-minute information on developments between Arnheim and the Ministry of War, the otherwise cool and efficient Sektionschef Tuzzi, has let them down.

Tuzzi has been misled over the nature of Arnheim's relationship with his wife – a 'Realpolitiker' like himself cannot conceive that Arnheim would place a deal on oil and arms in jeopardy by seducing the wife of an official whom he would need as an ally to settle the deal, if such a deal were really his objective. Tuzzi therefore assembles the facts he knows into a different pattern: the oil–arms deal is only a smokescreen for a supposed attempt by Arnheim, as an agent of the Tsar, to form a united front with those supporting pacifism in the 'Parallelaktion' (and, of course, Diotima is a key member of this faction) and thereby undermine the will of the Austro-Hungarian Empire to rearm and be in a position to defend itself. By the time Tuzzi realises that Arnheim's interest in his wife is in genuine conflict with his interests as an industrialist, the Foreign Ministry has lost much ground in its struggle with the Ministry of War, the plans for co-operation between Stumm and Arnheim are being consolidated, and a new threat has appeared in the form of Leinsdorf's insistence on some form of demonstrative action by the 'Parallelaktion'. The Foreign Ministry, fearing that Leinsdorf's militant pacifism will lead to war between the European powers, throws in its lot with Arnheim and Stumm and plots Leinsdorf's removal from the leadership of the 'Parallelaktion'.

So, in the time which Ulrich spends away from Vienna, the 'Parallelaktion' is shaped by a curious mélange of interests, ideas and emotions: Leinsdorf is pushing his desire for action to the point where it comprises his pacifist goal; Stumm wants rearmament but is prepared to tolerate pacifism to achieve it; Diotima is sublimating her frustrated desire for Arnheim, that 'Erotic coward!' (1036) as she now sees him, by reading all the available literature on the physiology and psychology of sex (such powerful stuff, indeed, that Bonadea discovers that even to describe it to Ulrich propels her inexorably into his bed!)[29]; Tuzzi, horrified by the tension inherent in the 'Parallelaktion', is moving towards the conclusion that the safest course is to throw in his lot with the Prussian arch-enemy (though this development is only recorded in a *Nachlaß* chapter).[30] Thus is the future of European diplomacy, and thereby the future of Europe, shaped by a curious love affair!

At the 'Grand Meeting' at the end of the published section of *The Man without Qualities*, Musil brings together most of the important members of the cast of characters he has used throughout the novel up to this point with the exception of Walter, Clarisse, Meingast, Linder, Hagauer and, of course, Moosbrugger. Everyone expects something decisive to be agreed, but the only motion passed is one which escapes the watchfulness of the leading figures. This is formulated as follows: 'Everyone should be free to die for his or her own ideas, but whoever causes human beings to die for the ideas of another is a murderer!' (1035); this carries a critical message from the author: the motion is a protest against a malignant tendency inherent in contemporary civilisation which the 'Parallelaktion' embodies: a tendency for things to be determined by a combination of chance and the scheming of people who are impelled by ruthless self-interest. This problem hinges, if we are to accept the narrator's position, on the relatively limp grip which the majority of people have on the direction of their lives – they live with great lassitude, they lack conviction, and they are therefore subjected to the curious effects generated by the nebulous will of the collective – a will often manipulated by the stunted passions of the unscrupulous and the emotionally unstable who see in the 'Parallelaktion' an opportunity to assert themselves.

What, then, does Musil achieve through the fictional device of the 'Parallelaktion'? There is a sense in which he takes up, in his narrative, the proposal for an 'Erdensekretariat der Genauigkeit und Seele' ('World Secretariat of Precision and Soul'): the 'Parallel-aktion' is a fragment of a 'Domesday Book', recording, if only within the compass of fiction, the secret feelings that find expression in human actions at this juncture in history – so, for example, Diotima's gushing enthusiasm for peace is traced back through relationships with her husband, Arnheim and Stumm, while Leins-dorf's dangerous bungling is placed against the backcloth of his hopes and aspirations. In each of the cases which Musil explores within the overall framework of the 'Parallelaktion', actions, statements and ideas are all followed through to their origins in some individual psyche; the totality of these cases makes up the instructive spectacle of folly, the small-scale 'inventory', that is the 'Parallelaktion'.

Through the medium of the 'Parallelaktion', Musil offers his readers a view not of what happened in Vienna before World War I but a kind of cut-away working model – a 'Seinesgleichen geschieht' ('The same kind of things happen again'). He brings forward for examination a set of people who see themselves – in the distorting mirror of 'Kakanien' reality – as representatives of Austrian 'Geist'; when seen in action through the transparent side of Musil's model, however, they are all revealed as misguided, self-seeking and spiritually impoverished.

Having examined aspects of the structure and content of *The Man without Qualities* we can turn to consider the very core of the work – Musil's attempt to contribute to the regeneration of contemporary civilisation by presenting, in fictional form, the sum of his insights, based on experiences gathered throughout his life. This is focussed on Ulrich – but Ulrich is best approached via the figure of the murderer whom he finds so compelling.

# 7

# MOOSBRUGGER – A STUDY IN APPLIED SUBJECTIVITY

Musil was rather wary of Moosbrugger, the psychopath and murderer; he preferred not to give public readings from the sections dealing with this character.[1] To have done so would have been to risk pandering to the public's taste for scandal and so to have given completely the wrong impression of his work as a whole. In *The Man without Qualities*, the study of sickness, affecting both individuals and society as a whole, is not an end in itself, but part of the search to heal civilisation. In civilised people, Musil argues, a layer of psychic processes responds to the demands of social life – this is the realm of self-images, of shared illusions and routine deceptions, of conventions of behaviour which Musil portrays critically in his studies of 'das Seinesgleichen'. In Moosbrugger, this layer is virtually absent and much deeper levels of feeling are constantly exposed to casual contact with the outer world. In this examination of psychopathic behaviour, Musil is following established practice among psychiatrists – he studies a mentally sick individual as a means to understanding mental processes which, though present in normal people, are much more difficult to detect there. Karl Jaspers, who was a psychiatrist before he turned to philosophy, points to the extraordinary immediacy of perception found both in the young and in some of the insane:

The very root of philosophising is seen in children and in the mentally ill. Sometimes it is [. . .] as if the fetters of general illusions were loosed and the individual were seized by truth. At the outset of some mental illnesses a person is shaken by metaphysical revelations [. . . ;] anyone looking on is overwhelmed by the impression that here a kind of covering under which we normally live out our lives [. . .] is being torn away. There is a profound meaning in the words 'Children and fools speak the truth.'[2]

The study of Moosbrugger provided Musil with a vehicle to study himself. Through Moosbrugger he could examine profound feelings and faculties which are part of the heritage of all human beings but which are usually overlaid by more superficial social skills. These include the operation of the will, and the intense fears and the welling anger that are provoked in the human organism's contact with outer reality. Once most individuals have learnt in childhood to control these powerful and ever-present psychic forces, they tend to repress awareness of them, and even to deny their existence.

The Moosbrugger-study provided Musil with a range of insights which he built into his text – the complex ways in which a person creates an image of how another thinks and feels. As we saw above, Musil starts out from a position of Machian sceptical subjectivism. How, he seems to ask himself, if my image of the world is formed simply from phenomena focussed in my head, can I hope to obtain objective, or even reasonably accurate, evidence of thoughts and feelings which find their focus in the head of another person?

It may seem that, in the context of a literary work, this is a pseudo-problem. Within *The Man without Qualities*, after all, there is not one man, Musil, thinking about another man, Moosbrugger; Moosbrugger, as a character, is totally encompassed within Musil's 'Gedankenexperiment'. There is no 'objective' Moosbrugger, existing outside the work, so Musil has the freedom to invent a 'Moosbrugger-mind' to which he has unlimited access – which he can know totally, in a way which no human being can know another human being in actual life. Musil, however, believed that he did possess, to quite a remarkable degree, the capacity to visualise the inner world of others, and, from the time of early adulthood, made a special study of actual cases of insanity, as we see in one of his letters:

[I] am concerned [...] with the scientific study of psychology [...] and [I believe] that, in the fine reports of the French psychiatrist, for example, I [...] can [...] both experience vicariously, and [...] depict every abnormality [...], transporting myself into the corresponding horizon of feeling, without my own will being seriously affected.       (*Briefe* I,24)

Karl Corino's recent researches prove that the figure of Moosbrugger was based on an experiment of the kind described here. Musil attempted to penetrate the inner world of a real murderer who lived in Vienna just before World War I.[3] In *The Man without Qualities*, Musil records, through the medium of Ulrich's preoccupations with Moosbrugger, his own experiences with that murderer. So comprehensive and self-critical was this undertaking that it is not only a record an obsession, but serves as a literary model for the functioning of the faculty of empathy in all human beings.

Moosbrugger has a vital place in the novel as a whole. The hero's concern with Moosbrugger in Part I and Part II requires a heavy counterbalance in Part III (and, presumably, Part IV). The counterweight to Moosbrugger is Agathe. From the time when Agathe makes her appearance in the novel, Ulrich's interest in Moosbrugger disappears almost completely. Moosbrugger is a figure from the period when Ulrich is a kind of urban thought-guerrilla – he wants to tap the resources of Moosbrugger's original vision of the world and his immense energy (resources available for the good as much as for the ill of society at large) and with this bring about change. The phase of *The Man without Qualities* in the course of which Ulrich is preoccupied with 'Wirklichkeit' is also the phase in which Moosbrugger plays a central part. Moosbrugger is, for the younger Ulrich, intellectual dynamite to blow up 'Wirklich-keit'. When no explosion takes place, not even a little one, Ulrich loses interest in the murderer; it seems likely that, even without Agathe's arrival his interest would have died a natural death. Moosbrugger is thus another of Ulrich's failures; it is, however, a magnificent failure.

To grasp how Musil sets about understanding a murderer we must expand our notion of the 'Gedankenexperiment' and here, I believe, the work of Edmund Husserl provides assistance. Husserl and Musil worked under the psychologist Carl Stumpf – Husserl when Stumpf was at the University of Halle, Musil after Stumpf had moved to Berlin; Musil's references to Husserl's work in his diaries indicate that he was wrestling with problems to which the philosopher had drawn his attention.[4] Husserl, in *Phänomenologische Psychologie*, examines the operation of human consciousness and its perception of objects.[5] One recognises in this work an approach which is similar to Musil's. Husserl takes as the starting point for his investigation of the world the awareness of the individual. According to Husserl, this can be purified by what he calls the 'phänomenologische Reduktion' ('phenomenological reduction'),[6] but the act of the philosopher is always, at root, the act of an individual mind. Daily life requires us to assess the thoughts and feelings of others. But how is this possible in the absence of any faculty that allows us insight into other people's minds? Husserl insists on the priority of subjective awareness. According to him, the only way open to us for direct experience of how others feel is how we feel within the compass of our own body. We draw analogies between experiences that we have had and the experiences of others. In other words, we do not so much 'put ourselves in another's shoes' as put them in our shoes – we transfer our perceptions of their situation, via an imaginative act (a sort of spontaneous 'Gedankenexperiment'), to our own body. Husserl expresses this idea as follows: 'With reference to the separate bodies of others and the separate life of the psyches which are associated with them, I can only have experience of these by making inferences about their separate corporeality which I experience through my five senses, *on the basis of the analogy with my own corporeality*' (my emphasis). This line of thinking is valid for Musil, too – and it is not only through Ulrich that we watch this kind of process at work.

Frank Kermode pays tribute to the way Musil explores the mind of the psychopath: 'it would be impossible to overpraise the imaginative achievement of Musil in the rendering of [Moosbrugger's] mind'.[7] In terms of *The Man without Qualities* as a continuing 'Gedankenexperiment' Moosbrugger is, indeed, Musil's 'imaginative achievement'; but, within the fiction, Moosbrugger is Ulrich's 'imaginative achievement', his 'Gedankenexperiment'; and several characters in the novel beside the hero speculate about Moosbrugger, though none of them speculates as deeply as Ulrich does. Of course, the fiction requires that there be a 'real' Moosbrugger; but it is impossible for the reader to thread his way to his 'real' character through the maze of speculation that surrounds him. The reader's attempts to understand Moosbrugger are based on the same kind of evidence as a man forced to assess another's character from impressions supplied by several correspondents; though each of these may believe that he understands the person in question perfectly, he supplies 'information' which does not tally exactly with that offered by any of the others. Let us consider the way in which the narrator transmits his creature, this recreated Moosbrugger, to the reader through the medium of the text itself.

#### Moosbrugger transmitted through the text

Ulrich, as we saw above, is not the only character in the novel who is preoccupied with Moosbrugger. Clarisse fantasises about him, as do Rachel and perhaps even Diotima's husband, Tuzzi; Bonadea, too, pleads his case. But here we are concerned with the Moosbrugger figure which emerges from the 'collaboration' of narrator and hero. This representation of Moosbrugger moves between the parameters of detachment and identification; at times the reader senses that the creative mind behind the reconstruction is fully aware of its own existence beneath the representation of Moosbrugger, at other times it seems to fall into a state of near hypnosis under the spell of Moosbrugger's mood. These two contrasting states are represented by the relative objectivity of standard third-person past-tense narrative, on the one hand, and, on the other, by the more subjective 'erlebte Rede' or interior monologue. Musil interweaves the two modes, interspersing them with transitional passages. In the following quotations, taken from Part II, Chapter 87, I have inserted letters in sequence to be able to refer more readily to points in the text:

[. . .] (A) In the meantime Moosbrugger was still sitting in an investigation cell of the provincial court. His defending counsel had a fresh wind in his sails and was trying hard to prevent the authorities from allowing the case to reach the stage of the final flourish of a pen.

(B) Moosbrugger was smiling at this. He was smiling out of boredom. Boredom gently rocked his thoughts. (C) Usually it extinguishes them; (D) but it gently rocked his; (E) this time; (F) it was a state resembling an actor sitting in his dressing-room waiting for his entrance. (G)

If Moosbrugger had had a big sabre, he would have now picked it up and cut off the chair's head [. . .] and the window's, the basin's and the door's. Then he would have put his own head onto everything that he had decapitated, (H) for in this cell there was only his own head, and that was beautiful (J).                                                                 (393–4)

Between A and B we have objective third person narrative – this gives expression to a mind fully conscious of its own existence, separate from the mind of the Moosbrugger figure it imagines. But, after B, this self-awareness begins to fade until, just before C, the reader senses that it is 'falling asleep' as the narrative takes on the rhythm of interior monologue. Between C and D, self-awareness awakes with a gentle start, indicated by the conscious act of comparison of this 'Moosbrugger'-state of mind with a normal state. Further fluctuations in narrative level follow, representing the mind in different phases of self-possession: it falls back into semi-consciousness from D to E; it sinks even further down, from E to F with a solitary word, 'diesmal', which is more incantation than rational statement; F to G it moves up sharply again with a simile which marks a mental effort set alongside the reverie; but it drops slowly from G to H at which point objective third-person narrative seems to have been subtly subverted by the half-mad mood of this strange inner monologue, which moves by the impetus of its own uncanny logic on to J.

When the narrative deals with Moosbrugger it is, if anything, more subtly modulated than when it deals with other characters (though there is certainly something of a similar rise and fall in the passages that explore other characters' minds as well). Let us look more closely at the way Musil creates these effects.

Between points A and B the reader is offered a glimpse of two scenes: a prisoner in a cell and a lawyer working on a case. There is nothing particularly remarkable about them. One imagines that the narrator had not so much seen prisoner and lawyer with his own eyes as read about them in a newspaper – which we now know, of course, was precisely what Musil had done – and was here giving a report based on a report. If the reader is to make anything of them he or she must, as when reading a report, call on his or her imagination to supply a background.

Immediately after point B the narrator begins to take on, as it were, the role of someone reading a newspaper, who, scanning the latest report on some sensational murder, allows free rein to imagination, whereupon a vision of the murderer in his cell arises in the mind's eye – his inappropriate and meaningless smile a fitting token of madness.[8] The narrator facilitates the imaginative act by changing from the sober tone of newspaper reporting to a rhythm which seems rather to belong to poetry. He takes a word, 'smiled', repeats it in conjunction with another, 'boredom'; repeats 'boredom' in a new combination with 'gently rocked', repeats 'rocked'. The whole has a soporific effect suggesting that the spell in prison has dulled Moosbrugger's mind which scarcely registers the sluggish flow of vacant hours.

With the word 'Usually' just after point C the narrator creates a kind of 'alienation effect'; he interrupts the reader's 'Moosbrugger-reverie' and forces him to consider that the way in which Moosbrugger's mind works is a deviation from normal behaviour. Perhaps an ironic twist is intended here, suggesting that readers who have in this passage intuitively grasped something of Moosbrugger's state of mind must be half-mad themselves. But from D to E the interrupted rhythm of the readers' recreation of Moosbrugger's thoughts is picked up once again. This reaches its most intense pitch at E to F with the isolated and emphatic 'this time'. At F to G the narrator intrudes with uncharacteristic abruptness, thrusting upon the reader one of his central concerns: he draws a theatrical analogy which is associated in the text of *The Man without Qualities* with 'Wirklichkeit'.[9] The analogy seems doubly out of place: surely no such image would be likely to occur to a simple working-man like Moosbrugger, and is it not the case that Moosbrugger is here the focus of attention because 'Wirklichkeit' is somehow too restricting a context for a man such as this? Perhaps the narrator is here imitating the way in which society, compelled to take action on the Moosbrugger case, reaches out towards the murderer and draws him, or, more precisely, the many-sided figure that it makes out of him, into its system.

Between G and H the cumbersome conditional form of the statements jars against the weird content they express; the narrator subjects the thoughts of the madman to a grammatical discipline which is as foreign to them as the routine of prison life is to the real Moosbrugger. But from H to J, with the shift from conditional to indicative, the reader moves back 'inside' Moosbrugger again. Of course here, too, the discipline of the syntax is still felt. Indeed what is perhaps the most hermetic statement of the whole novel, which follows shortly afterwards in the text, still embodies the point of view of the narrator whose attempts to explain and externalise his version of Moosbrugger's feelings are not concealed. Here maximum compression strains meaning to the utmost, but noun and verb still perform their proper functions:

The words he had were:– Hmhm, soso.
The table was Moosbrugger.
The chair was Moosbrugger.
The barred window and the locked door were himself.                    (395)

As it stands in the text, this is not Moosbrugger's experience. The above passage is preceded by a reservation. This, we are told, represents Moosbrugger's impression, 'even if he did not have the words for it' (395). Moosbrugger cannot find words to fit his mood; perhaps no one could find such words. Elsewhere, in conveying something of Moosbrugger's embarrassment when faced with the searching questions of the prosecution, the narrator remarks: 'Moosbrugger had the less favourable position because even a cleverer person would not have been able to express his strange and shadowy reasoning' (75). We are reminded that there is a hiatus in the work between the figure in the dock on whom so much of the attention in the narrative is focussed, the 'real' Moosbrugger, and the Moosbrugger who so frequently arises before us in the novel as the object of so many men's imaginative speculations.

The narrative modulations, the veering from identification with Moosbrugger to detachment from him, indicate the extent to which Musil is anxious that the reader be in no doubt about the process behind the creation of the figure of the murderer. In view of this, why is the overall effect of this so frequently distanced Moosbrugger-construct so powerful? The answer is partly that this process of self-critical creation is being carried out, in part at least, by the hero – it is integral to the fictional world of *The Man without Qualities*. But there is another reason of equal importance.

## Moosbrugger and 'das Gleichnis'

Similes are the main bridge between the narrator's imaginative reliving of Moosbrugger's experiences and the reader.[10] Musil, as we saw in our examination of *Acts of Union* was preoccupied with the dynamism of similes. For him, they unite the world of the average man, the poet and the scientist. Let us briefly consider their relevance in each of these contexts. In the hands of the 'Wirklichkeitsmensch' ('man of reality') they serve to break down arbitrary modes of thought and behaviour that otherwise appear absolute: 'It seems that the well-behaved, practical man of reality never loves reality quite without reservation nor does he take it completely seriously [. . .] as a boy he longs for the watch; as a youth with a gold watch he longs for the wife to go with it; as a man with watch and wife he longs for the senior post' (138). But once he has reached the pinnacle of this ambition 'his store of unfulfilled dreams seems undiminished. For when he wants to be uplifted, he uses a simile' (138). The simile is thus presented as the literary correlative for this restless shifting dissatisfaction with things as they are that drives mankind forward, or perhaps round in circles: 'Apparently because [the man of reality] sometimes finds snow unpleasant, he compares it with shimmering breasts and as soon as he starts to tire of his wife's breasts he compares them with shimmering snow' (138–9).

The simile is essential to the poet as well. Musil discusses in his 'Rede zur Rilkefeier' ('Oration in commemoration of Rilke') how, in Rilke's poetry, the simile challenges stereotypes of thought and pushes back the contemporary limits of awareness. He ascribes to Rilke's similes and images the leavening power of a moral yeast that transforms society.[11]

According to Musil, Mach believed that science, too, depended on the simile; in a letter Musil wrote: 'I think again and again of what Mach says of the analogy ['Vergleich']: that it is the root and the instrument of scientific thinking and that to make it progressively more precise is the aim [of such thinking]' (*Briefe* I, 88). Nor is this simply an aberration on Mach's or Musil's part: Max Planck is reported to have said: 'the pioneer in science [. . .] must have a vivid intuitive imagination, for new ideas are not generated by deduction, but by an intuitively creative imagination'.[12]

But this power comes from an intangible source; attempts to explain it lead to disappointment: 'usually [in such contexts] one has gained a little truth and lost the whole value of the simile' (593). The simile is alive; its life comes from the reader. However, in the way it reaches out to the reader each simile marks a momentary shift of register in the narrative as 'Gedankenexperiment' – a moment in which the work is switched directly into the reader's personal experience. Take the moment when the narrator says of Moosbrugger, who is attempting to come to terms with prison life: 'thus everything regained a certain order and calm, like the water over a dead rat which has fallen into it' (394–5). This is not a particular 'rat-in-the-narrative', a 'rat-seen-by-Moosbrugger'; it is the individual reader's accumulated personal experience of rats, his or her knowledge of rats, mixed up, perhaps, with fear and loathing, all immediately mobilised by the phrase 'water over a dead rat'. When used like this, the simile is indeed a Husserlian analogy. Even when the narrator breaks into the readers' reveries to remind them that this is not Moosbrugger thinking – 'Admittedly [Moosbrugger] [. . .] did not imagine it quite in terms of this image' (395) – this does not destroy the effect, so skilfully has Musil harnessed the readers' emotional energy to the narrative.

Through similes the narrator calls upon the reader to supply the apprehension or the elation, the boredom or the concern which is appropriate to his, the narrator's, particular purpose. The quality of the given emotion is given absolutely, for we as readers are both source and judge. Consider the moment in the fiction when Moosbrugger thinks back to all those times he has confronted authority: 'He saw before him what he had often seen: the inkwells, the green baize, the pencils, then the portrait of the Emperor on the wall and the way they all sat there' (394). Then he focusses his, and our, impressions in an image: 'in its arrangement it seemed to him like a steel trap, covered over with the feeling, this is how it has to be, instead of with grass and leaves' (394). In the brief span that the reader allots to a sentence of this length, images rush forward. He or she is spirited away to a limbo where the words of the narrator conjure up a knot of semi-private experiences: perhaps the memory of a man-trap exhibited in some museum, which in its turn provoked imaginings of the pain which that actual instrument might have caused, a sense of the barbarism of nineteenth-century justice, the curious paradox that makes property private even as the poacher exults in the freedom of the fields, and which culminates in that irrational deceit, the iron trap hidden in the grass, whose unfeeling jaws bite not into his flesh, but into ours.

At one point in the narrative we are given not only the simile, but its complete terms of reference as well. Ulrich, walking home one night, is accosted by a prostitute. This prompts him to ask himself what it might have been like for Moosbrugger to encounter the prostitute whom he was later to kill. Ulrich first imagines Moosbrugger's mood on the night of the murder: 'When the uncertainty of the walls of the street, like some theatrical backdrop, stood still for a moment, he had bumped into that unknown being which was waiting for him on the night of the murder by the bridge. What a strange recognising that must have been, [transforming him] from head to feet' (652). Here Ulrich provides the frame: 'Ulrich felt for a moment that he could imagine it' (652); and then comes the simile: '[Ulrich] felt something lifting him up like a wave. He lost his balance but he did not need it any more as he was carried along with the motion' (652). Caught up in their memories of bathes in the sea and the sensation of the immense power of the undertow which is utterly indifferent to all human strength, both Ulrich and the reader are placed in the proper frame of mind to examine the emotional turmoil and the deep compulsions that suspend Moosbrugger's helpless consciousness and make him the unwilling instrument in the murder. But before we examine the murder we shall consider Moosbrugger's problems with language, which are essential to an understanding of his mental state; in contrast to the experts whose use of language displays an uncritical self-confidence, Moosbrugger is perplexed by words. In this context the narrator's concerns and Moosbrugger's converge.

## Words that bend minds

Moosbrugger is in prison. He searches the faces of the officials who are in authority over him. His gaze moves from the doctor to the chaplain and on to the prison governor. 'He looked into the face of the doctor with its duelling scars, into the other-worldly face which had dried out from within, into the strict face of the administrator, tidied with bureaucratic efficiency, saw each of them look at his in a different way, and there was something in these faces which was beyond his reach but common to them and this something had been his life-long enemy' (235–6). He wonders what it is that marks these men out from him. He finds only the answer he always finds: 'In bitter anger, Moosbrugger sensed that each of them spoke as it suited him and that it was *this way of speaking* that gave them the power to do with him as they pleased' (235) (my emphasis). Language, for Moosbrugger, is an object of unfailing fascination. He knows that these men with their polite manners and comfortable jobs can both bend words to suit their meaning and can adapt his case to suit their convenience. Moosbrugger cannot fathom this; it is only in moments of ecstatic madness that the words which he uses have the power to shape the world. Usually words use him, spell-binding him with their allusive significances.

Moosbrugger is faced with a barrage of questions from the prosecution designed to prove his criminal liability for what he has done:

'Why did you wipe the blood from your hands? – Why did you throw the knife away? – Why, after the deed, did you put on clean clothes and underwear? – Because it was Sunday? Not because they were covered in blood? – For what reason did you go to a place of entertainment? So the deed did not prevent you from doing so? Did you feel any remorse at all?'

(75)

Ulrich who is in the courtroom believes he knows how Moosbrugger feels:

Ulrich well understood the deep feeling of resignation with which Moosbrugger at such moments laid the blame on his inadequate education that prevented him from unknotting this net woven from incomprehension, which, in the punishingly emphatic words of the judge, ran: 'you always know how to shift your guilt to others!'

(75)

The image of language as a net implies that the lawyers are not attempting to understand the way that Moosbrugger's mind works; they want merely to catch him, to catch him out. The same image recurs when the narrator shows how Moosbrugger is categorised and 'filed away' by the various departments dealing with his case:

Other Moosbruggers took their turn; they were not he; they weren't even like each other [. . .] It had been a sex offence [. . .], the deed of a madman, the deed of someone who was only half-responsible in law [eines nur halb Unzurechnungsfähigen] [. . .], a satisfying intervention by the detection service and the law [. . .]: such general and anaemic concepts, [. . .] caught up the incident which had been sucked dry of substance *at some point or other of its wide-flung net.*                    (532) (my emphasis)

Such an 'anaemic concept' is that of 'Unzurechnungsfähigkeit' ['legal non-accountability'] which is of considerable importance in this novel. The lawyers probe Moosbrugger's extraordinarily complex case with the notion originating over two thousand years ago, that man, as a rational being, has the power to hold his animal nature in check.[13] But since Moosbrugger is evidently prey to hallucinatory states where he cannot behave rationally, they try to establish exactly how his mind was functioning on the night of the murder to allow them to judge whether he is to be accounted 'zurechnungsfähig' ('legally responsible') or not. In other words, they start out from an abstraction which developments in modern research have tended to discredit; and, knowing full well that Moosbrugger is quite incapable of giving a coherent account even of what is passing through his mind at the present moment, they rely on Moosbrugger's erratic recollections of his feelings on a night which is now weeks, perhaps months, back in the past. Such activity the narrator dismisses as being like the 'pedantic exertions of an idiot, trying to pierce a bird in flight with a pin' (248).

Moosbrugger affects indifference to the whole legal world. When he is aware that people are looking at him he begins to smile. The words the reporters use in their descriptions of Moosbrugger's smile chart their unconvincing and contradictory efforts to seize the connection between the man and the deed: 'It was, by turns, an embarrassed smile, or a cunning, an ironical, painful, insane, blood-thirsty, uncanny one:– they were clearly groping for expressions which contradicted each other and seemed to be desperately seeking something in this smile, which they obviously found nowhere else in the whole honest phenomenon' (68). They must find words to put in their reports which will allow a court to decide what kind of man he is. Yet, even when he stands before them in the flesh, Moosbrugger is indefinable. In other words, they face the same kind of problem which the narrator of *The Man without Qualities* must solve.

How is the narrator to speak of a man whose deeds[14] set him apart from other men? In the following passage the narrator describes the ride in a carriage from one prison to another, apparently as Moosbrugger experiences it:

A confused jolting came from the wheels through the bench and into his body; behind the bars of the grille the cobblestones ran backwards, heavy carts were left behind, occasionally men, women or children whirled diagonally through the bars, from far behind a hansom-cab pressed closer, grew, came nearer, began to scatter life like an anvil throwing off sparks, the heads of the horses seemed to be about to burst through the door, then the clattering of hooves and the soft sound of the rubber wheels ran on behind the side [of his carriage]. Moosbrugger slowly turned his head back and looked at the roof again [. . .]                                                    (212)

Somehow here an element essential to a normal human perspective has disappeared. The shapes glimpsed through the iron bars at the window have lost their proportion – as if the images passing through the eye were not organised by the brain, but simply recorded by some distinterested apparatus. A normal man sitting in a moving vehicle would subconsciously compensate for the movement of that vehicle; he would be subliminally aware that as an object moves closer to the eye it seems to become larger and the sound it makes increases in intensity. His brain discounts these sense distortions;[15] it has learnt to do so. But Moosbrugger's senses are all the sharper because he has had such difficulties in learning. His vision, like an infant's, is uncoordinated and extraordinarily vivid. The sense data are stripped of familiarity, each vivid visual or aural image makes its distinct claim on his attention. It seems that consciousness, for Moosbrugger, is not always a dialogue between brain and world, but sometimes simply a stream flowing without intermission; and Moosbrugger does not watch the stream – in some sections of the narrative he is simply a part of it. When he turns away from the barred window it is as if, wearying of the ceaseless confusions of experience, he wants to rest his eyes against a blank space. The stream does not stop, it will stop only with death, but now at least it flows more smoothly.

In the passage we have examined, the words which the narrator uses serve one purpose but subvert another. In telling of how Moosbrugger saw things as well as saying what he saw, the narrator may be attempting to set the normal perspective on its head but he still approaches Moosbrugger from an angle which is not radically different from that adopted by the lawyers. As they do, he snares the Moosbrugger phenomenon in the net of his syntax. We may ask ourselves – indeed Musil's critical narrative invites us to ask ourselves – whether in this private moment those were really 'horses' that Moosbrugger saw, and not rather a dancing rhythmic pattern of movement; we may ask whether the passers-by were identified as such in his mind – surely it is more likely that they appeared as mere shapes? Why should such bright confusion be guided secretly by principles that are analogous to the grammar of the sentences in which it is supposedly expressed? In a film, with skilful use of camera angles and sound effects, a more faithful version of this vision might have been evoked, though in that, too, the observer would still have the sense of looking at a screen, of seeing at second hand through a medium, rather than of being shapes without an eye and sound without an ear. Language, as a medium, betrays the intervention of mind in the world, editing Moosbrugger's experiences.[16] But the narrator does not simply use language as a means of 'getting inside Moosbrugger's skin' and recording his impressions; he also shows how Moosbrugger himself is linguistically active, exploring the world through words to which he attaches private meanings.

In his attempts to grasp the world Moosbrugger is as naive as Ulrich is sceptical. Ulrich speculates that, for God, the world is 'an image, an analogy, a figure of speech' (357) and that it would be wrong to take God literally: 'we ought not to take God at his word' (357–8). Moosbrugger does take the world literally. His senses channel to him an unusually faithful representation of things. But Moosbrugger makes a fateful mistake for he pays words the same naive respect as he does sense data. He understands that, for some, language is a smoke-screen to cover up the injustice of their actions; but, in his usage, words are hieroglyphs, an embodiment of what they represent, charged with a mystical power and individually meaningful. What we, looking from 'outside', recognise as thinking in associations[17] is for Moosbrugger, who sees these from 'inside', simply the ongoing flow of life. He knows that in some areas a squirrel is called 'Eichkatzl' ('oak-kitten') (240), in others 'Baumfuchs' ('tree-fox') (240); each of these words somehow brings forward from the image of a squirrel the features which it has in common with cat and fox respectively. It is, in his view, quite consistent with his experience as a much-travelled man to say to the psychiatrists who have put before him a picture of a squirrel: ' "That is probably a fox or perhaps a rabbit; it might also be a cat or some such thing" ' (240). The reader imagines the remembered words suggesting just such a succession of images which pass quickly through Moosbrugger's consciousness. The narrator explains: 'if an oak-kitten is not a cat nor a fox and in the place of a horn has teeth like the rabbit which the fox eats, one doesn't need to take the thing too literally, but it is somehow or other sewn together from all these things and goes running over the trees' (240).[18] This looks as if Moosbrugger has the kind of control over language which Sartre claims for the creative author: the freedom to choose the words that the individual experience itself demands rather than those which convention requires.[19] But in fact the reverse is the case. Moosbrugger does not choose the words appropriate to the images in his memory; words here control his consciousness by controlling the central images that pass through it.

When Moosbrugger deals with abstractions, words cause him even greater problems. Asked to add fourteen to fourteen, Moosbrugger answers ' "roughly twenty-eight to forty" ' (240). The association between the word 'twenty-eight' and the words 'twenty-nine', 'thirty' and so on, that normally follow it, is stronger for Moosbrugger than the abstract notion of addition. Moosbrugger knows 'that one comes to twenty-eight if one goes fourteen further than fourteen, but who says that one has to stop there?!' (240). He gets similarly muddled when he tries to puzzle out what men mean by the 'Law': ' "Right," he thought extraordinarily slowly, in order to define this concept, and thought in such a way that it was like talking to someone, "that is when you don't do wrong, or something like that, isn't it?" ' (236). Here the mind is working sluggishly, waiting for the association that will move it forward. This does indeed come: 'suddenly it occurred to him: "Right is Law" ' (236). Looked at objectively the substitution of one word for another hardly seems a striking discovery. But, for Moosbrugger, 'Law', drawing life from this new context, comes with the shock of unfamiliarity. Moosbrugger turns this over in his mind, slowly making himself familiar with it, the possessive adjectives marking a literal taking-possession-of the new notion. 'That was it; his Right was his Law!' (236). A few moments later the 'idea' is there in its totality, weighted down by its significance: 'His Law had been denied him!' (237).

In the narrator's version of how Moosbrugger's mind works, words are flaws on the retina of consciousness. In Part II, Chapter 59, Moosbrugger sits in his cell with nothing to do. In the following passage we find him just after he has 'woken up', so to speak, from one of his extended day-dreams, his mind becoming conscious once more of the walls that surround him: 'He felt like someone who has dropped a key on the ground. But he could not find it; the soil and the corners became as grey as daylight and sober again, where they had, a moment ago, been like a magic soil where suddenly a thing or a person grows *when a word falls there*' (237) (my emphasis). The loss of the word – and this is not just a key-word, but a literal 'word-key' – halts the flight of memory.

At this moment of boredom Moosbrugger decides to explore his memory and review his attacks of schizophrenia. Moosbrugger prepares this mental effort with what is presented as a verbal imperative, a summons to the words that constitute experience: 'Moosbrugger gathered *all his logic* together' (237) (my emphasis). He remembers that his attacks start invariably with a bad mood; his eyes are drawn to follow any women who pass the place where he is working. What then happens was examined earlier in *The Man without Qualities*:[20] he watches one woman, and when she is out of sight, waits for another to appear; however long this takes, Moosbrugger's interest in women, the simple fact that he is waiting for the next woman to appear, makes the ultimate arrival of another woman seem as necessary as a mathematical progression. But Moosbrugger is not aware of this; he does not notice the fact that he is waiting; he concentrates exclusively on the arrival of the next woman. In his present frame of mind (and, of course, he is not always in this state) the secret pathological imperative demands that there be a connection between the women – some plot directed against him. Something working subconsciously within his brain transforms a chance sequence into a conspiracy. This is the prelude to schizophrenia. The next symptom is that his ability to communicate becomes impaired in inverse proportion to his appreciation of the evocative power of individual words. The person he is talking to cannot understand that, as far as Moosbrugger is concerned, the sharing of a word means the sharing of an elemental experience: 'and [...] when he was speaking to someone, it happened that the person suddenly looked at him in astonishment and failed to grasp how much a single word meant when Moosbrugger slowly brought it out' (238). Words made heavy with meaning take on physical substance for Moosbrugger: 'precisely at times when he needed them most urgently, words spitefully stuck to his palate like gum and then sometimes an immeasurable period of time passed before he tore a syllable loose and made progress again' (238).[21]

After perhaps days of such embarrassing difficulties comes the relief of hallucination, where perception and imagination come together in harmony: the outer world flows inwards, the inner outwards: 'The important thing was that it is of no importance whether something is outside or inside; in his state this was like bright water on both sides of a transparent glass wall' (239).

In the following passage a word-key, 'Rosenmund' ('rose-bud mouth'), makes metaphor come grotesquely alive for Moosbrugger:

And, in the course of his life, it had also happened that he said to a girl: 'Your dear rose-bud mouth!', but suddenly the word parted at the seams and something very embarrassing happened: the face became grey like earth covered by mist, and, on a long stem, a rose emerged; then the temptation to take a knife and cut it off or to give it a blow so that it drew back into the face again, was immensely strong. (240)

The face of the girl is hidden behind the image of the rose, which was itself born of a word, a cliché of endearment uttered in innocence. Moosbrugger loses contact with the world. It is at such a moment that the crime is committed for which Moosbrugger is imprisoned, and in his lunatic pride Moosbrugger feels that the crime is a token of his superior vision.[22] Of the actions which he performed that fatal night, Moosbrugger boasts that they were done 'fluently': 'as if he had suddenly spoken something fluently in a foreign language which made him very happy but which he was not able to repeat' (242).

Why does Musil spend so much time and effort on the portrait of such an unfortunate man? Such a question may itself seem extraneous to a work of art which does not have to answer for its utility; but there can be no doubt that, in ethical terms, Musil was treading here on dangerous ground.

## Moosbrugger and the question of freedom

Wayne Booth in his work, *The Rhetoric of Fiction*, pointed to the confusion which may arise when characters are presented 'through the seductive medium of their own self-defending rhetoric'.[23] The crime which Moosbrugger commits is seen from his point of view; the narrative provides something of an apology for his action; in view of this it is hardly surprising that Musil was dubbed a perverse writer in his time.[24] But to write an empathetic account of how a psychopath commits a murder is not to condone murder done in cold blood. It is essential to see the murder framed in Ulrich's interest. The critical presence of the healthy mind provides the central, if implicit, perspective for this section of the narrative. The narrator traces a negative image – the way in which Moosbrugger becomes embroiled in his compulsions; but from this the reader provides the positive – a vision of human freedom.

Why is it necessary to explore the realms of compulsion to find out how men are free? Under normal circumstances the decision to move a limb results so spontaneously in the corresponding action that the individual gives no thought to how it came about; nor,

perhaps, could even the most brilliant neurosurgeon explain precisely how the action was prompted by the brain. The free will,
functioning freely, is both mystery and fact. The activity of the will
becomes interesting, and more readily observable as a phenomenon, in instances where its operations are impaired. Even in
healthy human beings such cases can be identified. In conversation
with Agathe, Ulrich takes as an example a common experience
which illustrates how difficult it is to pinpoint how a man actually
comes to carry through into action something that he has set his
mind to do. 'Just think,' he says, 'how difficult it is to turn over in
bed at night!':

'One is dissatisfied with one's position; one thinks constantly of changing it
and makes up one's mind time and again to do so without carrying out this
intention; finally one gives up: and all at once one has turned over! In fact
one really ought to say one was turned over. This is the exact pattern both
in matters of passion and also in long-planned decisions.' (737)

On the one hand there is the will to act, on the other the physical
world in which one's body belongs and where the will to act takes
effect. At times, especially when the mind is half-asleep or affected
by sickness or drugs, the 'lines of communication' between mind
and body may seem impaired or broken. Then the effort to
'transmit a message' along these lines becomes highly perceptible.
Ulrich watches Moosbrugger making such an effort. The murderer
is, I believe, Ulrich's psychic 'test-bed' for the operation of the
nervous system; in the reconstruction of the night when Moosbrugger murders a prostitute we can detect Ulrich probing into
what it is that inhibits the normal exercise of will power in this
unusual subject. Moosbrugger has been drinking. He feels a
nervous pressure building up within. 'Even when one is not drunk
the world may be unsafe. The walls in the streets shake like scenery
behind which something is waiting for the cue-word before making
an appearance. At the edge of the town things get quieter where
one comes out into the open moon-lit field' (73). Here we are
offered not so much the external image as an internal sketch of
what it is to be this man. We are drawn into an account of thoughts
and feelings in which not reason but paranoia dictates the interpretation of natural phenomena: 'even when one is not drunk' – a
drinker assures himself that he is sober and that it is the world which
is starting to shake to its very foundations; 'is waiting for the
cue-word before making an appearance' – Moosbrugger prepares
to succumb to the rule of language which (according to the law that

free association of ideas is not free but bound within the complexes of the individual mind) will lure him surely towards his obsessions; 'where one comes out into the open moon-lit field' – the sense of freedom is held in check by the mad pull of the moon. With the interior monologue, readers are drawn into the scene, identify with the strange psyche at its centre, their pulses quicken as they run the gauntlet of the dark city streets, eventually slowing to a calmer beat as the tension eases. Moosbrugger still has his bearings: 'There Moosbrugger had to turn around to make his way home by a circular route' (73); his powers of judgement are intact as he assesses the girl who accosts him: 'It was the kind of girl who sells herself to men down in the meadows, a runaway out-of-work serving-girl, a slip of a person' (73). But at the end of the sentence a note of emotion is struck, anxiety perhaps, or suspicion: 'a slip of a person, of whom one could only make out two enticing mouse-eyes beneath her head-scarf' (73). Moosbrugger takes evasive action: 'Moosbrugger told her to go away and quickened his step' (73); the girl persists: 'but she begged him to take her home with him' (73). His anxious suspicion is magnified by her pursuit: 'Moosbrugger walked on; straight ahead, around the corner, finally helplessly to and fro; he took great strides and she ran alongside him; he stopped and she stood like a shadow' (73).

If we step back from the narrative the scene is very bizarre: a huge powerful man trying to shake off the attentions of a tiny prostitute because he is frightened of her. But here Moosbrugger is losing his grip on the external world; his internal preoccupations are starting to interfere with his ability to match response to a given external stimulus. But since the narrative perspective is provided by Moosbrugger's perception of what is happening, the reader can understand the internal consistency behind his actions.

There may be sound reasons for fear; perhaps the girl has a male accomplice intent on robbing Moosbrugger. But this is not the cause of Moosbrugger's fear. In a normal man one would look for a balanced reaction: indifference or irritation mingled with caution. But there is no equilibrium in Moosbrugger. The next sentence reveals what Moosbrugger feels is happening: the girl has somehow attached herself to him: 'He was pulling her along behind him, that was it' (73). For the reader reliving Moosbrugger's thoughts and actions these words are the figurative equivalent of his feeling. There is a sense of discovery here, Moosbrugger almost breathes a sigh of relief at a puzzle solved: 'that was it' – this is the emphatic statement of a man who has discovered a 'truth' he will not henceforth be prepared to question.

Kurt Michel, in an article entitled 'The Utopia of Language', suggests that, in Musil's work, what he calls 'the image of the world of the senses' is co-extensive with 'the reflected image of the psychic state'.[25] Musil does indeed trace the way that experiences find their focus in the mind; the narrative of *The Man without Qualities* is sensitive to those delicate states where the individual is uncertain whether his feelings are properly his or are rather a function of an external situation. But, at another level, the narrative transcends the subjective point of view. In the course of the passage we have discussed above, the reader cannot fail to be aware of a decline in the quality of Moosbrugger's awareness of things. Between the point where the girl first appears: 'There [...] by the iron bridge, the girl came up and spoke to him' (73) and the cryptic words: 'He was pulling her along behind him, that was it' (73), something has evidently gone wrong with Moosbrugger's perception. That the reader can see this clearly is an indication that Moosbrugger's vision of the world – his 'world of the senses' intermingled with the 'reflected image' of his internal condition – is not the sole perspective here.

On occasions we can detect the operation of the mind shaping the reconstruction – Ulrich conducting his private Moosbrugger-'Gedankenexperiment'. I believe that we can make an educated guess at the conclusions that are drawn from this experiment. We know that Musil read a treatise by Ernst Kretschmer, *Medizinische Psychologie*[26] which argues that human awareness is formed by two interwoven strands: a man sees himself as if from 'without', as a creature of flesh and blood and prone to those influences of nature and environment which he readily observes in other men around him – this form of consciousness he calls 'objective'; but he is also a consciousness 'inside' experiences, the feeling centre of a universe that moves when he moves – and this form of consciousness is called 'subjective'. These two states of consciousness carry on a continuous dialogue with each other in the normal individual. Mental health stems from constant self-criticism by the mind of its interpretation of reality. The loss of self-criticism means that the individual, in losing grip of his or her own emotions, loses the freedom to choose between different courses of action. Private feelings become a tyrant that brooks no resistance.

Looking from Kretschmer's perspective, we can see that, in this passage, the subjective mode is starting to drown out the other. As this happens, the dualistic feeling of being in the world – which Karl

Popper vividly describes as the feeling that, if one kicks a stone, the stone kicks back[27] (a lesson which, as we saw, Ulrich had to learn from his contact with 'Wirklichkeit') – gives way to a monistic sense of being the world – a kind of 'applied pantheism', as if the ego were somehow permeated with a sense of being an organic extension of the whole of creation. When the girl first speaks to Moosbrugger his loathing for women is aroused and he instinctively feels fear and suspicion. But at first he can distinguish between what comes from without and what originates within; at this stage perception and emotional response are maintained as separate modes of experience. As his fear grows, his ability to differentiate between these declines quickly. His responses to the girl's actions cease to be comparable with those of a normal person in such a situation (relief, perhaps, at not being attacked by anyone, or irritation at the girl's persistence) to the point where somehow the tension of waiting to see what she will do is lost in a deeper horror, the certainty that, whatever she does, it will be no less than the confirmation and embodiment of his dread. If only in the clarity with which Moosbrugger's confusion is perceived, we recognise the stamp of the mind of the observer behind the reconstruction who watches the process whereby a free man becomes unfree and all objectivity is put to flight by the panic that precedes the surrender to compulsive action.

We take up the account of the evening's events again as Moosbrugger seeks refuge in a café. He drinks coffee and three glasses of brandy and sits there for a while. But his fear has not abated: 'when he paid, the thought was there again of what action he would take if she had waited for him outside?' (73–74). His fear is made our fear by the simile: 'Such words are like thread and entwine themselves in endless loops around arms and legs' (74). Moosbrugger gets helplessly enmeshed in this fixation. The act of taking refuge indicates that Moosbrugger has not completely surrendered to his fear; but the appearance of such a thought after the respite in the café indicates how panic has undermined the proper processes of thought and is tracing its own mad pattern. Ulrich's father sets down clearly what, according to legal tradition, constitutes free action: 'A willed action is [. . .] always one connected with thought, not an instinctive action [. . .]. Willing is precisely not something from the realm of chance but a self-determination issuing necessarily from our "I" ' (317). Whether we take this point of view as our criterion or rely on more recent theories which see consciousness as simply the latest state in an evolutionary development and subject to the distorting influence of emotions, Moosbrugger cannot be said to be acting as a free man.[28]

Moosbrugger leaves the café. 'And he had scarcely stepped out into the dark street when he felt the girl at his side. She wasn't submissive any more but cheeky and sure of herself; she also didn't ask for anything any more but was silent' (74). The girl's silence (the reader may interpret it as resignation or despair) Moosbrugger sees as proof that she is sure of her power over him. In the next few sentences the first climax of subjectivity is reached. Moosbrugger is seized by the conviction that she is organically part of him. Having projected his fear into her, he becomes her quarry in a nightmare chase. Moosbrugger has transformed an experience that properly belongs in the objective mode – the girl following him – into a purely subjective one where he has willed himself into a situation of claustrophobic powerlessness: 'Then he recognised that he would never get away from her because it was he, himself, who was pulling her after him. A tearful loathing constricted his throat. He walked, and this thing, half a step behind him, was also him' (74). His fear has reached a new pitch. This we can gauge by comparing the earlier statement 'he was pulling her along behind him', where 'he', Moosbrugger, is subject and 'her', the girl, is the object, with the statement in this new context: 'und das, halb hinter ihm, war wiederum er' ('and this thing, half a step behind him, was also him'), where 'das' ('this thing'), an impersonal demonstrative pronoun refers to the girl, the subject of the clause, and he, Moosbrugger, 'er' ('him') is merely the complement, a predicate of the girl-subject!

Moosbrugger's crime appears to the prosecuting counsel as an act of conscious choice, the deliberate seeking out and cutting down of a victim. For the narrator, the murder is committed at the moment when Moosbrugger's consciousness of the outside world is nil, when he has become totally lost in his fear. Nor is the thought from which the murder stems one of murder, for now Moosbrugger's mind is functioning in pure associations.

The passage continues with the stirring of a memory; we are not told why this memory appears; suddenly without warning it is there: 'He had once cut a big splinter of wood out of his own leg because he was too impatient to wait for the doctor' (74). Then a foreign object found its way into his body; now a girl gets 'under his skin'. The analogy is quite unambiguous. The cure, now as then, is surgery on the self with a knife: 'in a rather similar way he now felt his knife again; long and hard, it lay in his pocket' (74). Something of the meaning of that hermetic statement about Moosbrugger's vision of his actions becomes clear: 'In the eyes of the judge, his deeds issued from him, in his they had come flying up to him like birds' (75). Deeds have ceased to be his deeds, originating in his own subjective wilfulness and have become 'events' or 'happenings'; they are confused with elements of objective perception. We see the whole nexus of association moving through Moosbrugger's mind: 'girl, mouse eyes, ugh! Hate them all! She's following me! Must get away! She's still there, she's pursuing me, can't shake her off, she's part of me, under my skin . . . a splinter . . . splinter? . . . knife!' These flowing thoughts submerge in a nightmare where one is powerless to affect what happens.

But Moosbrugger makes a final effort, although he is now deeply enmeshed in the nightmare, to fight his way back into the waking world and establish the distinction of subject and object: 'With a positively superhuman exertion of his morality, Moosbrugger had recourse to another line of escape' (74). Here is precisely that effort of the will which society insists, retrospectively through the stern reassessment of a law court, that a criminal ought to have made in order to resist temptation (and we should bear in mind that most men are not prone to compulsions as strong as the one which has now seized hold of Moosbrugger).[29] He tries once again to escape:

Behind the boarding which bordered the path lay a sports-field; no one could see anybody there and he turned and entered it. He lay down in the narrow ticket booth and thrust his head into the darkest corner; the cursed soft second 'I' lay down beside him. So he pretended to fall asleep in order to be able to creep away again later. (74)

Moosbrugger has here managed to suppress his panic and the drastic solution it had suggested and has recourse to a feasible method of escape. It is a final attempt to break back into an objective state of mind. By what is described as a moral effort, an 'exertion of his morality', Moosbrugger succeeds, if only for a few moments, in lifting himself beyond his fear.

But when his will is spent, Moosbrugger slips back into his role as the executioner of plans that his fear, or his desire, or whatever deluded emotion this was,[30] had brought forth:

But when he crept out softly, feet first, it was there again and twined its arms around his neck. Then he felt something hard in her pocket or his own; he dragged it out. He didn't know quite whether it was a pair of scissors or a knife; he drove it in. She had insisted that it was only a pair of scissors but it was his knife. She fell head-first into the booth; he dragged her out a little way onto the soft earth and stabbed at her until he had completely separated her from himself. Then he stood beside her for perhaps a quarter of an hour, watching her until the night became calmer again and strangely smooth. Now she could not insult or attach herself to any other man. Finally, he carried the corpse over the street and laid it before a bush so that it might more easily be found and buried, so he asserted, for now she could no longer be blamed for anything.    (74)

This study of insanity is, at the same time, an enquiry into human freedom. According to John Wilson in an article entitled 'Freedom and Compulsion', 'Free action occurs when the "cause" or "origin" of the action is "within" the agent.'[31] In terms of the above definition Moosbrugger's murder of the prostitute seems to be an 'inside' action – one for which he is responsible. The court, we are led to believe,[32] will come to this conclusion and condemn him. The analysis of the murder given in *The Man without Qualities*, however, presents Moosbrugger as being under the influence of a force which he knows nothing of and over which he has no control.

John Wilson puts the problem clearly. He asks two questions: ' "How can we be quite sure that those whom we now regard as responsible and blameworthy are not really suffering from an unknown compulsion?" ' (p. 61), and ' "Can we set up criteria for free and compelled action that will be permanently valid?" ' (p. 61). Such questions, he argues, are justified because our methods for assessing actions vary widely. As we find out more about the way the mind functions, we come across forces which we rarely perceive directly. The realm of freedom seems to be reduced by each new advance in psychology – or, to put it in Kretschmer's terms, 'outside' motivations seem to be replacing 'inside' ones.

According to Wilson this is indeed the case if we take, for example, Plato's definition of man as our criterion: 'For Plato, the true self is the rational self; anything which interferes with this counts as compulsion' (p. 65). For Plato, rational motivations are 'inside' motivations; irrational ones, 'outside' motivations. Plato postulates an inner self, reason, which is the seat of freedom and an outer self, the passions, which makes for determined action.

In the narrator's view, the institutions of the law embody a Platonic view of mankind.[33] This, he believes, is now out of date. His account of the way that Moosbrugger's mind works suggests that the stuff of experience is much too complex to be explained in terms of a division into the realms of reason and impulse. But he does not argue that men are not free, rather that they should alter their view of what freedom is, to incorporate the influence of irrational forces. The narrative suggests that freedom is the activity of consciousness in its critical appraisal of the importance and weight of the impressions and impulses that flash across the screen of the mind.

The narrator thus takes the reader through all the steps that lead up to the moment when Moosbrugger murders the prostitute and helps to explain how the way Moosbrugger sees things affects what he does. Even readers who have no knowledge of psychiatry can see what is wrong with Moosbrugger. Their clearer perception and awareness of the extent to which their actions would have differed from Moosbrugger's run in parallel to their vicarious reliving of Moosbrugger's predicament; readers repeat the 'Gedankenexperiment' and, from their own inner resources, provide the measure of Moosbrugger's madness. Here Musil adapts the neurologist's method for the study of moral issues – abnormality supplies the critical perspective for a consideration of normality.[34] As the narrator traces the path from perception to action in a sick man, he throws light on the connections between perceiving and doing, between the realms of understanding and morality, in a healthy person. Musil noted in his diary about 1920: 'Consciousness = to stand in a context. The object being stared at is, at best, half-conscious. It is only [...] the relationships that are established which give the conscious experience' (Tb1, 452). A *sine qua non* of responsible action is the critical activity of consciousness establishing its dialectical relationship with the data of experience. We have seen the way in which Moosbrugger loses his distance from the 'object being stared at', we see how this is abolished, absorbed in the image of the splinter that once penetrated his flesh. As the proper perspective of this psychic situation slips away from him, Moosbrugger relinquishes the freedom which a normal man in a similar situation would possess. He no longer has the sense of the necessary separation of self and world and, losing his grip on the polarity of subject and object, he can no longer freely determine what he does. When he murders, Moosbrugger has surrendered his freedom. He is merely an executioner, blindly obeying the directives of wayward impulses.

Musil, in his study of Moosbrugger, does not look into such questions as the need for a society to protect itself against men like Moosbrugger. Like von Mises, who defended his positivism by arguing that he was not responsible for the viability of the institutions which he criticised, so Musil seems not to concern himself with the question of how a society would survive if it actually based its legal system on the kind of insights which Musil's account of this murder offers. Musil is content with provoking thought and discussion of the issues, without pointing the way to solutions. Musil does not offer any suggestions for a revision of the methods used by society to assess criminality. But, in showing the inconsistencies in the way in which the Austrian judiciary deals with Moosbrugger, in drawing this coherent picture of the confused mind of the murderer, in identifying the way in which his will becomes impaired, Musil is not suggesting that free will is a redundant concept which should be rejected with all the other archaic impedimenta of the legal system. On the contrary, he clearly distinguishes between the sick mind which bears little or no responsibility for the actions it prompts and the healthy mind which bears full responsibility for them.

Walking home late one night, Ulrich is approached by a prostitute. We are not allowed to overlook the similarity between this experience and Moosbrugger's: 'And, even as Ulrich spoke to the girl, he was reminded of Moosbrugger by way of a patently obvious thought-connection. Moosbrugger, [...] the hunter and exterminator of prostitutes, who had walked through that unhappy night in just the same way as he did today' (652). Ulrich responds in a very different way to the challenge she presents. Caught off his guard for a moment, he quickly recovers his composure and thrusts into her hand a sum of money 'corresponding approximately to the amount for one visit' (652), then goes on his way; in other words, Ulrich, keeping a grip on the objective world, counters this jolt to his inner equilibrium economically and efficiently. The contrast with Moosbrugger – this character who has been recreated in Ulrich's psyche – could scarcely be more marked.

### Moosbrugger and 'das Seinesgleichen'

We have seen how shadowy a figure the 'real' Moosbrugger is. The lawyers misunderstand him; Ulrich insists that he has no certain knowledge of the murderer;[35] the narrator merely encourages the reader to usurp Moosbrugger's consciousness, to play out a Moosbrugger role. However Moosbrugger can be seen quite clearly from one angle – the interest which society, in particular bourgeois society, displays in him.

In an essay, 'Die Gegenwartsbedeutung des kritischen Realismus' ('The contemporary meaning of critical realism'), George Lukács argues that there is a deadly sameness and monotony about bourgeois society.[36] Musil would probably not have quarrelled with this description; the image he provides for the morality of the age, 'bourgeois over-indulgence in goodness' (958), is a depressing comment on the quality of bourgeois existence. Musil would almost certainly have approved of the next step in Lukács' argument: that the bourgeois craves a vital experience which his self-indulgent 'goodness' denies him. Lukács argues that in *The Man without Qualities*, as in many other works, 'the eccentric forms a [...] necessary complement, a polarity to the average, and with this polarity attempts to exhaust all possibilities of human existence' (p. 483) – the bourgeois secretly desires what he publicly deplores; there is no need here to emphasise that this indeed corresponds to that relationship between the official disapproval for Moosbrugger (whom Lukács discusses in his essay), and the private fascination that helps to sell the newspapers which carry reports on him.[37] Ulrich's thoughts turn to this aspect of contemporary existence after his chance meeting with the prostitute. He recalls the theory of depth psychology that unfortunate creatures like Moosbrugger are 'the embodiment of suppressed urges [...] which all participate in, their thought-murders and their imagined rapes made flesh' (653). The visit to Moosbrugger's prison by Ulrich, Clarisse and Stumm von Bordwehr in Part III, Chapter 33, is clearly prompted by an interest that is more than merely philanthropic.

Lukács argues that the figure of Moosbrugger symbolises the decadence of bourgeois society; the fascination that Moosbrugger exerts on so many of the characters in *The Man without Qualities* anticipates, in Lukács' view, the 'flight into neurosis as a protest against vile reality' (p. 483). For Lukács, Moosbrugger is, in fact, the bourgeois as he existed at the time of Musil's novel, but without his mask.[38] Indeed, Lukács would have been presented with even stronger evidence for this interpretation of Musil's novel had an earlier version been published. Here the hero, Ulrich's 'predecessor' so to speak, is even more deeply preoccupied with Moosbrugger than Ulrich and makes an unsuccessful attempt to rescue the madman.[39] But in the present novel the plot is less extravagant and the hero is more prone to compromise (and perhaps, by that same token, more of a bourgeois) and eventually refuses to have anything more to do with Moosbrugger.[40]

Moosbrugger, even for those who find him fascinating, is only one pole of an emotional complex. The bourgeois subject their eccentricities to the strictest controls. To imagine oneself as Moosbrugger is one thing; to do what Moosbrugger does is another – a powerful taboo guards the gate to actual actions.

This line which separates involvement in Moosbrugger's world from horror at his deeds is finely drawn in the scene where Ulrich holds up to Bonadea a mirror in which she sees the image of her bourgeois conduct. The narrator makes it perfectly apparent that this scene is set against the background of Moosbrugger's crime.

Bonadea finds Ulrich sexually irresistible. He knows this. Bonadea knows that he knows. When she comes to visit him privately at his home there is no doubt about what she has come for. She pretends to herself that her visit is an intercession on Moosbrugger's behalf, but she senses that it would be wise not to ponder her motives too deeply. She looks at Ulrich and scenes from their past relationship act as a warning to her. The narrator focusses the vague sense of self-alienation that Bonadea experiences in a theatrical image – which here as elsewhere in the text points to the idea of 'das Seinesgleichen' – and this is, in turn, fused with the theme of madness: 'what one has before one are stage eyes, a stage moustache, theatrical costume buttons opening, and the moments between the time one enters the room and the dreadful return to sobriety again are played out in a state of consciousness which has stepped out of the head and covers the walls with a papering of madness' (259).[41] In this scene within a scene, played out entirely in Bonadea's imagination, Ulrich, the bourgeois-actor, tempts her into a frenzy which touches him too. The actual situation is destined for a similar dénouement. Lady and gentleman meet in the privacy of the latter's home; they are freed from the formal restraints of a code which both frequently break in private – Ulrich as a matter of principle, Bonadea when opportunity coincides with inclination – and are faced with a sexual temptation from which nothing appears to hold them back. Temptation is linked, at a symbolical level, with the madness of Moosbrugger.

There are, however, restraints of a personal nature. Each has private reasons for wanting to resist. Ulrich wants to avoid any further entanglements with women in the interests of his 'Urlaub vom Leben' ('leave from life'). Bonadea wants to impress the man whom she has decided will henceforth be her only lover with her strength of character and self-control. What actually happens?

Ulrich's first action is to stall by pouring them both a glass of whisky. Bonadea misinterprets this as an improper move, assuming the woman she was rather than the lady she has now become: ' "A lady doesn't drink whisky in the morning" ' (258) she protests, but accepts the whisky nonetheless. Alcohol slowly infiltrates their respective resolves.

Bonadea says that she has come to ask him to intervene on Moosbrugger's behalf; Ulrich refuses and tries to explain why. He asks Bonadea to imagine Moosbrugger working as a carpenter at her home: ' "You are alone in the house with him and he begins to roll his eyes this way and that" ' (262).[42] Bonadea thrusts aside Ulrich's suggestion as thoroughly improper. She will campaign for a good cause, but to put the man she wants to help into such a personal context is to look the gift horse of her charity in the mouth. Her words suggest the repression of powerful feelings: ' "It's dreadful what you're asking of me!" ' (262). But Ulrich's reference to Moosbrugger and to a scene even more compromising than the present one increases the suggestiveness of the moment and the tension between Bonadea's desire and her determination not to throw herself at Ulrich. She takes the respectable middle way of coquetry: 'Bonadea needed to adjust something on her stocking and felt forced to look at Ulrich as she did so with her head slightly tilted back, so that on her knee, unsupervised by her eye, there emerged a contrasting still-life of lace hems, smooth stocking, tensed fingers and softly yielding pearl-sheen of skin' (262). Ulrich is thrown off-balance; he quickly lights a cigarette and keeps on talking. Bonadea in disappointment at his failure to respond takes another sip of whisky, which further undermines her resolve. Ulrich explains why it is impossible to do anything for Moosbrugger: ' "Basically, all these cases are like hanging threads, and if you pull at them the whole social weave begins to unravel" ' (263). This simile deserves some attention. We have, on the one hand, the cloth with its interwoven strands, on the other, society with its interconnecting human relationships. The temptation to pull at a broken thread corresponds to the humanitarian concern for someone who has broken the law through no fault of his own. But the awareness that to pull at the cloth will cause damage corresponds to the self-protective caution of the man or woman contemplating the consequences of breaking society's rules; to study the links between the abnormal and the normal, between a Moosbrugger and a gentleman or lady, is to break the rules. Secret desires are to be kept secret; to ask questions about human motivation is to put at risk the settled notion that humans are essentially rational beings. The fabric of society might be unravelled if this were found to be untrue.

Ulrich typically 'pulls at the thread'; Bonadea tries to find some way of tempting him away from intellectual to more tender pursuits: 'Bonadea lost a shoe in some mysterious way' (263). She knows that gallantry will require Ulrich to pick it up. 'Ulrich bent to pick it up and the foot with its warm toes came towards the shoe in his hand like a little child. "Leave it, leave it, I'll do it myself!" said Bonadea, holding her foot out to him' (263). Here again the inward frame of reference of the narrative is seen to be Moosbrugger – as Ulrich puts her shoe back on he tries to concentrate on what he is saying 'while, from the leg, the fragrance of diminished responsibility ['verminderte(. . .) Zurechnungsfähigkeit'] reached his nose' (263). At this delicate moment, words used by lawyers in their exploration of Moosbrugger's mental state, are diverted to describe Bonadea's condition which is now being communicated to Ulrich.

Bonadea makes an even less ambiguous move:

> Bonadea unclenched his fingers and spread them out over her breast. Her accompanying glance would have touched a heart of stone; in the next few moments Ulrich thought he could feel two hearts pounding in her breast like the confusion of clocks striking together in a clockmakers' shop. Summoning all his will-power he set the breast to rights and said softly: 'No, Bonadea!'                                                    (263–4)

The rhythm of the present scene follows closely that of the section of the narrative dealing with the night of the murder. Both scenes involve a woman giving blatant signals of sexual intent, in both the man displays initial indifference, which is gradually overcome; since in contemporary mores sex was seen in terms of conquest and surrender, both scenes can be seen to culminate in violence – the murder and the act of sex respectively. But there is a decisive difference between these two scenes. Ulrich brings this to the surface with the observation: ' "It's a strange thing. A remarkable difference: the person who is responsible in law ['Der zurechnungsfähige Mensch'] can always do something different, while the person who is not ['der unzurechnungsfähige'] can never do so!" ' (265).[43] Here the hero confirms that normal men possess a freedom of choice which Moosbrugger does not have. It is this, Ulrich tells Bonadea, that marks Moosbrugger out from people like them.

Ulrich has gently but firmly pulled his hand away from Bonadea's breast; Bonadea matches his sense of purpose with hers: '[Bonadea] had resolved, if need be, to remain seated on her chair, in hat and veil, to the very end, so that he would realise that he had before him someone who, when it was required, knew how to control herself just as well as her rival, Diotima' (266). They take up their positions, decorously apart, separated by 'Zurechnungsfä-higkeit' ('legal accountability'). There the narrator might have left them, but, instead, he brings the scene to an ironic close, confirming as he does so that Moosbrugger's act stemmed from compulsion, Bonadea's and Ulrich's from choice. Bonadea sits still, tortured by her decision to do nothing; tension mounts within her when 'suddenly a corporeal illusion came forth in a sudden twitch, a flea' (266). The narrator makes it quite clear that this is, indeed, an illusion and that Bonadea knows that it is, however life-like the sensations involved may seem:

She felt a shiver in her brain, an improbable impression as if one idea there had freed itself from the shadowy confinement of the others but was still only an illusion; and, at the same time, an indubitable, true-to-life shiver on the skin. She held her breath. When something comes, tripp, trapp up the staircase and one knows there's no one there, and still one hears quite clearly tripp, trapp, that's how it is. (266)[44]

She feels a bite, screams, Ulrich comes to help her find the offending insect as Bonadea removes articles of clothing, but of the flea no trace, of course, can be found.

The last few lines of the chapter are suggestively vague: ' "I don't know what that was!" said Bonadea.

Ulrich smiled in an unexpectedly friendly way.

Then Bonadea, like a little girl who has behaved badly, began to cry' (266). Here the Moosbrugger-like self-abandonment is part of the montage, the bourgeois camouflage of intention. When this is lifted to one side we can see what really happened. An Ulrich who in the end was more than half-willing, has been skilfully, willingly and wilfully, seduced.

Ulrich is more fully aware of things than the average man; the emotions which the out-and-out bourgeois represses he examines dispassionately: 'His inner conflict was different; it involved, to be precise, his not repressing anything' (653). But what this 'psycho-analysis' of his own emotions reveals is the image of the bourgeois who plays out in imagination acts that he dare not perform in real life. In conversation with Arnheim, Ulrich is seized by the desire to plunge his pocket-knife deep into the other's neck.[45] He thinks through all the movements he will have to make to do so; but this Moosbrugger-like impulse runs its course in the medium of imagination. Ulrich does nothing.

The fascination which Moosbrugger holds for the bourgeois who finds himself 'more deeply preoccupied with Moosbrugger than with the progress of the career that was his own life' (69) is echoed in Ulrich who realises that the murderer affects him more profoundly 'than his own life' (121). But fascination is not the same thing as the desire to emulate what Moosbrugger has done. Ulrich explains to Bonadea that people can feel a certain sympathy for Moosbrugger, but that it is inappropriate to try to do anything for him. The bourgeois is not prepared to lift a finger to help Moosbrugger; he sees in Moosbrugger someone whose thoughts and actions are too much of one piece. In Moosbrugger there is sometimes no gap between thought and deed; it is essential to bourgeois society, indeed to all societies, that there should be such a gap.

Towards the end of Part II, Bonadea pays a visit to Ulrich at Diotima's salon and begs him once again to do something for Moosbrugger. As she pursues the plan she conceived earlier the reader recognises that her motives are far from altruistic.[46] Ulrich says that there is no basis on which he could legitimately argue Moosbrugger's case – his position on Moosbrugger has shifted a long way from that in the scene with Graf Stallburg in the opening chapter of Part II when he had interceded on Moosbrugger's behalf. Although Ulrich has apparently been preoccupied with the murderer he feels he knows nothing of him: '"What do I know of him? I have seen him once fleetingly in a hearing and I've read a few other things that have been written about him"' (580). What has masqueraded as concern for another has, in fact, been involvement with himself. When he reflects that 'Moosbrugger, for some unknown reason, concerned him more directly than the life he led himself' (121), this 'Moosbrugger' might well stand in inverted commas, for 'he' has been nothing more than a focus of feelings that Ulrich has found in his own nature. The 'Sektionschef' ('Head of Section') played out a private Moosbrugger-game with his wife; Ulrich has explored, with the help of Moosbrugger's revelations, his own subconscious. Ulrich gently turns down Bonadea's request with the strange rebuff: '"It is as if I had dreamt that the tip of your breast was like a poppy leaf. Am I allowed to think, because of that, that it really is one?"' (580). Moosbrugger is no more than the stuff of dreams, 'An escaped simile of order' (653).

Where does this leave the 'real' Moosbrugger as he sits in prison awaiting the outcome of endless appeals? Ulrich has washed his hands of Moosbrugger but society cannot do the same. Ulrich knows 'that the state will, in the end, kill Moosbrugger because, in such a half-baked situation, it is simply the clearest, cheapest and safest thing to do' (245). Just as the private moral hygiene of the bourgeois[47] seems to require the stimulus of the horrific, so the public hygiene of bourgeois society at large requires that Moosbrugger be eliminated.

The gross injustice that will be done to Moosbrugger is expressed in graphic detail when Ulrich describes to Bonadea his inevitable fate:

'Two men will put the noose around his neck without feeling the slightest stirring of ill-will towards him but merely because they are paid to do so. Perhaps a hundred people will watch, some because this is officially required of them, some because everyone wants to have seen an execution once in their life. A solemn gentleman in top hat, tails and black gloves, draws the noose tight and at the same moment his two assistants hang on to both of Moosbrugger's legs so that the neck breaks.'          (119–20)

The passion of a hot-blooded murder done in a moment of frenzy by a mentally deranged man is answered by a formalised, premeditated killing in cold blood in which the whole of society shares by default – Bonadea typifies the refusal of most people to think seriously about such matters, and Ulrich surprisingly ultimately displays a similar indifference despite his initial role as a secret judge of the murderer.

Moosbrugger, the innocent, must die; though he can in no way be held responsible for what he has done he has touched the taboo object and brought into the open the secret guilt of society, its repressed passion and violence. Ulrich, sick at heart, turns away both from Moosbrugger and the society that condemns him. Here, as elsewhere, Musil is a provocative critic, not a social engineer. Musil makes no proposals for changes in the legal system to cater for his findings in this case. We should, however, remind ourselves of what he does achieve.

First, his narrative is an outstanding literary achievement in itself – it offers an extraordinary portrait of a psychopath. Second, Musil makes full use of the freedom available to a creative author to develop his investigations into contemporary society in a direction which is entirely his own. Even the freedom he would have enjoyed if he had become an assistant to Alexius Meinong would have been, in practical terms, far more circumscribed by the requirements of academic research. No psychology professor would ever have given him his head for such a wide-ranging investigation of the mind of one madman, no research board would have considered supporting for one minute, let alone for the months, perhaps years, which it required, a study of this kind, based as it is on newspaper reports and conjecture rather than empirical data. However – and this leads to my third point – Musil's 'Moosbrugger'-project has something of the self-critical quality of a scientific enterprise. With scrupulous concern for accuracy, Musil explores the phenomenon of empathy, the faculty for intimate understanding of the life of another human being – and this is surely a suitable topic for serious investigation since, without it, all social relationships would cease as each human being was marooned on his or her own island of psychic solitude. In Musil's project, empathy is transformed from the status of mysterious intuition to a faculty which is closely examined and precisely described.

Fourth, Musil, working through his hero, uses the figure of Moosbrugger to focus his thinking on the drives hidden beneath the surface of civilised human life. Musil assumes that Moosbrugger is different from other men only in the strength of his passions and the weakness of his critical faculty; thus, in Moosbrugger, the hero is confronted with the image of feelings which pulse unseen through his own psyche. In the sick mind, the working of the unconscious is part-transparent. What is it, Musil asks, that divides mental sickness from mental health? (The answer implicit in the narrative, as we have seen, has to do with the nature of the relationship between objectivity and subjectivity, between spontaneity and self-criticism.) Why, Musil further asks, is the life of this man so intense while that of civilised men and women seems anaemic – could some of Moosbrugger's energy be redirected along safer channels to regenerate a civilisation that seems to have lost its way? (To this question, no answer is given, as far as I can see.)

Finally, as we have seen, the figure of Moosbrugger provides a focus for Musil's reflections on free will. Through him, Musil seeks an answer to the question 'Can human beings determine actions themselves, or is freedom an illusion?' The answer from the narrative is 'Yes, human beings *are* free agents.' If the answer had been 'No', the hero's search for authentic morality, which is at the centre of the whole novel, would have been meaningless.

# 8

# ULRICH AS 'MAN WITHOUT QUALITIES'

As an older man looks back over his earlier life, he forms an opinion of it, seeing and judging his younger self from the vantage point of experience and hindsight. However, as we have seen in our examination of the theme of 'Wirklichkeit', Musil does not always manage in Part I and Part II of *The Man without Qualities* to make this historical and moral judgement sufficiently clear to his readers.

We can see that Ulrich, this relatively young man living in Vienna in 1913, is suffering from a surfeit of unproductive thought; his intellectuality is too inward-looking and has become a prison. No thought seems reliable, no belief tenable, no action worthwhile. Though Ulrich, at the outset of *The Man without Qualities*, does not represent the intellectual and moral position of the mature Musil, the fact that many critics think that he does – that they believe that the kinds of things which Ulrich thinks and says throughout *The Man without Qualities* can be put together to form the 'Collected Wisdom of Robert Musil' – is sufficient indication of a failure by Musil to make his mature position stand out. Perhaps this is partly because Musil did not finish *The Man without Qualities*. Part I and Part II make up by far the larger section of the material which Musil published; these Parts of *The Man without Qualities* present, as I shall show below, the hero before his attitude to the world matures. Perhaps only when Part III and Part IV had been finished would the balance have been restored and the hero have been seen 'in the round'. It is vital that we notice those passages in the text of the first half of the work where Musil presents his hero in a critical light, thereby preparing the ground for his hero's change of heart and mind.

Musil introduces his hero in an ambiguous pose: it is clear that we have a scientist before us, for he stands at the window of his Viennese home conducting impromptu statistical experiments on the movement of traffic and pedestrians outside.[1] Ulrich stands seperated from the outside world by glass,[2] symbolising his detachment from the things he studies, whether they belong to the outside world or to the inner world of feelings. Here, at the beginning of the novel, the 'aperture' of Ulrich's consciousness is opened to its widest extent allowing a flood of data to rush in; he measures the movements with a stop-watch in an attempt to find formulae that will make this teeming world fall into a knowable order. This symbolises the predicament of a scientist who wants not only to work under controlled laboratory conditions but to apply his scientific skills to life at large, and who then discovers how impossibly complex a task this is. For not only is there too much to deal with, but it is also not possible to distance oneself from the world and study it with aseptic detachment. At the beginning of the novel the glass of the window seems to seal Ulrich off from the queer 'world experiment – Kakania'[3] but, as we have already seen, this 'man-camera' has, in the course of the plot, to become part of the 'film' that is his own life.

Ulrich feels alienated both from the outside world at large which he cannot control and even from his own body which seems to be 'out there' in the physical world, almost beyond the reach of his mind.[4] He observes things with scrupulous concern for objectivity but he cannot exert much influence on the external environment through which his alienated body must move. He is in a dilemma. On the one hand he is convinced that, without self-awareness, modern life is pulled into a vortex of unmeaning – that, in other words, 'Seinesgleichen geschieht' ('The same kind of things happen again'); on the other hand, to reflect is to isolate oneself and to feel the impotence of reason in the hectic world of living experience. Despite this, Ulrich wants, and is determined to achieve, what F. G. Peters calls a 'direct and necessary connection between thought and life'.[5] He wants to discover no less than the principle that imbues a man's life with meaning. His scientific training has been rigorous and thorough and determines the way in which this search is carried out: it is to be conducted with a scrupulous concern for objectivity. But it quickly becomes apparent that the pursuit of objectivity and the search for meaning are difficult to reconcile.[6] It seems that the more Ulrich understands of the world around him, the less significant he feels himself to be; the more he grasps about the nature of human motivations, the less he feels constrained to take a particular course of action himself. In view of this he accepts Walter's name for him, 'Mann ohne Eigenschaften' ('man without qualities').[7]

Ulrich finds that this title gives expression to his feeling that there is no pattern to his experiences; they do not seem to bear the signature of any personal intervention on his part. He tries to probe the problem of identity, but both question and answer are rhetorical, they come from the same source, his own self-conscious intellect: 'Was he a strong person? He didn't know [...]. But certainly he had always been a person who had confidence in his strength' (149). Words are here not the means to dispel the fog of ignorance, they are part of the fog itself. What unchanging measure can be found against which 'strength' can be measured? The oracle of consciousness is Delphic: it reflects no more than the hopes and doubts of Ulrich himself. The problem of personal identity is part of his general moral predicament: 'Why, then, did he live in a vague and indecisive way?' (153). For this question he is able find a satisfactory answer: 'Without doubt [...] [it] was none other than the urge to free and to bind the world that is called [...] intellect [Geist]' (153).[8] The incorrigible intellect recognises that the root of his uncertainty is also the root of his intellectual existence. Hume, who may be seen as one of Ulrich's antecedents, was fully aware of the fascination of such self-defeating self-questioning: 'I never can catch myself', Hume insisted.[9] Attempts to identify precisely who and what one is are bound to fail.

Here, a question of self-perception is relevant to moral issues. This problem bears directly on the search for what Ulrich calls 'das [...] rechte[..] Leben [...]' (255) ('the [...] right way to live'). Try as he will, Ulrich cannot catch sight of the inner connection between thinking and doing.[10] 'If I knew what I was', he seems to say, 'I would know what I ought to be – I would know what to do.' Sometimes he glimpses within himself the shadow of an individual impulse to action but he never sees the whole picture, the guiding life-principle, that should shape all his activity. (The so-called 'utopias' that preoccupy him seem to be a kind of synthetic substitute for moral purpose. They are the hero's attempt to design a structure to give shape and purpose to his actions, but they are structures which prove too flimsy to withstand the incalculable pressures, the natural accidents, of daily life.)

As I have indicated above, it is the narrator to whom the reader looks for a critical judgement on the hero and for some indication, however indirect, of where Musil himself stands. What does the narrator say about Ulrich, this man who is hamstrung by too much reflection? He has very little to say that is not ambiguous, and he seems to delight in refraining from any substantial moral evaluation of the hero's conduct. This can be seen particularly clearly in a sample of text from Part I, Chapter 11, where the narrator presents Ulrich's attempt to apply his knowledge of mathematics to wider existential problems.

The narrator starts with the promise which mathematics appears to hold: 'here is the new theory of thought itself, intellect ['Geist'] itself, here lie the wellsprings of our time and the origin of an immense restructuring' (39). He presents the appeal of mathematics – this purest of the pure sciences – with apparent enthusiasm. The reader may perhaps feel that he has recognised that the narrator shares Ulrich's enthusiasm for mathematics. This view seems to be confirmed after a few more lines of text when we read 'all people who have to know something of the soul ['Seele'] because, as clergymen, historians and artists, they derive a good income from it, aver that it has been ruined by mathematics' (40). The wry suggestion by the narrator that some of the critics of mathematics conceal their material interests behind a cloak of spirituality appears to indicate that his sympathies lie with the mathematicians. But then, without warning, he switches to criticism: 'mathematics, mother of exact science, grandmother of technology [is] also the great-great-grandmother of that spirit ['Geist'] [...] from which, in the end, poison gases and fighter-pilots issued forth' (40). In this account neither mathematician nor non-mathematician escapes unscathed: the mathematician is presented as dangerously oblivious to the general good, while the non-mathematician's public protests about the evils of science are devalued by his private self-indulgence. There, with even-handed criticism, the narrator leaves the matter; he offers the reader no readily identifiable opinion about Ulrich's plans and way of living.[11]

The narrator, in Part I and Part II of *The Man without Qualities*, presents Ulrich's dilemma; he does not, as we saw earlier, make explicit his judgement on the hero's attempts to solve it. The narrative of *The Man without Qualities* reflects the riddle of the structure of human existence as Musil construed it.[12] Ulrich, having rejected all forms of authority, finds it impossible to establish whether what he undertakes has any meaning; the narrator, in apparent deference to Ulrich's views, declines to act as an authority. The diffidence of the narrator mirrors the difficulties which Ulrich experiences in establishing who he is and what he should do. Just as Ulrich must piece together fragments of insight from diffuse experiences, so, it seems, readers are left to assemble their own evaluation of the hero on the basis of his encounters with Austro-Hungarian reality in Part I and Part II. In fact, however, close attention to the narrative does reveal the narrator's attitude to the hero.

Chapter 11 opens with an account of Ulrich arriving home, badly beaten, with torn clothes and his wallet missing. We start at what, in terms of the temporal sequence of the events recorded in the chapter, is very nearly the end, for these sentences are the setting for Ulrich's private reconstruction of what has happened to bring him to this sorry state, as he recovers in bed and thinks over what happened. Here, like Proust's hero, Ulrich is 'à la recherche du temps perdu' – though in Ulrich's case it is the immediate, rather than the distant past that he wants to recover. We have here the first of a number of temporal shifts, the 'signature', so to speak, of Ulrich's intellect at work. But this act of taking possession of experience is simultaneously a sign that the reader is being taken one remove away from the events described. He is made aware that this is experience at second hand; or, to use Husserl's notion, this is existence between intellectual brackets.[13]

Ulrich commands the immediate past to appear before his memory to allow him to sift through it and catch its meaning. But in this internal narrative something has changed. Of course, no retrospective intervention can alter the experience itself. What has changed is the context in which the experience is placed, the question of how it is to be interpreted.

While walking in the streets of Vienna, he has inadvertently brushed against a passer-by. Suddenly three heavily-built men have surrounded him. Now, as Ulrich thinks back over what happened, their hostile intentions are perfectly apparent; but then, called upon to make a decision 'on the spot', he hesitated. As Ulrich mulls over the links between the external situation and his internal reactions to that situation, he suggests an interpretation which may strike the reader as rather a curious conclusion for an intellectual to draw. Ulrich blames thought, the act of reflection itself, for his hesitation: 'He seemed [. . .], when faced with three rogues, *to have spent a little too much time thinking*' (26) (my emphasis). He is set upon and beaten into unconsciousness; but, in retrospect, what seems to him important is not the nausea, the splitting pain as the world spins on its axis within his head, but the sense of being an impartial onlooker at some aesthetic spectacle: 'Ulrich [fell calmly asleep] [. . .] with the same delight in the spirals of ebbing consciousness which he had been subliminally aware of already during his defeat' (27). The reader is left with the impression that, at least in a situation like this, the intellect is out of phase with the body to which it belongs.

This impression is borne out when Ulrich reexamines the way the intellect regains its imperfect control over the body as consciousness slowly returns: he is aware of a cab stopping and the driver attempting to assist him. The hero's faculties seem partly restored, but as his eyes start to focus again it is evident that his mind is still affected: 'a lady bent over him with the expression of an angel' (28); he finds himself 'as if in the world of children's books' (28). The world of children's books is often untroubled by reality; the irony is that this vision of feminine perfection cannot survive the harsher scrutiny of that reality: the lady is Bonadea, the nymphomaniac. Childhood innocence recedes as the lady's perfume insinuates itself into his senses and awakens adult layers of consciousness. 'So that he knew immediately [. . .] that he couldn't have been seriously hurt, and did his best to regain his feet' (28). However, Ulrich is a little unsteady and is offered a lift home in the carriage. Here he quickly recovers – so quickly, in fact, that Bonadea fears she has compromised whatever reputation she may still have left – and he begins to explain to her how he came to be lying in the gutter.

In telling Bonadea what has happened, and in re-relating it to himself resting at home in bed, Ulrich has, in one sense, made the experience his own; yet, at the same time, the narrative records his original feeling of alienation from what took place. The narrator dwells not only on the way the intellect suffered the embarrassment of unconsciousness but how this state resulted directly from its own inefficiency.[14] The anti-intellectual climax follows: even as Ulrich lies in bed preoccupied with arranging events in logical order, a lady is announced. She proves to be the beautiful stranger who helped him when he lay injured and who has returned, allegedly to enquire after his health. The reader knows that Ulrich is busy investigating the connection between the realms of intellectual and corporeal energy; what Bonadea sees is a handsome male lying helpless in bed. The chapter ends with a statement that mocks the temporal contortions which have charted Ulrich's attempts to come to terms with the attack: 'Two weeks later, Bonadea had already been his mistress for a fortnight' (30). Thus the narrator suggests that intellect is routed: for even after the fog of unconsciousness has cleared and Ulrich's mind has established its retrospective 'control' over existence it seems not to have learnt any lesson. Here, back in the present, it is seen to be without defence against direct sensual ploys which it can accurately diagnose and minutely describe, but which it does not know how to resist. In short, the critical attitude of the narrator to the hero is discernible on close examination of the text, but is not as clear to the reader as it might be, indeed as it ought to be.

These mental gymnastics form part of the 'Urlaub [vom] Leben' (47) ('leave from life'), an incorrigible intellectual's approach to moral issues, a scientist studying the phenomenon of moral impulses in the subject most readily to hand, namely himself. He resolves to go through the motions of living his life more or less as he has done before but from now on without conviction; he proposes to be both an actor in the play of life and somehow also out in the auditorium watching his own performance. This curious experiment demands not only detachment but the opportunity to withdraw and reflect. As we have seen, Bonadea repeatedly makes demands on the hero which are difficult to reconcile with rigorous objectivity and studied non-involvement! The narrator describes such scenes with gentle irony and thereby indicates to the reader that Ulrich's experiment will fail, even though Ulrich himself continues for much of Part I and Part II of *The Man without Qualities* to see detachment as the key to understanding the nature of morality.[15] When Clarisse taunts him over his failure to become deeply involved in any enterprise whatsoever, his response is to reflect: 'On no account does God mean the world to be taken literally; it is an image, an analogy, a figure of speech, which He has to make use of for some or other reason and, of course, always for an insufficient reason; we must not take Him at His word, we have to find the solution to the puzzle which He sets us' (357–8). Here the 'Urlaub vom Leben' takes on quasi-theological form. Ulrich imputes to God the attitude to creation which he has chosen himself: 'Life is not something valuable in itself', he argues, 'it is a vast problem that we must set our minds to solving'.[16]

G. E. Moore, a philosopher of whom Bertrand Russell was a pupil, wanted to find a scientific basis for the study of moral problems. He suggested that in order to test the value of actions it would be necessary to construct a model of the universe in which all the effects of an action could be examined. Ulrich originally seemed to belong in the same tradition of thinking about moral questions but he evidently believes that he can achieve the results which Moore expects of his model universe by using the real world as a model. In conversation with Diotima, Ulrich suggests that people attach far too much importance to what they happen to be doing at a given moment. They should learn to disregard the sense of urgency that attaches to activity in the real world, or, to use Ulrich's own term which we examined above in its specific context, they should be forced 'to abolish reality'.[17]

But the effect of this theory is to be seen most clearly in Ulrich's attitude to Moosbrugger, the murderer. Ulrich relives in imagination the crimes which Moosbrugger commits, he meditates on the scenes in a courtroom where Moosbrugger is being tried, he examines the murder and its implications from the social, the philosophical and the legal angle. But time and again we are reminded that his interest moves almost exclusively on a theoretical plane. His initial concerns do not seem to impinge on the living world which he tends to keep at a distance.

Ulrich holds the view that nothing compels him to do anything for Moosbrugger because his speculations about the way in which Moosbrugger was driven to commit murder are, precisely, speculations not facts. It may be, he argues, that he has not understood the murderer at all; for all he knows Moosbrugger may indeed be the callous scoundrel that his accusers present in their depositions to the court. But what is the reader expected to make of such reservations? Doubts are two-edged; the man may be guilty, but equally he may be innocent. Here is the call to action – the bridge to the real world. Ulrich does not cross the bridge. In the very act of doubting his own ability to establish that Moosbrugger is innocent, he places in doubt the ability of the court to find evidence to substantiate Moosbrugger's 'guilt'. At the very least, he should use his newly won influence with the Austro-Hungarian establishment to ensure that the legal definition of responsibility, 'Zurechnungs-fähigkeit', is re-examined in the light of modern developments in knowledge about human consciousness.[18] Clarisse sees the opportunity offered by Ulrich's access to the leading figures of the 'Parallelaktion' and makes her view perfectly clear: '"Something must be done for Moosbrugger [...]"' (213), she says. The challenge to action is unequivocal. But Ulrich side-steps it (evidently feeling that to become involved would be to interfere arbitrarily in the field that he has chosen for his experiment).

Later Clarisse reminds him of what she has said but this time makes her statement much more personal: '" You've got to do something for [this murderer]"' (217). (Clarisse, incidentally, has plans not only for Moosbrugger but for Ulrich as well. She believes that she knows what is wrong with the hero; she wants to force him to become involved in things, to thrust him forward into a position from which he will be unable to retreat.)[19] When Ulrich asks what he should do, her laconic answer is simple and categorical: '"Free him"' (217).[20] Clarisse is convinced that injustice has been done, this must be put to rights in the most direct way possible, by breaking into Moosbrugger's prison and setting him free. Ulrich is taken completely aback; he is unable to fit Clarisse's words into any context: 'Ulrich looked at her. He did not quite understand. He must have missed something she said; a comparison or some "as if" which made her words meaningful' (217). Ulrich tries to find in Clarisse's statements the kind of reservations that would have restrained him if he had felt a similar impulse. In juxtaposing the tentative hero with the absolute Clarisse, the narrator implies that there are things in this world undreamt of in Ulrich's 'philosophy'.[21]

The narrator shows that his understanding extends beyond Ulrich's when he describes the one time that Ulrich does do something for Moosbrugger. During his interview with Graf Stallburg in the first chapter of Part II of *The Man without Qualities*, Ulrich blurts out a plea on Moosbrugger's behalf. As the narrator makes quite clear, the words slip out before they can be censored by Ulrich's intellect and cause the hero no little embarrassment.[22] It is surely significant that this action of Ulrich's leads to a review of Moosbrugger's case.[23] Ulrich's bad conscience about Moosbrugger is part of a flow of emotion within him which, when the dam of the 'Urlaub vom Leben' is breached, begins to transform his whole life. We shall explore this further in our examination of Ulrich's life after his meeting with his sister, Agathe.

The 'Urlaub vom Leben' was intended to be a means of discovering the best way to live but, as Musil shows us here, cutting oneself off from fellow human beings is merely an evasion. Ulrich may have seen the 'Urlaub vom Leben' as an opportunity for the exercise of freedom – but freedom without commitment is vain. This should have been made clear to readers but it is not. Obviously Musil's failure to finish the novel was one reason for this, but there are others, in particular a decision by Musil about the design of the novel which seems to me to have been a mistake. This requires detailed examination.

### A flaw in the design of 'The Man without Qualities'?

Johannes von Allesch,[24] who knew Musil from the time when they were students together in Berlin, suggests that Musil's trust in the powers of the intellect derived from his scientific and technical training. Von Allesch argues that, as early as his schooldays, Musil was introduced to a mode of thinking which was 'characterised by a striving for naturalness, clarity, accessibility and a corresponding simplification, indeed a touch of naiveté'. Von Allesch continues: 'this rational attitude [...] was constantly available to him as a potential mode of thinking [...] a potential way of solving the tasks which life sets'.[25] Von Allesch states that Musil gave up a career in engineering in order to see whether this approach would actually work when used to tackle human problems. Von Allesch's view of Musil is formed essentially, it seems to me, from the powerful impression which Musil made on him when they were both students. Later Musil began to doubt the wisdom of militant intellectuality as a way of tackling existential problems. The narrator looks from a mature vantage-point on the attitude of the hero who repeats the extravagances of the young Musil. Watching over Ulrich's shoulder, so to speak, as the hero carries out his intellectual experiments, the narrator knows for certain what Ulrich himself only suspects[26] – that they will prove futile.

For the reader who is alert to the way in which the hero's intentions are thwarted at every turn by the situations he meets there may be no need for the narrator to resort to explicit statements about the hero's plans. The irony in the narrative is a pointer to Ulrich's continual failures and his need to change direction.[27] But Musil evidently felt that this had to be expressed more prominently. On 10 February 1930 he made the final changes before publication which he thought would serve this purpose: 'I am reworking Chapter 61 [and] redistributing its components into Chapter 61 [and] 62, extending a part [and] that is very time-consuming but very important for the novel because now the U[lrich] problem will be almost finished up to the turning-point at the end' (Tb1, 700). However, it seems to me that, far from clarifying any problem, these two chapters disturb the balance of *The Man without Qualities*.

Chapter 61 deals with what is described as 'Die Utopie der Exaktheit' ('Utopia of Exactitude') and Chapter 62 with 'Die Utopie des Essayismus' ('Utopia of Essayism').[28] These 'utopias', as we saw above, are intellectual blueprints, designs for living in an age which denies the individual any sense of moral certainty. The two utopias in question represent the quintessence of Ulrich's thinking at different points in his life. Up to this point in the narrative the narrator, too, has kept silent on the limitations of Ulrich's present 'utopia'; his deeper knowledge of the mis\kes which Ulrich is making is expressed only in a quizzical irony – it is almost as if the 'Gedankenexperiment' had exacted from the narrator a vow of silence on his views of the hero; but now, the narrator breaks this vow, rising up to a vantage-point from which he surveys the whole of Ulrich's life since maturity and passes judgement on it. I believe that this 'narrative betrayal', though intended to help the reader, tends to confuse.

The 'Utopie der Exaktheit' is a programme which appears to embrace the whole of the hero's life up to this stage in the narrative; it is a general theory about the way a person should shape his or her life, given the problems, and the opportunities, of the world in the twentieth century. (The 'Urlaub vom Leben' is Ulrich's attempt to apply the theory in the context of his immediate existence in 1913.)[29] But the approach is, of its nature, unworkable. There is an essential flaw about it which David Pears neatly characterised: 'Archimedes said that he could move the world, if he could find a point in space which would serve as the fulcrum for a sufficiently long lever. His idea can be used as an image to illustrate the origin of philosophy. Philosophy originates in the desire to transcend the world of human thought and experience in order to find some point of vantage from which it can be seen as a whole.'[30] Ulrich's approach is philosophical in this sense; it is also scientific, and here is another central problem. The experiments on which scientific knowledge is based can be tried out by other scientists. But human life cannot be approached this way. The scientific experiment is, of its essence, repeatable. Human life is not. In the moral field, experimentation is ruled out because human existence is, at every moment, unique. As we are shown in the text, the 'Utopie der Exaktheit' is inoperable. Moral detachment is not a practical *modus vivendi*.

The other utopia, that of essayism, though narrower in scope, is presented by the narrator as definitely superior to the 'Utopie der Exaktheit'.[31] It is not concerned with the problems of living in general but with the individual in specific situations; according to this utopia, the source of morality is found in restricted but substantial moments.[32] In recognising that moral problems are unique, that each human life is unrepeatable and so not a suitable subject for scientific investigation, the 'Utopie des Essayismus' is quite different from the 'Utopie der Exaktheit'. In fact, it is incompatible with the 'Urlaub vom Leben' which, as we saw, was derived from Ulrich's desire for 'exact' living. It is linked with the experiments in more active living which we find when Agathe comes on the scene in Part III. We are thus faced with an unfortunate anachronism in the structure of the novel, a hiatus between the reflective commentary by the narrator and the stage which the hero has actually reached in the plot itself.

At a point less than halfway between the beginning of Part I and the end of Part II, Musil stands back from his hero for the first time and produces a sketch of his outlook on life not as it is at this point in the narrative but as it will be only towards the beginning of Part III of the novel. The reader, grappling with the complexities of the 'utopias', is thrown into confusion in an attempt to square what the narrative now says about the hero with the hero's present behaviour and present attitude. In fact, the observations about the 'Utopie des Essayismus' seem to me to be in the wrong place – they belong some seventy chapters further on in the text of *The Man without Qualities* at a point where Ulrich realises that the 'Urlaub vom Leben' holds no more meaning for him.[33] I can only explain this lapse in terms of Musil's haste to satisfy his publisher; it has made it difficult for critics to understand how much Ulrich's outlook changes in the course of the work.[34] Even as sensitive a critic as Michael Hamburger, for instance, misses Ulrich's development; he states that 'the hero does not proceed from a given way of life to a different one, either chosen or imposed'.[35] I shall argue below that the hero does change, in response to stimuli that are both external and internal.

### Abandoning the 'Urlaub vom Leben'

Setting aside this lapse on Musil's part, we can say the following about this aspect of *The Man without Qualities*: at each point in the hero's progress the narrator has the whole course of Ulrich's development in view. But as he looks 'over Ulrich's shoulder' at each moment in the novel he understands and, to a certain extent, sympathises with what the hero says and thinks and does as a part of this development. The value of each undertaking, the affair with Bonadea, the appointment to the 'Parallelaktion', the conversations with Diotima, may be measured against an inescapable necessity – that Ulrich must come to terms with existence, by giving up sceptical detachment and developing an awareness of an innate moral sense. As we have seen, the narrator does not explicitly judge and condemn, but subtly, almost imperceptibly at times, measures the extent to which Ulrich resists this simple truth by the degree of irony in his treatment of the hero.[36] So, in the earlier stages of the work when Ulrich strays far away into intellectuality and abstraction, the narrator dwells with some delight on the confusions that beset the hero. The narrator does not expatiate on Ulrich's folly in formulating the 'Urlaub vom Leben'; he merely intimates that the hero has forgotten to take account of time which alters the individual's perspective as inevitably as it redistributes his energy and interest. One imagines the narrator wearing a wry smile as he produces an analogy which withdraws credibility from that undertaking:

if one upholds a demand for a long time without anything happening to it, then the brain goes to sleep in exactly the same way as the arm goes to sleep if it holds something up for a long time, and our thoughts can no more be at a perpetual stand-still than soldiers can stand still at a summer parade; if they have to stand too long, they simply fall down in a faint.     (255–6)

On the other hand, in the later parts of the novel, above all in Part III when the hero is moving in the right direction, the ironic distance between hero and narrator disappears and the reader senses an identity of perspective in the search for the right way to live.

There are scarcely any references to the 'Urlaub vom Leben' in Part III of *The Man without Qualities*. That it drops out of Ulrich's life almost without trace is an indication that it has been left behind as unwanted intellectual baggage which is not needed for the journey 'Ins Tausendjährige Reich' ('Into the Millennium'). On one occasion, however, Ulrich does refer to it in Part III, albeit obliquely. He is trying to explain to Agathe a particular philosophical point of view.[37] He asks her to imagine a bench in the mountains in front of which a herd of cattle grazes: '"Just imagine that some official or other is sitting there in 'Lederhosen' which have come straight from the factory and which have green braces with 'Grüß Gott!' embroidered on them; he represents the real content of life which is on leave."'' (767). There can be little doubt that the leather trousers with their folksy greeting are a disguise; this is really Ulrich's caricature of himself on his 'Urlaub vom Leben'. The hero is looking back over the last few months of his life – the period covered in Part II of the novel – and at once giving Agathe an account of his thinking during these months and offering his own critical assessment of it. Here Ulrich performs the role which Peter Nusser described as that of 'narrator of his own self'.[38] As he talks to his sister he expounds for her something from his personal intellectual history and he adopts the ironic pose, the detachment that, earlier in *The Man without Qualities*, was adopted by the narrator himself.

Ulrich has chosen the Austrian dignitary on holiday to illustrate the kind of transformation of consciousness which the 'Urlaub vom Leben' required. Seated on his bench in the mountains the worthy gentleman relaxes the faculties which make him a force to be reckoned with in the office: '"[...] When he looks at the herd of cattle, he does not count or calculate, he does not estimate the live-weight of the animals grazing before him, he forgives his enemies and thinks kindly of his family. For him, the herd has changed from a practical to a *moral object*, so to speak [...]"' (my emphasis) (767). The term 'moral object' is ironic. This describes Ulrich's misguided attempt to marry the scientific attitude and morality in the 'Urlaub vom Leben'. Surely, the reader is invited to respond, morality is incompatible with detachment – it cannot be merely an extension of the scientist's attitude of scrupulous impartiality. Morality involves commitment.[39] But, as I have indicated, in this scene Ulrich is here parodying his earlier point of view.

It was towards the end of Part II of the novel that understanding had dawned in Ulrich himself.[40] We see evidence of this in Part II, Chapter 12, where Ulrich confronts his rival, Arnheim. Each seems to want to dominate the other by force of personality as well as argument.[41] Arnheim concedes that Ulrich's idea of treating life as something provisional has a certain eccentric charm but asks '"what happens, for example, with wars and revolutions? Can one wake the dead again when the experiment is finished and is deleted from the work schedule?!"' (636). Ulrich defends his theory, saying that a man who lives 'life in the experimental mode' is unwilling 'to accept a responsibility which, in a certain sense, is limitless' (636). Borrowing an idea from Nietzsche he asserts that, where conscience is not firmly anchored in belief, it becomes redundant – it must be jettisoned with the dogma from which it sprang.[42] (The resemblance between this notion and the 'Urlaub vom Leben' is not accidental.) This does not mean, as we shall see later, that Ulrich advocates hedonism. Arnheim calls Ulrich's bluff with a demand that he consider a practical problem: he asks what Ulrich would do about Moosbrugger, would he let him escape if he had the opportunity to do so? No, Ulrich says, he would not; but then he reconsiders his answer. He is not sure, he says, '"I don't know. I don't think so. I could, of course, make the excuse that in a world which is set up wrongly it is not possible for me to act in the way that I think is right; but I'll simply admit to you that I don't know what I would have to do"' (636).

This answer marks a tentative, but significant, move by Ulrich towards reaching the position where his view matches the narrator's. Here he is beginning to question the value of his intellectual experiments. He all but concedes that consciousness cannot anticipate some of the finer promptings of the moral will. It is not possible to predict how one will behave in the future until one stands in the nexus of circumstance. Only then will one know, through the agency of some moral intuition beyond the reach of reason and analysis, what to do. In short, the answer which he gives Arnheim shows that he is about to abandon the 'Urlaub vom Leben'. Musil marks this shift in attitude with a surprising offer to Ulrich from Arnheim. He asks the hero to join him as private secretary with the prospect later of a senior position in his business empire. '"And to what qualities ['Eigenschaften']", Ulrich asks, "do I owe this suggestion [. . .]?"' (642). Arnheim replies: '"It is [. . .] your character, your human qualities that for certain reasons I should like to have constantly at my side"' (642). Ulrich points out that others have a quite different view of him from Arnheim: '"My qualities? [. . .] Do you know that my friends call me a man who has no qualities?"' (642). Apart from this, however, Ulrich raises no objections to what is effectively Arnheim's denial that he is a 'Man without Qualities'. It is almost as if Musil were suggesting that the title of the novel no longer applies to the hero from this point onwards.

At this point Ulrich is seen to be changing from a 'free spirit', immune to the call of any moral imperative, to someone who is concerned to find out which feelings, at the deepest inner level, bind and hold him fast. He is shown to be moving from amoral rationality and detachment to concern with the way men and women are guided by some innate ethical sense. We can judge what has happened here more clearly if we look briefly at a passage much later in the text. A tram-journey in Part III provides a parallel, and a contrast, to one in Part II when Ulrich tried to think out how he might explain to Clarisse why he was so inactive. On this second ride, he looks at the shops, the people, the carriages, the bustling vitality of the capital, and experiences another moment of awakening to the challenge of life beyond the pose of intellectual detachment: 'Ulrich now knew where the weakness of his reflections lay. "In the face of this self-sufficient splendour, what is the meaning", he wondered, "of asking for a result that is supposed to be above, behind, beneath it?! Is it supposed to be a philosophy, then? An all-embracing conviction, a law?"' (873). The self-evident answer is 'No!'.[43] In the final chapter of Part II clear evidence is offered of the change in Ulrich.

Here, Clarisse is waiting for the hero when he returns home after the meeting with Arnheim. Clarisse plans to make a different man of him – the first step is to seduce him. Gently but firmly Ulrich resists her passionate advances.[44] Surely the appropriate response from a 'Man without Qualities' would have been to let things take their course – to allow this curious Austrian experiment to shape his life as it wants to? After Clarisse has left, Ulrich becomes aware that he is changing: 'between himself and his environment, a deep feeling spreading out like ground-water on which the [...] buttresses of sober perception and thought usually rested seemed to shift' (664). What this change is, Ulrich is not able to identify – but there can be little doubt that Musil is indicating to the reader that deep emotional upheaval in the hero which is mirrored at a reflective level by the change from the 'Utopie der Exaktheit' to the 'Utopie des Essayismus'. Here – in the final chapter of Part II of *The Man without Qualities* – the narrator is attempting to show the reader that, when Ulrich sets out 'Ins Tausendjährige Reich' ('Into the Millennium') in Part III, he is no longer the man who was introduced at the window, looking out on a busy Vienna street, in the second chapter of Part I. Ulrich himself records the change as he reflects: '"It is a different kind of attitude; I'm changing into another person and so everything which is connected with me is changing, too!"' (664). Here, in this chapter entitled 'Die Umkehrung' – which Kaiser and Wilkins translated as 'The Turning-Point' in their English version of *The Man without Qualities* – a process of maturing is seen to be complete. This man who had earlier drawn a curtain of reflection between himself and the world will henceforth be far more willing to act spontaneously in accord with subtle feelings which rise up from levels of selfhood that he accepts cannot be approached by intellectual effort.

Perhaps the shift in self-awareness which we have identified in Ulrich towards the end of Part II might have been followed by a change in activity in Part IV. Though this is speculation on my part, I wonder if the 'Wendung des Schlusses' ('turning-point at the end') might have been yet another step in the process whereby Ulrich merged into narrator and so into author by becoming a creative writer?[45] His interest in such activity surfaces in Part II, Chapter 91, where Tuzzi asks Ulrich if he has ever been a writer. Ulrich answers flippantly: '"I am disturbed to admit that I never have [. . .] I have resolved that, if I don't soon feel the urge to write, I shall kill myself as a person of thoroughly abnormal predisposition!"' (418). This apparently light-hearted remark is given prominence in the text, through the following image: 'this joke [rose up] out of the flow of conversation [. . .] like a stone emerging from the stream which has covered it' (418). It is evident that the narrator wants the reader to take careful note of the moment. Later, Gerda actually suggests to Ulrich that he write about his experiences on the 'Urlaub vom Leben'.[46] This would have been no light step for any hero of Musil's to take. For Musil, writing was a commitment to the highest order. I do not believe that he would have permitted his *persona* the illicit luxury of remaining a dilettante sceptic, rehearsing his criticisms of the world for one or two of his friends and acquaintances but never presenting them in the form which would reach a wider audience and so make a significant contribution to the evolution of culture. Certainly, Ulrich, the intellectual drone of Part I and Part II, is launched on a nuptial flight in Part III.

Even though my suggestion that Ulrich may have become a creative writer towards the end of *The Man without Qualities* – thus supplying a 'missing link' between author and hero – is only speculative, the change in the hero's awareness which I have identified is irrefutably part of the fabric of the novel. To understand fully the messages throughout the narrative which express Musil's *Weltanschauung*, it is vital to grasp the way in which the subject at the centre of the novel develops. It will be helpful to review this development briefly below.

The text itself covers only a period of roughly one year when Ulrich is about thirty-three years of age, but it is possible to reconstruct an earlier phase in his life. In early manhood this man has taken an unusual step – he has done his best to cut the umbilical cord, so to speak, which joins him to the world of Austria-Hungary. His links with the world around him seem no longer visceral; he filters impressions, thoughts and feelings through the alienating medium of his critical mind. From the point of view of his close friends, Walter and Clarisse, the hero's self-mutilation has left him crippled: his intellectuality has transformed his life from indicative to conditional, his constant mental reservations inhibit any spontaneous actions. From the point of view of Arnheim, his rival, Ulrich is hopelessly impractical – all his schemes would fail the reality-test. In Part I and Part II the narrator affects a pose of critical impartiality: he singles out Walter, Diotima, Arnheim, Leinsdorf and others for close ironic attention – but Ulrich, too, is not exempt from his irony. In one respect, however, Ulrich is set apart from the others: his distancing himself from the surrounding world is seen in a positive light. Alienation is a necessary step, an assertion of freedom, an exercise of the will to break with the tyranny of contemporary patterns of living. But Ulrich seems incapable of making any use of his freedom; all ways lie open to him, but in the absence of any compelling pressure, he goes nowhere; he is frozen in a state of passivity which, while preferable to most of the meaningless activity around him, is not a satisfactory permanent attitude to adopt.

We find him, in the earlier sections of the novel, in the throes of an inner crisis: the intellectual approach signalled in his ambivalent escutcheon, 'Man without Qualities', seems to have led him into a cul-de-sac. The role of secretary to the 'Parallelaktion' orders the outward course of his life, filling it with trivial duties. But his spirit is in turmoil: 'As he let himself be moved to and fro in the petty and foolish activity which he had taken on, as he talked, indeed took pleasure in an excess of talk, living with the desperate perseverance of a fisherman who casts his nets into an empty river, he waited' (256). In the waiting, an agonising inner pressure builds: 'He waited behind his personality, in so far as this word refers to that part of a human being which is shaped by the world and the course which life takes, and the calm despair he dammed up behind it rose higher day by day' (256–7). The 'Urlaub vom Leben' – an experiment which coincides roughly with Part I and Part II of the novel – is an attempt by the hero to force his own hand, to bring intellectuality to some conclusion. This experiment, described as we have seen with telling irony, is abandoned as a failure in Part III but it has one positive result: the hero begins to rediscover within himself feelings that will henceforth be at the very centre of his attention. In other words, alienation from those who accept the rule of conventional thinking and feeling brings the hero into intimate contact with layers of selfhood within him which he has hitherto overlooked. These layers, though present in all humans, are commonly overlaid by more strident concerns. Here, at last, a way opens to him which, in contrast to other ways, he feels a compulsion to take. Part III will lead the hero along the path of self-discovery 'Ins Tausendjährige Reich' ('Into the Millennium'); this involves not an 'Urlaub *vom* Leben' ('a leave *from* life') but what we might call a period of leave *in the midst of, and for, life*, an

'Urlaub *im* Leben' ('leave *within* life'), an exploration of the most intimate areas of human experience while marooned on an island of isolation from the world of 'das Seinesgleichen'.

An argument can be advanced that, from Part III onwards, Ulrich has ceased to be a 'Man without Qualities' at all.[47] Perhaps Ulrich quietly lays down his claim to his 'escutcheon' in the exchange with Arnheim which we examined above, where he appears to distance himself from the judgement made by Walter, and goes in search of those spiritual qualities within himself which Arnheim finds so intriguing. On the other hand, it might be felt that he simply enters another, equally distinctive, stage in his life where the intellectuality implicit in the 'ohne Eigenschaften' ('without qualities') label is still present but subordinate to his new involvement in the life of the emotions. In Part III the narrative certainly enters a new phase – where earlier the irony in the account of the hero's experiences is a measure of his 'distance' from the narrator, from Part III the perspectives of narrator and hero virtually merge, one into the other.

Musil asked his reader to read the *The Man without Qualities* through twice. A second reading does, indeed, reveal the detail of the narrator's deeper insight into things: half-hidden in the text, we recognise the evidence of the perspective of that older and more mature consciousness which, through surreptitious interpretations and the subtle prompting of certain images, traces out a pattern of coherence which Ulrich fails to see. (If, indeed, the 'Wendung des Schlusses' ('turning-point at the end') was to be Ulrich's transformation into a writer, then the narrative would be his own autobiographical account, the older self looking at life over the shoulder of his younger, less observant, counterpart.)

In the following section, we shall examine important passages and themes from the novel in which a sense of significance and shape to the world underlies the insecurity, the Machian discomfort, of the 'ohne Eigenschaften' mode. This is the world seen from what I believe might be called 'the perspective of the mature Ulrich' but which I shall refer to below as 'the perspective of the narrator'.

# 9

# A REVIEW OF 'THE MAN WITHOUT QUALITIES' FROM THE PERSPECTIVE OF THE NARRATOR

## 'Gewalt' and 'Liebe'

Perhaps the most fundamental notion of *The Man without Qualities* as a whole is that, in its simplest and most original form, life can be seen as the intertwining of two elemental principles: 'Gewalt' ('violence') and 'Liebe' ('love'). This conception is expounded most fully in Part II, Chapter 116.[1] Here Ulrich is undergoing the central transition in attitude which we have just examined. Ulrich sees with sudden conviction: 'that life is a rough and dire condition in which one cannot afford to give too much thought to the morrow since one has one's hands quite full enough with today' (591). This, as we have seen, is incompatible with his earlier attitude to life. He now sees that it was folly to consider that any observer could be completely impartial and his insights totally objective. Life spawns ideas, not ideas life. Ulrich reproaches himself for his shortsightedness earlier: 'How could a good observer fail to see that this life-mix of concerns, urges and ideas, which at best exploits ideas in order to justify itself or uses them as a stimulus, has of its very nature the effect of shaping and binding [the ideas] which take from it their spontaneous movement and their limits' (591). The narrator follows Hume who argued that, whenever one examines a thought closely, one finds the emotion in which it originated.[2] There is no such thing as disinterested research;[3] all discoveries are predicated on a person's interest in the object of his or her enquiries. This central principle of human existence is translated immediately into a universal law: ' "In a word" thought [Ulrich] [. . .] "creation did not emerge in response to a theory but" and he was going to say from violence ['Gewalt'], but then a different word from the one he expected leapt in and his idea ended as follows: "but it comes from violence and love ['Liebe']" ' (591). Ulrich here extrapolates from his own development to the constitution of all things. He has been misguided, he reflects, in treating existence as if it were an intellectual puzzle for him to solve. In his enthusiasm for things of the mind he has lost sight of the primacy, not of intellect, but of emotion. And what is the original emotion, the very source of creation? He supplies the answer immediately: the source is 'Gewalt'. Then, straight away, he modifies this statement and asserts that to explain existence we must admit a second elemental principle interworked with the first, namely 'Liebe'.

That this is, indeed, as far as Ulrich is concerned, a new insight is borne out by study of earlier passages of the novel where the evidence of such elemental duality is brought before the hero, but where he fails to set it into any coherent picture of human existence. This is the case in Ulrich's dealings with Moosbrugger: one of the features of Moosbrugger's illness is to make the emotions he feels unusually apparent to the skilled observer.[4] Moosbrugger is introduced as a good man. He has, we are told, 'strong [. . .] good-natured paws' (67). 'Good-natured strength and will to do what is right were also written on his countenance' (67). To the reader who misses the force of the 'Gewalt'–'Liebe' duality, it must appear inexplicable, first that such a man is capable of murder, second that in the act of murder there is a hint of manic self-destruction.

We remember that Moosbrugger, in his madness, attacked the girl as an extension of himself. The vicious knife-thrusts disembowel the girl-self: 'She fell headfirst into the booth. [Moosbrugger] dragged her a little way out onto the soft earth and stabbed at her *until he had completely separated her from himself*' (74) (my emphasis). Here Moosbrugger hacks away at flesh of his flesh; the blood that flows is, in his deluded vision, his blood – this murder is a kind of suicide. But when he has killed her, another feeling comes over him: 'Then he stood beside her for perhaps a quarter of an hour, watching her as the night became calmer again and strangely smooth [. . .]. Finally he carried the corpse over the street and laid it before a bush so that it might more easily be found and buried' (74). Having attacked the girl with pathological ferocity, Moosbrugger holds a vigil at her side, then picking her up and carrying her as gently as a father might his sleeping child, sets her down reverently by the side of the road. Here we are back with the image of Moosbrugger as a good man. Thus it is suggested that Moosbrugger is not simply an incarnation of the principle of violence; he is prompted, too, by love. If Ulrich is schizoid, then so is Moosbrugger, and since Moosbrugger, according to the narrator, is 'a distorted arrangement of our own elements of being' (76), so is humanity at large. Ulrich sees within Moosbrugger this unhappy juxtaposing of feelings in violent disagreement with each other, but it is only at that moment of enlightenment which we examined above that he is able to make sense of it.

## Contemporary sexuality

Moosbrugger fascinates not only Ulrich but many other bourgeois as well. The narrator hints that even a 'Head of Section' may ask his wife as they go to bed: ' "what would you do now if I were a Moosbrugger ... " ' (69). Here the narrator is presenting a paradigm of contemporary behaviour. Something prompts this gentleman to put on a 'Moosbrugger-mask'. Is it not because he is embarrassed by his own feeling for his wife? That it does not fit his image of behaviour appropriate to someone with his position and responsibility? Is this not, to use Freud's term, a 'repression' of natural inclination? Or, to express this in terms of the 'Gewalt'–'Liebe' dichotomy, it seems that here love is distorted, is forced into an artificial shape by what must be interpreted as the need to submit to society's codes of practice which reach even into such an intimate scene. To perform the act of love, this anonymous Viennese gentleman (his title suggesting that he may be Diotima's husband, Tuzzi) pretends to be someone else, thereby making his wife into the prostitute-victim of Moosbrugger's violence.

The notion of a connection between violence and sexual passion is a recurrent theme of *The Man without Qualities*; the following example is taken from Part II, Chapter 68: 'Nothing stimulates bourgeois love as much as the flattering experience that one has the power to drive another human being to an ecstasy which involves such mad behaviour that one would positively have to become a murderer if one wanted to find a second way to become the cause of such changes' (284–5).[5] The narrator further argues that a central feature of the bourgeois code is the suppression of overt sexuality and that this makes for hypersensitivity to sexual stimuli. He intimates that in the natural order of things the sexual act is one way in which love expresses itself directly; but in an unhealthy social climate it becomes the primary focus of every casual encounter, and the taboo associated with sex assigns it to the realm of the furtive, the criminal and the violent.[6]

Here, I believe, is to be found the key to Ulrich's statement about the link between 'Gewalt' and 'Liebe': it is typical of bourgeois behaviour, he reflects, that these elements 'are usually brought togther in the wrong way!' (591). Such coupling is wrong: ' "[...] the usual connection between these two is wrong!" ' (591). Ulrich and the narrator both express their revulsion for the sexual mores of the day. The narrator's view of contemporary sexuality is seen most clearly in the examination of the relationship between Gerda and Ulrich. Here, as elsewhere, we are given the impression of an older man passing judgement on his younger self but recognising, too, that the mistakes he once made originated in 'das Seinesgleichen' – that they were conditioned by the state of society as a whole. When alone with Bonadea, Ulrich displays the sexual appetite of the bourgeois, as one might expect from a man who, for the duration of his 'Urlaub vom Leben', has suspended personal moral commitment. Ulrich's relationship with Gerda, though more intellectual, is also plagued by sexuality: his immorality and Gerda's complexes prevent any happy union.

Gerda's love for Ulrich is hedged around with external pressures which mainly have to do with her family background. Her mother, Klementine, comes from a 'good' upper-middle-class family. Gerda is not allowed to forget this and is expected to embody an ideal of decorous and close-bridled femininity; in other words, Klementine is one of those Viennese mothers who unknowingly nurtured in their daughters the neuroses that made Freud's livelihood as a practising doctor. Klementine's demands of her husband are no less inhibiting. She expects that her compensation for marrying a Jew, Leo Fischel, will be the status and financial rewards that will flow from his brilliant career in banking. When no meteoric rise materialises she begins to despise him; this feeling is compounded by anti-Semitism, which is no longer only a lower-class phenomenon with no weight in her circles, but is now becoming something of a fashion among 'cultured' acquaintances as well.

Fischel can make no sense of his wife's behaviour; he takes a classical liberal position and has no sympathy with irrationality, however bourgeois its pedigree. But, as a sensitive person, he cannot help but be hurt and rather bewildered. Gerda, an only child, suffers more deeply still. She has grown up in the shadow of her parents' quarrelling, which has been intensified by her mother's frigidity – her own disposition, a union of her father's sensitivity and her mother's inhibitions, make her awkward and unhappy. She is already at that difficult age when friends and family are wondering why she is not yet married. She knows that, unless something happens soon, she will remain a frustrated spinster for the rest of her days. To these feelings, Musil adds the hesitant defiance of an incipient feminist.

In her emotional and intellectual confusion, Gerda comes to visit Ulrich, knowing that he will see this as a sign that she expects him to seduce her; this, at least, would be a token of her liberation from taboos on sex which she senses at home. Thus her coming to Ulrich is not a spontaneous act of love or desire but the ambiguous outcome of a tug-of-war between anxiety and resolve. Fear has drained her face of all colour and prettiness, making her look 'almost like a dead woman' (618). Gerda's arrival at Ulrich's door is an attempt to rise above herself and be emancipated; it is a febrile act of will. For Ulrich, the expectations which Gerda places on him as a man with the reputation of a sensualist put him under an unpleasant obligation – for him there is no pleasure in this love-making and certainly no spontaneity either. He feels: 'that it was extraordinarily unpleasant to have to carry out everything that was involved in this' (620). The fear of sex proves stronger than Gerda's desire to break with the past and to emancipate herself; she has an attack of hysteria at the very moment when Ulrich takes her to his bed. The unwilling seducer, thwarted, finds himself confessor and comforter.

By setting this meeting against a background of family tension, on the one hand, and eccentric intellectual experiment, on the other, the narrator demonstrates how 'Gewalt' becomes a usurper in the realm of 'Liebe'. With evidence such as this the narrator justifies his antipathy for contemporary society. Ulrich is moved by Gerda's condition; the ugliness of this episode teaches Ulrich a lesson. It helps him to see that intellectual experimentation with feeling is wrong. He realises that he must disown his bourgeois 'alter ego', inherited from the world of 'das Seinesgleichen', and start to take heed of the quiet voice of authentic morality within him.

Ulrich is not the only character in the novel to need moral tuition – but whereas he proves an able, if initially obtuse, pupil others seem incapable of learning; the pressure of 'das Seinesgleichen' – destructive of original feeling – is too strong in them. The account of the love of Arnheim and Diotima is, from this perspective, a sad moral tale – a further study of the way love is deformed by bourgeois society.

## Arnheim and Diotima

Arnheim, a Jew by birth, is by upbringing and personal choice, 'Prussian Orthodox'; he has a brilliant mind and refined sensibility. His moral code, like his clothes, has been chosen with such deliberation and impeccable taste that he looks almost uncomfortable within it.[7] Diotima, too, has been spoilt – her affectations are documented with ironic detail:

It may be that there was once something authentic in Diotima, an intuitive sensibility which was then rolled up in her propriety, a dress worn thin by much brushing, to which she had given the name 'soul' ['Seele'] and which she rediscovered in the batik-metaphysics of Maeterlinck, in Novalis, but above all in the nameless wave of adulterated Romanticism and yearning for God which, for a while, the machine-age sprayed out as an intellectual and artistic protest against its own self. It may also be that this authenticity in Diotima was to be identified more precisely as a vague stillness, tenderness, devotion and kindness which had never found its way properly and which, through the process of cast-making in lead which fate performs with us, had taken on the peculiar shape of her idealism. (103)

Diotima is, indeed, as one critic has expressed it, an 'eclectic countess of the soul'.[8] In her salon she has discovered that a classical education has practical uses, helping her to project an image of unparalleled refinement. This, once firmly established in the mind of her cultured public, will later provide (when the 'affair' with Arnheim enters its final stages) a cover for her brazen research into the arts of sexual fulfilment (which earns her the wide-eyed admiration of Bonadea who has spent all her adult life trying to reconcile moral theory with sexual practice). Diotima's experiences as a married woman have revealed the anarchic drives of sex in a society which wanted to wish it out of existence.[9] In the development of their attitudes to the other sex, both Arnheim and Diotima are shown to have suffered emotional damage.

Diotima knew neither love nor passion before meeting her husband; now she has a hearty sexual appetite[10] which is not fully satisfied by a husband who brings to the marriage bed the seductive skills which might be expected in a conscientious civil servant; but Diotima's reading of authors like Maeterlinck and Novalis has convinced her she is suffering from romantic rather than sexual starvation. This is the moment when she first meets Arnheim.[11] She is quite unaware of what is going on behind the scenes. Tuzzi, her husband, seeking information about Arnheim's reasons for visiting

Vienna, actively encourages his wife to cultivate Arnheim.[12] Diotima combines expediency and her growing passion in one inspired idea: Arnheim is the man to lead 'her' 'Parallelaktion'! It does not seem to occur to her that some might look askance at a Prussian being in charge of the supreme expression of Austrian patriotism. Thus, when seen from Diotima's perspective, this affair is inextricably intertwined with her public ambitions. Arnheim, too, has other motives besides the pursuit of love. As we saw earlier, he is attending meetings of the 'Parallelaktion' because he wants to bring the oil-fields of Galicia, an outpost of the Austro-Hungarian Empire, under his control.[13] These peripheral desires 'corrupt' the passion between Arnheim and Diotima. Diotima sees their love as timeless; but by choosing a business-man and celebrity as her lover she has bound herself to this age with its pseudo-morality of appearance and convenience. She exults in Arnheim's present inaccessibility, clasping his hand and pouring out her feelings – but she does not forget to lay in a store of adventurous underclothes against future eventualities.[14]

In the course of time, their feelings for each other do reach a pitch where some action is demanded. Their respective decisions indicate a basic failure of communication between them: Arnheim wants marriage, Diotoma adultery. Each senses the other's commitment to the relationship:

but they did not know how they should give expression to this wish, for happiness swept their souls ['Seelen'], created for this very purpose, to such heights of solemnity that they were in fear of ignoble gestures – a state which is only to be expected in people who have a cloud beneath their feet.

(504–5)

As we have seen, the intense antipathy of the narrator towards these two people is prompted by the sense that they have not been true to their feelings for each other, but have allowed these to be affected by external forces – ambition, status and greed. The moment captured above proves to have been the zenith of their love; soon Arnheim lets his idea of marriage drop and, with the instinct of the incorrigible business-man, shrinks from any capital investment of 'soul' in something as risky as this relationship.[15] ' "A man who is conscious of his responsibility", said Arnheim to himself with conviction "when he makes a gift of his soul ['Seele'], may only sacrifice the interest and never the capital!" ' (511). Diotima, disillusioned and disgusted, turns away from him.

## The 'logic' of contemporary 'morality' and the language that reveals its operations

Nietzsche described morality as 'one long duress';[16] Musil seems to agree, presenting contemporary morality as a system of repressions, at odds with the irrepressible energy of life. Arnheim is fascinated by sculptures of men who had been martyred for their unswerving loyalty to intuitions of the moral law that conflicted with the prevailing codes.[17] Now, Arnheim reflects with regret tinged with relief, men live by a 'morality' of appearances. He finds that it is 'good business' to be good. A show of virtue, not virtue itself, is rewarded.

Using Arnheim as example, the narrator explores this 'businessman's morality' in Part II, Chapter 106, interrupting one of Arnheim's reveries with his own commentary: 'Moral ersetzt die Seele durch Logik' (506), ('Morality replaces soul ['Seele'] with logic'). Musil, as we saw in our examination above of this curious statement,[18] forces the reader to think about different possible meanings for the term 'Seele', using it in the above context to refer to the spiritual and biological energy of individuality but, immediately afterwards, using the same term as an ironic label for Arnheim and Diotima's image of themselves. Continuing this interruption of Arnheim's reflections the narrator describes the pseudo-moral calculations that lie behind all that Arnheim does:

When a soul ['Seele'] has morality then there are actually no more moral questions for it to answer but only logical ones; it asks itself whether what it wants to do falls under this precept or that, whether its intention is to be interpreted in one way or another, and other similar things, which is all rather like a madly rushing throng of people being subjected to gymnastic discipline and, at a signal, performing a sweep to the right, arm thrusts and deep squats.                                                                    (506)

The reader learns to interpret the important message in such ironic commentary: the narrator stresses that what passes for 'morality' in the contemporary world is something so regimented and repressed that it is poles apart from morality in its natural state. It is yet another example of the way in which 'das Seinesgleichen' distorts the behaviour of mankind.

Arnheim's decision not to have an affair with Diotima is presented as typical of the way his mind works. What appears to the world as noble renunciation is presented to the reader in another light.[19] For Arnheim a union of 'souls' is acceptable but a liaison would flout the self-protective principles of his 'morality'. If he were to abandon them he would be utterly disorientated,[20] it would unbalance his 'System des Glücks' ('system of happiness'). On a purely practical level, too, there is a major objection: an affair would prejudice Arnheim's dealings with Diotima's husband and thus adversely affect his plans for a deal with the Austrian government over Galician oil. Considerations like these mean that Diotima and Arnheim's relationship, far from being an affair to eclipse Tristan and Isolde's, ends in bitterness and regret. Thus is passion hedged about with contemporary constraints.

The decision to renounce Diotima is so painful that Arnheim is unable to overlook the base calculations which govern his decisions. As he stands, a lonely man at his hotel window looking down on the street below, he reflects dejectedly: 'This need for single-mindedness, repeatability and firmness which is the precondition for success in thinking and planning [...] is always satisfied in the realm of the soul ['auf seelischem Gebeit'] *by some kind of violence* ['Gewalt']' (507) (my emphasis).

Arnheim's pessimism shapes his thoughts: 'Whoever wishes to build on stone in a human being may only make use of the base qualities and passions, for solely that which is most closely linked with egotism endures' (507). Up to Part III of *The Man without Qualities*, Arnheim and Ulrich, in their different ways, are both intellectual exiles from life. The narrator shows that Arnheim's conviction that men are at root evil has come from his sacrifice of life and love; from evidence later in the narrative it seems that he will not break free from this conviction.[21] Ulrich, by contrast, in Part III of *The Man without Qualities*, comes to reject the ideology which holds him fast – his inhibiting sense that all things are relative – and does attempt to escape it.

## Wilfulness

There may seem to be little connection between the correct and self-conscious Arnheim and the erratic and impulsive Clarisse. They are, however, alike in their wilfulness; each binds the capacity for love in a straitjacket of purposefulness. There are several stages in Clarisse's development: her early infatuation with Walter as a man of potential genius; her obsession with intellectuality, culminating in her unsuccessful attempt to seduce Ulrich; her preoccupation with Meingast as the philosopher who urges a Dionysian self-forgetting in action; and, in *Nachlaß* chapter-drafts, her descent into madness. As we saw above, Ulrich has given her the works of Nietzsche as a wedding present and she has so completely absorbed the Nietzschean message that she has made herself – as far as it is possible to translate a philosophical insight into a mode of living – an embodiment of Nietzsche's 'Will to Power'. She is obsessed with Nietzsche's idea of the redemption of mankind by the chosen few. Trying to coerce Walter to join this elite, she force-feeds his 'genius' by denial of sexual satisfaction.[22] Her attempt to seduce Ulrich is part of a deranged emotional calculation: she wants to compel the indecisive Ulrich to take a decisive step;[23] she feels an overwhelming urge to fling the weight of her body onto what she visualises as Ulrich's infuriating intellectual insubstantiality;[24] she wants Walter to be goaded by jealousy into frenzied aesthetic production. The tug of lunacy is always felt in her presence. As she throws her arms around the resisting Ulrich she seems, as far as it is possible to distinguish any sense in the words she utters, to be invoking Moosbrugger. But there is method here, too, for, as we read later in The Man without Qualities, she understands madness to be 'none other than what is called "will", but in a particularly intense form' (910). Clarisse is a person who does not know her limits, indeed who refuses to recognise any limits. Wilfulness, virtually unattached to any remotely reasonable aims, racks her small body. She suffers the manifestations of her will ecstatically and publicly; Arnheim's sacrifices are more private and less theatrical. Both characters exemplify forms of self-denial and self-discipline which the narrator presents as 'morally unhygienic'.

## Images as a system of pointers to the narrator's viewpoint

'Gewalt' and 'Liebe', as we have seen, are not only fundamental to Ulrich's mature vision of things, but are crucial to the narrative itself. A pattern of images throughout the text provides recurrent reminders of the narrator's perception of these twin urges and of his sense of the worth of a given action or institution. Sometimes 'Gewalt' assumes the shape of a wall. Walls are hard, solid and man-made; they separate, and form artificial partitions. All these areas of significance are brought into play in The Man without Qualities to express the narrator's disapproval. Ulrich compares Moosbrugger's trial to 'the struggle of a shadow *with the wall*' (76) (my emphasis). Moosbrugger's attempts to justify himself are of little use. He is the 'shadow'; the institutions of justice with its esoteric language and traditions shut him up and cut him off from others and we watch as his perceptions flicker and flutter across the hard surface of the walls that surround him. There is no doubt that the narrator's sympathy lies with the prisoner, and not with the system.

The image of the wall also plays a part in the evocation of Clarisse's experiences. Clarisse has plans, but these are constantly baulked. Her frustration is given symbolical shape in the following passage:

[she] saw [. . .] a black wall with white patches on it; black was everything she did not know and although the white ran together in small and larger islands the black remained unchangeably unending. From this black went out fear and agitation [. . .] Between the white patches she could now see thin grey paths: [. . .] these were events; departures, arrivals, animated debates, struggle with parents, the marriage, the house, incredible wrest-ling with Walter. (146)

There is evidence here of the vividness of Clarisse's impressions and imaginings: notion becomes image, abstraction metaphor. But the narrator, as he records Clarisse's thoughts and impressions, hints at how they are to be interpreted: onto an inner wall she projects the incomplete map of her achievements and hopes. Shades of light measure the intensity of her comprehension, and experiences, half-understood, stand out against the black background: 'Between [. . .] white patches [. . .] grey paths: [. . .] these were events' (146). But ignorance, spawning fear and tension, is blackness: 'black was everything she did not know' (146) – and the wall, this wall inside her mind, is also black. For Clarisse and Moosbrugger there is something hostile about the walls which their minds make.

Then, extending the image, the narrator shows that what he rejects many people applaud: in fact many build 'walls' for the sake of their peace of mind. Such a person 'believes in ideas not because they are sometimes true but because he has to believe. Because he has to keep his emotions in order. Because he has to stop up the hole *between the walls of his life* to prevent his feelings escaping in all directions' (1037) (my emphasis). Here the image of the wall expresses the notion of a corpus of familiar ideas, beliefs and habits of mind with which a person's inner world has been furnished; these walls stand between him or her and the *Angst* of emotional disorientation.

Like Clarisse, Ulrich finds such 'security' intolerable; for him it is simply a self-restriction. In Part II, Chapter 40, Ulrich reflects on the restlessness that harasses him whatever he does. In this context the symbolic 'wall' is the substantial presence of the world as a man-made environment shored up with systems and ideologies – a world that hems the enquiring mind in on all sides. The effect is like some Edgar Allen Poe nightmare tale: 'At the very centre of the frozen, petrified body of the town he felt his heart beating. Here was something within him that had not wanted to remain anywhere, had felt its way *along the walls of the world*, thinking as it did this that there are *millions of other different walls*' (153) (my emphases). Then towards the end of the passage another image follows. Hemmed in at the centre, alive but half-stifled, we find the 'slowly cooling "I", a laughable droplet, which did not want to relinquish *its fire, this tiny glowing core*' (153) (my emphasis).[25]

The image of fire appears as the complement of the image of the wall in just the same way as, after the mention of 'Gewalt', 'Liebe' stole in of its own accord. The image of fire functions in *The Man without Qualities* as an infallible sign of the narrator's approval. Fire symbolises the vital protest within Ulrich at the state of the world; though this protest has lost some of its energy with the passage of time and the failure to achieve any breakthrough, it is still active within him. The narrator shows even Arnheim to be a sensitive man; but, because Arnheim does not trust to his better instincts, he is a target of the narrator's hostility. The following passage describes Arnheim's experience of love which is so complete that it alienates his present from his former self: 'Since he had once again encountered the *fire* that made his tongue feel dry, he was overwhelmed by the feeling that he had forgotten a path which he had originally taken, and that the whole ideology of the "great man" that filled him was merely a makeshift replacement for something that he had lost' (383–4) (my emphasis). Love is fire (the fire image is proof of the authenticity of Arnheim's love); ideology is restraint. But Arnheim dare not commit himself; he cannot bring himself to surrender to this noble passion: 'The very moment when he wanted to hurl himself *into the flame of his feeling* or felt the need to be as great and as unalloyed as the figures of primeval times [. . .] a voice bade him restrain himself. It was the voice of reason, making itself heard at this inappropriate juncture' (510) (my emphasis). The mockery in this passage, one feels, affects only the surface of the man, his compulsive concern with appearance, his moral façade; it is evident that the narrator feels some sympathy for the suffering of a man divided against himself – and a man who fully appreciates his own dilemma. (It is easy to overlook the importance of Arnheim as a character in whom Musil has perhaps invested more of himself than is immediately apparent.) Arnheim finds his life poor by comparison with men of earlier times: 'He felt how, originally, *an ineffable fire had glowed* in morality, at the sight of which even an intellect ['Geist'] such as his could do little more than stare *into the burnt-out coals*' (187) (my emphases).

Instead of deriving inspiration from the evidence of belief in earlier time, Arnheim feels burdened by the deadweight of the history of civilisation. In the following passage the narrator indicates, again using the imagery of fire, how decadence has spoilt 'Seele' in adopting the compromised moral ethos of the contemporary world:

As soon as a soul ['Seele'] has morality or religion, philosophy, a deeper form of bourgeois culture and ideals in the realm of duty and of aesthetics, it is presented with a system of regulations, conditions and procedural instructions which it has to fulfil before it can think of being a noteworthy soul ['Seele'], and *its molten flow is channelled like that of a blast furnace into neat rectangles in sand.* (186) (my emphasis)[26]

Here, fire, the sacred element which consumes what it will, is transformed by an impious act into a mere source of industrial energy and so symbolises the divorce of inner feeling and outward behaviour, the hybris of mankind in the modern world.

But perhaps the most striking example of the fire image is found in Part III, Chapter 12, where Ulrich expounds what might be described as his 'creed for a man who does not believe in anything'. Here we read: '"I believe that none of the [precepts of our morality] are right.

Another meaning flickers behind them. *A fire which ought to melt them down*"' (769) (my emphasis). Here we are at the core of Ulrich's belief – a belief shared with Heraclitus of Ephesus.

This may seem an unlikely connection – the pre-Socratic philosopher and the post-Machian thinker. But there is evidence in *The Man without Qualities* to support this juxtaposition. Heraclitus's teaching has been handed down in aphorisms which later Ancient thinkers included in their work. The fragments of philosophy that have survived in this way have been surprisingly well-received by minds schooled in the sceptical tradition of the era of science[27] – for, in their present shape, they stir the imagination without offending the intellect. Each of Heraclitus's statements seems to claim a special status – they are 'signs of the macrocosm' rather than part of a coherent argument. They fuse elements of philosophy and poetry – Heraclitus demands that we make a concerted effort of imagination and eye and look about us for the tangible proofs of his statements.

Heraclitus is commonly regarded as the philosopher of flux,[28] but he is also the philosopher of fire.[29] Fire, giving off warmth and light, searing and consuming, flaring up and burning low, is for him the elemental stuff of the changing universe.[30] For Heraclitus, this is more than a mere literary effect; his physics moves in concert with his philosophical insight: fire is flux, the world burns now quickly, now more slowly, and where the eye cannot discern this combustion, the imagination can. Ulrich's words from Part III, Chapter 12, quoted above, recompose Heraclitus's aphorism: 'The order of this world [...] was always, and is, and will be, eternal living fire, glowing according to measure and dying away according to measure.'[31] This measure is to be found in *The Man without Qualities*.

A concealed quotation from Maeterlink in Part II, Chapter 32, seems particularly difficult to reconcile with any moral stance: '"The soul ['Seele'] of the sodomite could walk through the midst of the crowd without noticing anything, and in its eyes would be the transparent smile of a child; for everything depends on an invisible principle"' (122). This recalls Heraclitus's aphorism: 'For God, everything is beautiful and good and just; but human beings assume one thing to be unjust, another to be just.'[32] People make judgements, expressing horror at acts which have been tabooed by society since time immemorial; God sees at once that everything is relative to all other things and that the whole of creation is held in an absolute balance. Ulrich's 'invisible principle' and Heraclitus's 'God' seem powerless onlookers at the chaotic spectacle of creation. But Karl Popper, in his assessment of Heraclitus's thought, discerns a sense of necessity underlying the conception of universal flux.[33] Popper presents Heraclitus as a man bemused by the troubled times that he lived in, but predisposed by those very disturbances to put his trust in an absolute and unchanging cosmic order. Thus the philosopher who professes the relativity of all things, the philosopher of flux, is also the philosopher of the absolute measure, the immutable law.

This paradox can perhaps best be understood by reference to Heraclitus's notion of the qualities of actions. Take an action, 'A'; let this action be bad in the eyes of a man, 'x'. 'Ax' is accordingly a bad action. But Heraclitus argues that the action is not changed by its epithet. In other words, another man, 'y', may see the same action, 'Ay', as a good action, though the change of epithet from 'bad' to 'good' has made no change to the action itself. Heraclitus illustrates this with the surgeon's cutting and burning his patient. From one perspective the action is bad, because it is painful, from another perspective it is good, because it is intended to heal. Since normal men cannot appreciate the whole context of things, they tend to place individual actions now in the one category, now in the other. Relativism is thus an appropriate theory for the individual, but the operations of the universe – manifest to the philosopher through the fiery principle – conform to an absolute law. Something of this paradox is to be found in *The Man without Qualities*. There is, on the one hand, a show of relativism:[34] 'Humanity produces bibles and guns, tuberculosis and tuberculin. It is democratic, with kings and aristocracy; builds churches and then universities to pit against the churches; makes monasteries into barracks, but then assigns field-chaplains to the barracks [...] It is the well-known matter of contradictions' (27). But the narrator insists, on the other hand, that these moral dilemmas are signs of decadence, they are a product of contemporary moral thinking. The goodness of a man like Ulrich's brother-in-law, Hagauer, is only a superficial judgement on the basis of convention and appearances; how can such a man be really good when, as we shall see, he makes his wife so utterly miserable? When Ulrich contemplates the effects that breaking the law might have, he argues that, under certain circumstances, this could be a force for the good. In fact the narrator and Ulrich ultimately appeal to an incorruptible standard against which action can be measured absolutely. This surely is the '"other meaning [...] [the] fire, that ought to melt down [the precepts of our morality]"' (769). Nowhere are we told what this standard is to be. The passage we examined above in which Ulrich comes close to formulating his basic belief was a protest against the shape of the world; it was not a positive statement of faith. However, from the scenes which we have considered, it is possible to distil the central conviction implicit in the narrative: only impulses which come direct and unimpaired from the passionate heart of creation – from 'Liebe' before it is distorted by 'Gewalt' – can be considered an authentic guide for mankind. To explore this principle further we must look at later stages of the novel.

# ULRICH AND AGATHE

### Ulrich falls in love

Having been informed of the death of his father, Ulrich returns to the family home in a provincial town. Here he meets his sister, Agathe, with whom he has not been in close touch since childhood. They spend some time together and become inseparable. Part III of *The Man without Qualities* is concerned to a large extent with their love which is placed in a mystical context to which Musil's title for Part III refers: 'Ins Tausendjährige Reich' ('Into the Millennium'). Let us set aside for a moment the question of the incestuous nature of their relationship and consider it as if it were a normal heterosexual affair, for, as we shall see, it is not unreasonable to see it in such a light.[1]

Reflecting the change in Ulrich, the tempo of the narrative slows considerably. Brother and sister withdraw from the world outside, establishing an almost monastic routine of reading, meditative walks in the garden and intense discussion. Ulrich's life has become quite different from life in Vienna with its countless interruptions: Bonadea knocking at the door, Stumm ringing up for advice, meetings with Fischel, and the round of 'Parallelaktion' chores. The simplicity of life devoid of such external pressures allows Ulrich to focus his attention entirely on the feelings which are stirred by Agathe's presence. Take the following passage in which Musil describes the effect on Ulrich of touching his sister. The scene takes place in the library of their father's house: 'Agathe had climbed down [. . .] from the ladder on which she had been sitting, and had put her arm around [Ulrich's] shoulder [. . .]. This was an unaccustomed act of tenderness. His shoulder could feel the beauty of her arm simply by its static weight-distribution and, on the side which was turned towards his sister, he felt the shadowy proximity of her blond arm-pit and the contour of her bosom' (749–50). This contrasts strongly with, indeed is deliberately contrasted with, other skin contact in *The Man without Qualities*. Moosbrugger and the prostitute pressing her body against the murderer's – a contact from which he shrinks in a horror which culminates in the cutting away of this alien self, this 'soft, cursed second "I"' (74), from his own self; Bonadea, wriggling like a harpooned fish when Ulrich makes love to her; the moment of unwonted proximity to another male when Arnheim puts his arm around Ulrich's shoulder and the latter feels the urge to stab him through the neck with his pocket-knife.[2]

I have argued above that all these experiences – even the reconstruction of Moosbrugger's inner world – are enhanced by Musil's creative imaginings; he has picked up emotions from the very periphery of his consciousness and amplified them by studious concentration. The emotions themselves are familiar; it is only the deliberate effort to find a language in which they can be directly communicated that is extraordinary. The evidence from Musil's diaries, as well as from his creative work, shows that he was adept at spotting what Freud termed the 'primary thought processes', the ongoing day-dreaming activity of the otherwise unoccupied mind through which, in Freud's theory, the ego pays its continual tributes to the id. But Musil was not a follower of psychoanalysis – he treats this as 'data', not as evidence for a theory. If there is any theory it is that these are responses to the frustrations of living as a member of this society. These pressures have been internalised to form part of the structure of each personality: for Moosbrugger, physical contact with the other sex may provoke a violent defence response; for Bonadea, stripping off the encumbrances of contemporary fashionable clothing is a delicious foreplay to surrendering to the will of a gentleman who, on taking off his clothes, leaves behind all other impedimenta of culture as well and reverts to the level of beast. Both acts, the brutal attack, the surrender of the body, are at the end of a maze of social strategies which inhibit the natural flow of feelings and redirect them down channels of artificial behaviour. In the account of the feelings of Ulrich for Agathe, Musil – like a Rousseau wandering through the purgatory of Freud's Austria – is attempting to recover natural emotion, to catch 'Liebe' before it is rechannelled and reshaped by 'Gewalt'.

When Agathe comes to stay with Ulrich in the capital, his bachelor home is transformed by her presence; Ulrich strains his mind to fix the new range of data which his senses register:

Where earlier there was stillness, he heard [...] her voice for minutes on end, and what was her voice like? Waves of fragrance accompanied the movement of her clothes, and what was this scent like? Her movements were now knee, now delicate finger, now a lock of hair that would not stay in place. The only thing one could say of this was: that it was there. It was there, where before nothing had been [. . .] as when a shady place is filled by the sun with warmth and the fragrance of opening herbs! (897)

Even the more overtly sexual encounter with Agathe whom, in the absence of any lady's maid, Ulrich has to assist with dressing after her bath is charged with a delight which surprises this experienced seducer:

As he bent close to her shoulders, the skin of which was supple, delicate and yet suffused with life, [. . .] Ulrich felt the slightest touch of a sensation which could not properly be expressed in words unless one were to say that his body was assailed by the sense that, very close to him, there was a woman, and yet no woman; but one might equally have said that he was indubitably standing firmly in his own shoes but yet felt drawn out of himself as if he had been given a second, and far more beautiful, body. (898)

Such delight is born of a recaptured innocence; none of Ulrich's encounters with women for many years have brought him such unalloyed pleasure. He has fallen in love. The sense of the separateness of the other person has gone; to express this in the words of Martin Buber, the 'I', so long isolated within the realm of the 'it', has made contact with the 'thou'.[3] The prison of individuality, constructed in response to the pressures of civilised living, has been broken open; at last, in this private context, the curse of detachment has been lifted. Love brings Ulrich a heightened awareness of what it is to be alive.

For Schopenhauer, Musil's teacher's teacher, the 'Will' behind all things, in manifesting itself in things, became fragmented. Because of this 'principium individuationis' each separate existent is necessarily separate. This principle holds for Nietzsche's thinking too. But Musil modifies this pessimistic basic belief and shows that Ulrich's self, in losing itself, is not lost. Ulrich merely changes perception and steps from the field of 'Gewalt' to the field of 'Liebe'. This change is mirrored in the structure of the novel: Part I and Part II show Ulrich's intellectual and emotional evolution and his direct confrontation with the spirit of 'Kakanien' a few months before World War I. At this stage he maintains a pose of scepticism and arrogant detachment as if to say, 'I did not make this world and I will accept no responsibility for it or within it.' Part III presents Ulrich in a new phase in which falling in love brings about a change in him; since Ulrich is the prime consciousness in the novel the focus of the work shifts to take account of this change.

Love is, without warning, simply there. The change is so sudden that some readers may feel that it is insufficiently motivated; however, it involves not something new and alien, but a potential within Ulrich which was once familiar but which he has long forgotten, suppressed by the self he had become. But why did Musil choose to make a potentially or actually incestuous affair[4] the vehicle for love in *The Man without Qualities*?

### Agathe–Martha

Musil mentions in his diary that his parents had had a daughter, two years before he was born, who died in infancy. She fascinated him.[5] In early entries in his diaries Musil recorded his sense of the utter isolation of the individual psyche – this isolation continued into early manhood. Then, while studying for his doctorate in Berlin, he met Martha Marcovaldi, née Heimann. His love for her transformed his perception of himself. In drawing up a balance sheet for the period 1905 to 1910, Musil wrote '[Martha] ist [etwas] das ich geworden ist' (Tb1, 226) ('[Martha] is [...] something that has become "I"'). Man and wife were scarcely separate individuals. After the parting in World War I, they rarely spent more than a couple of hours away from each other.[6] Martha neglected her considerable talents as painter and artist to give her husband total support in his work; he, in turn, came to rely on her sure judgement in literary matters.

Despite Martha's giving up her own career for her husband, this relationship did not involve Musil subordinating another individual to his will: it meant rather a new way of thinking and feeling. Once, when Musil wished to conceal Martha's identity – she was already married to him – he referred to her, on a postcard, as 'my married sister Frau Heimann' (*Briefe* I, 70), thus playing on Martha's maiden name. Musil's portrait of Agathe is drawn with Martha standing as model. Though Musil was not discreet in his exploration and exploitation for *The Man without Qualities* of the experiences of friends and acquaintances, he evidently felt that his most precious human relationship should be disguised when transposed to *The Man without Qualities*. But there can be no doubt that the love affair of Ulrich and Agathe is Musil's own marriage in transfigured literary form.

Transforming marital love into a brother/sister affair also gave the novel a quality which, in Part I and Part II, had been supplied only at the periphery of the action in the portrayal of Moosbrugger – the appeal of a strong sexual taboo. Indeed the unifying theme of Part I and Part II of *The Man without Qualities* – the 'life between intellectual brackets' which Ulrich calls his 'Urlaub vom Leben' – is less vigorous than the temptation of incest which is present throughout the incomplete Part III.

The plot as a whole needed just this kind of impetus from within; Ulrich shares most of his creator's gifts, but lacks his application. Ulrich's intellect is pure but sterile; his rich inner life has no practical outlet in the world around him. This is how the reader finds him, at least, at the beginning of Part III. The leopard cannot change his spots; Ulrich does not become an activist of his own volition. Now, however, the author forces Ulrich's hand, manoeuvring his hero into situations in which, if only through the power of circumstance, he will be forced to take decisions. The relationship with the sister, with its implicit challenge to social orthodoxy, gives Ulrich's life a far stronger charge of intensity than he has known hitherto; this has to do in part with Agathe's greater spontaneity, her tendency to turn some of Ulrich's ideas into direct action.[7]

Conflict with society becomes inevitable; the relationship of brother and sister is a challenge to the world of 'das Seinesgleichen'. Where, in Part II, Ulrich had been on the sidelines of society, the passive observer of its absurdities, here in Part III, through the agency of Agathe, he becomes a potential target of society's censure and hatred. Ulrich and Agathe's attitude to society grows out of an unspoken agreement to resist the world which their father represented and upheld – both in a professional capacity as an establishment lawyer and privately as citizen of Austria-Hungary. In failing to act in accordance with their father's will, even over instructions which he gives about his medals,[8] Ulrich and Agathe are challenging the tradition which the father supported in life and now enters in death. The corpse represents a civilisation which, for Ulrich, is itself dead – we are reminded of what was, in effect, Ulrich's funeral oration for that civilisation, which we examined above: 'Not only is Father dead, but the ceremonies which surround him are also dead' (696). Traditional patterns of behaviour seem to invite Ulrich and Agathe to do their bidding, to follow principles which reach out through and in death – in a manner reminiscent of Ancient Egyptian culture. As brother and sister stand next to the dead man, however, Agathe announces that she will not return to Hagauer, the husband in whom her father found a son-in-law entirely to his taste.[9] This is the first of several acts of symbolical defiance by brother and sister including Agathe's placing a garter from her leg in the pocket of the dead man's jacket; more significant will be the altering of the father's will itself and, finally, the most important of all their actions, the experiment of living together. All these acts spring from the intense protest of son and daughter against their father: it is an instance of those generation conflicts which spring up repeatedly in the course of civilisation, reappearing in particularly virulent form around World War I in Germany. But, whereas many of Musil's contemporaries in the Expressionist movement sacrificed clarity for intensity, in his work the intensity remains entirely coherent and clear. Here, in *The Man without Qualities*, the programme sketched in *The Enthusiasts* – Musil's attempt to break the mould of bourgeois existence – is in evidence again. Ulrich and Agathe make a stand for love, and for life, against cold convention shrouded by the sanctity of law, habit and custom which is represented here by the corpse and which will later be upheld by Hagauer. Agathe's husband will mobilise the law in pursuit of his interests in his father-in-law's will – his instinctive sense that he has been wronged is indeed correct, for Agathe, imitating her father's handwriting and striking herself out of the will, thereby ensures that no money from her father's estate will pass into Hagauer's control.

Ulrich is concerned to develop an understanding of feelings that can withstand scientific scrutiny. He has brought with him from home the works of mystics which he now uses as a source of comparison with his own inner experiences. (Ulrich uses the records of what other people have experienced as supplementary evidence of a specific human potential – he takes a cautious, even scholarly, approach to the subject.) In Part III, Chapter 12, 'Holy conversations. Varied continuation', he points some of these books out to Agathe and says:

'These are Christian, Jewish, Indian and Chinese records; more than a thousand years separates some of them. Yet in all of them one recognises the same structure of inner feeling which diverges from the every-day but yet has a homogeneous structure. Virtually the only difference between them is that which derives from the connection with a system of theology and knowledge of heaven under whose protective roof they have taken shelter. So we may assume that there definitely exists a second and unusual state [. . .] to which a human being has access, and which is closer to the source of things than the religions [. . .].                    (766)

This is what Musil elsewhere calls 'der andere Zustand' ('the other state'). Agathe has experienced the ecstatic loss of self which 'der andere Zustand' involves, but it is Ulrich who gives it form in words where passion and precision are in harmonious balance:

'It is similar to the experience of looking out over a wide reflecting expanse of water: everything is so bright that the eye is confused and sees darkness and, beyond, on the far bank objects appear not to stand on the ground but hover in the air, so delicate and yet uncommonly clear that it is almost painful and bewildering. There is, to this impression, both an enhancing and a losing. One is part of all things and one cannot come close to anything. You are on this side, the world is on the other, the I and objectivity are transcended but both clear to the pitch of pain, and what divides and binds these otherwise commingled elements is a dark flashing, an overflowing and extinguishing, a rising and falling pulse. You move like a fish in water or a bird in the air, but there is no shore and no branch and nothing but this moving!' (751)

There is no doubt that Ulrich's feelings for Agathe have strongly influenced his choice of reading. What he feels for his sister corresponds closely to the experiences described in the words of the mystics. What concerns him is not the label which attaches to the experience – whether this is love for one woman or an intimation of divine love – but the experience itself. And what is the experience? It involves a loss of definition, a diminution of the distinct shape of individuality, and thereby a waning sense of the separateness of self from the world as a whole. It can be compared with the way, so Ulrich imagines, that simpler creatures than man sense the world they inhabit. For them, relatively less precise perceptions, and virtual absence of the ability to draw abstract inferences, are compensated with a richer sensuous involvement. But 'der andere Zustand' is also connected, on the other hand, with heightened spiritual sensitivity, with the relationship between mankind and creation as a whole. Musil was intuitively certain that Love, in its purest form as experienced here, held the potential to transform those who felt it, to set them, inwardly, on the right path. Thus, in this state, we also glimpse the energy behind '[das] rechte [...] Leben' (255) ('the right way to live') – and this, of course, was the moral goal which Ulrich ceaselessly pursued.

'Der andere Zustand' is fleeting; Ulrich cannot hold it fast for more than a moment. He is aware of the incongruity of the spectacle of himself, as scientist, pursuing a quasi-religious quest, but he is convinced of the importance of what he is doing. Though he will not get closer to the state than the feeling which finds expression in the passage we have examined, his search takes precedence over all other concerns.

Thus, though Musil's thinking is based on the rational and scientific tradition with its roots in Classical humanism and the Enlightenment, his intellectual curiosity embraces areas of experience that are commonly seen as belonging to other realms – those of Christian mysticism and Romanticism. This is so in the case of hermaphroditism – a subject familiar to theologians and Romantics.[10] From the midst of the emotional upheaval that meeting his sister has meant, Ulrich senses within himself two modes of feeling that are commonly seen as characteristic of the two sexes: 'For one can be hard, selfish, belligerent, jutting out into externality, on the offensive, so to speak, and one can suddenly, though still the same Ulrich Soandso, feel quite the opposite, sunk into one's own depths, a selflessly blithe being in an indescribably sensitive and somehow also selfless state of all surrounding things' (687). Part III, Chapter 25, 'The Siamese Twins', describes what happens after Agathe arrives in, indeed 'invades', her brother's bachelor house: Ulrich, having given up his bed, 'crept into his room and, there, for the two hours during which he was unable to work, was introduced to the state of being hemmed in by consideration' (908). When man and woman live together in close proximity – as any couple will confirm! – much foresight and anticipation of the feelings of the other are essential to a relationship of tolerable harmony. Though at first unused to the emotional needs of the woman who shares his life, a man will develop a degree of empathy through the daily experiences of that shared life; similarly, a woman will learn to anticipate, to live out in advance in her imagination, the emotions of her male partner. Musil suggests that, in psychological terms, every heterosexual relationship involves both partners in practical hermaphroditism. Two become 'one flesh'. Agathe remarks, jokingly, that they are 'Siamese twins'[11] and Ulrich is fascinated by this notion of an uncomfortable, permanent fusion of brother with sister, a grotesque but natural coupling of male and female. He is, indeed, so taken with the idea that he tells General von Stumm about it.[12] The inevitable result of Ulrich's indiscretion is that the idea is broadcast around the circles his sister and he frequent. (The reader is left to speculate whether this was a simple slip on Ulrich's part or whether he deliberately circulated the '*mot*' to throw down the gauntlet to society.) Wherever Ulrich and Agathe go they are seen as the 'Siamese Twins'; this evidently leads to gossip about their relationship which will eventually reach Agathe's husband. As far as their friends and acquaintances are concerned the term 'Siamese Twins' is a euphemism for the strong suspicion of incest.[13] In this context the love of brother and sister takes on the taint and mystery of a mortal sin.

Denis de Rougement examines *The Man without Qualities* from this perspective in *Myths of Love*.[14] The overall theme of his work is passion. Why, de Rougement asks, are there few tales of real passion in modern literature? One reason, he suggests, is the mechanism of passion itself – it needs a resistance, or, to be more specific, it needs the kind of obstacle that faced Tristan and Isolde – the profound taboo of adultery in an age when religion, the awe of kingship, the obligations of chivalry, were undisputed elements of the social fabric. What modern taboo could take the place of the passion between Tristan and Isolde? Certainly not adultery since modern society is too approximate in its judgements to give such behaviour the absolute mark of sin. In the view of de Rougement only two possibilities remain: love between a mature man and a young girl or 'nymphet' (de Rougement analyses the case of Nabokov's *Lolita*) and incest (and here de Rougement's example is *The Man without Qualities*) since to both of these crimes powerful taboos still attach. De Rougement sees the love of Ulrich and Agathe in *The Man without Qualities* as something as aesthetically potent as the love of Tristan and Isolde since, despite the modern context, this love is absolutely forbidden. In the love of Ulrich and Agathe the desire for consummation is met head-on by the incest-taboo. De Rougement believes that, having experimented in earlier versions of the work in which Ulrich and Agathe commit incest, Musil found that the tension essential to the high passion then immediately left the work. So, in the place of the so-called 'Reise ins Paradies'[15] ('journey to Paradise') which is, in the physical as well as spiritual sense, a honeymoon for brother and sister, he set a mystical inner journey 'Ins Tausendjährige Reich' ('Into the Millennium') in which Ulrich and Agathe do not make love.[16]

Describing the relationship of Ulrich and Agathe as portrayed in the later *Nachlaß*-chapters of the *The Man without Qualities*, de Rougement argues that their love is 'no longer egocentric, but allocentric'. This reminds de Rougement of 'Buddhist detachment'; 'it could also manifest', he continues, 'the redemption of passion by true love' (p. 64). He goes on to argue:

At this point, passion gives way to presence, the suffering of desire to mutual ecstasy – but also the novel to the poem [. . .]. But doesn't this blissful presence in shared love also suggest a more intimate mystery, another redemption of Eros by Agape? Mightn't the fascinating prohibition of love between brother and sister have been the disguise – quite unconscious, I'm convinced – of a love too real to dare speak its name in a novel? Happy love has no history, as everyone knows since novels were first written – novels that arouse passionate interest. But wasn't this literary convention, condemning the fulfilled marriage, a taboo quite differently fearful, for both writer and reader, from any sort of incest of blasted passion? The eroticism of marriage is a terra incognita for Western literature. Perhaps Musil has unwittingly approached it closer than anyone else [. . .]                                                                    (pp. 64–5)

In the love affairs in earlier works Musil often focussed on some significant flaw, infidelity, for example, in *Die Vollendung der Liebe* (*The Perfecting of a Love*) or, in *Die Portuguiesin* (*The Woman from Portugal*), illness. In *The Man without Qualities*, Musil creates dramatic tension through a brother/sister relationship fatally flawed by incestuous desire and, in so doing, draws (quite consciously, in fact) a portrait of his own marriage. The sections of Part III which were published in Musil's life contain such overt warnings about incest that it seems likely that, in 1933 and possibly later, Musil intended that brother and sister would physically make love as they had done in the drafts of the novel to 1927. The most striking of these warnings is the following from Chapter 12:

[. . .] whoever has not already recognised the traces of what was happening to brother and sister should put this report away for in it an adventure is described of which he will never be able to approve: a journey to the edge of the possible, skirting past the dangers of the impossible and unnatural, indeed of the repulsive, and perhaps not always quite past them.   (761)[17]

But, in the last few years of his life, Musil may have come to the conclusion which de Rougement suspects he did – namely that the avoidance of incest is essential to the narrative in the latter part of the novel. De Rougement's view parallels that of Kaiser and Wilkins whose interpretation of *The Man without Qualities* revolves around their conviction that Ulrich and Agathe do not commit incest.

### Clarisse in 'The Man without Qualities' – Part III (1933)

A glance at the *Nachlaß* of *The Man without Qualities* confirms the vital role of the sub-plot which centres on Clarisse. Musil sets the relationship between Ulrich and Agathe against the background of

Clarisse's path towards insanity. Even in the 1933 edition of Part III it is evident that Musil balances the Ulrich/Agathe plot under its aegis of 'Liebe' with the Clarisse-plot with its variations on 'Gewalt'. It is significant that the Moosbrugger sub-plot, with its undercurrent of violence, is kept alive in Part III not by Ulrich but by Clarisse who nags Ulrich to arrange for her to visit the murderer in the asylum. Indeed 'responsibility' for the murderer seems to pass completely to Clarisse.[18] Common sub-themes provide further evidence of the interdependence of the plots: the bane of near-incest which is attached to Ulrich and Agathe has not escaped Clarisse who as a girl was sexually molested by her father;[19] though it is less powerful than that between brother and sister there is an undercurrent of sexual attraction between Ulrich and Clarisse too; Clarisse no less than the 'Siamese Twins' has hermaphroditic feelings. This latter element is vital to the integration of the Clarisse- theme into *The Man without Qualities*, Part III (1933) and the *Nachlaß* of *The Man without Qualities*.

In Part III, Chapter 14, Ulrich, Meingast, Walter and Clarisse watch, with varying degrees of embarrassment and fascination, an exhibitionist who has hidden in the bushes of their garden and who, without knowing that he is being observed from the house, waits for a passer-by before whom to expose himself.[20] This incident is important for its revelations of how Clarisse sees things. A normal reaction to this incident would be to see the appearance of the man in their vicinity as mere chance, but Clarisse is convinced that this perverted sensualist has been attracted by the aura of lustfulness that hangs about her home – in other words, that she, through denying Walter sexual satisfaction, has filled her house with the magnetism of frustrated animal passion.

We remember why she does this. In torturing Walter by denying him sex, she does not consider herself to be sadistic; she is helping him to store sexual energy because she sees this as a potential which men and women can redirect for their own specific purposes – this is, no doubt, another of the unforeseen consequences of Ulrich's wedding present, since one detects here yet another of Nietzsche's ideas! At such points we are reminded how far Musil's views have made themselves independent of his first teacher's – for there can be no doubt, precisely through the comparison established with Ulrich and Agathe, that Musil condemns this practice. Whereas Ulrich and Agathe are, so to speak, the apprentices of their love, learning from it and seeking to register its subtlest promptings, Clarisse does violence to love when it touches her, reshaping it to her ends. '"One must be on this world to some purpose [...]"' (921), she says; this purpose she sets herself.

Unlike Ulrich and Agathe who seem to be waiting for some mystical sign about what they should do and how they should behave, Clarisse impatiently seizes responsibility for herself and sets her own course through life. Ulrich and Agathe take up an attitude of humility towards the mysteries of human experience; Clarisse behaves almost like a Sartrean existentialist, insisting that no one but she herself can make her own world. While Ulrich and Agathe seek the passive inwardness of mystics, trying to lose themselves in the wonder of love, Clarisse, as Walter eloquently expresses it, makes her world just as he paints a canvas: 'In some unknown way a picture, too, excludes every and colour and line which does not harmonise with its basic form, its style, its palette and [...] draws what it needs from the hand according to the laws of genius which are different from the normal ones of nature' (927). It is difficult to imagine a stronger image for Clarisse's intense individuality – she has detached herself from the natural bed of her life, making it into merely an object which she creates in repeated acts of wilfulness. Her world has become, in Nietzsche's sense, dominated by an aesthetic design; it is shaped by her own creativity. The dangers inherent in such an attitude to reality are self-evident; they are of a piece with Moosbrugger's viewpoint when his phobias get the better of him and imprint their visions on his perceptions. The difference, with Clarisse, is that her imaginings are, to a large extent, conscious expressions of her will. Even madness is fitted into the total picture: 'she [understood] [...] by madness nothing other than what goes under the name of "will", but in a particularly intense form' (910),[21] so she makes herself mad, rejecting sanity as the trap of mediocrity. Clarisse, with her reckless stress on will, her single-minded commitment to ill-thought-out action, her desire to change the world whatever the cost might be, has at least as many attributes of a Nazi personality as the figures of Reiting and Beineberg in *Young Törless*. Ulrich puts this cult of action into a sane perspective: "It is so simple to be energetically active and so difficult to seek a meaning to action!" (741).

Clarisse's wilfulness has blasphemous overtones. Her fascination with Moosbrugger springs from an association she makes between him and Christ. Since both Christ and Moosbrugger were carpenters, Clarisse assigns to Moosbrugger the role of 'redeemer'.[22] Some kind of erotic fantasy is involved here – for, in Clarisse's mind, it is men who change the world, so she, to change the world, must become a man. Various men, including Ulrich, Meingast and Moosbrugger, play roles in her inner life but the transition from the private realm of the imagination to the public world at large can be problematical – as we saw above in Clarisse's failure to seduce Ulrich.[23] As figures in her imagination they are totally at her disposal; as real human beings they are liable to offer resistance to her schemes for them. It seems, however, that her madness is trying to find a way round even that obstacle, for, to her delight,Clarisse discovers that she is developing signs of hermaphroditism. This offers her the promise of enhanced individuality and independence. Meingast says to her: '"You have the air of a boy about you"' (919) and this remark, objective enough in itself in view of Clarisse's slim limbs and underdeveloped chest, thrills Clarisse with a sense of portent. She grips the arm of this man whom she reveres as the 'Master' and, immediately, her powerful creative imagination is at work on this simple action:

While this happened, she was overcome by the sensation that she was pushing a part of herself over to him and, in the slowness with which her hand disappeared into his sleeve, in this surging slowness, circled fragments of an incomprehensible lust which were derived from the perception that the Master was keeping still and letting himself be touched by her.

(919)

Under the powerful influence of Clarisse's will, Meingast's mind is seized by an irrational panic at this reversal of masculine and feminine roles: 'But, for some reason, Meingast stared in dismay at the hand which thus held his arm in its grip and which climbed up it like a many-legged creature mounting its female' (919). In other words, Clarisse seems to be moving towards a condition in which she, as an individual, can become independent of other people by uniting in one personality the qualities and powers of man and woman.

However, the contrast between Ulrich and Agathe, on the one hand, and Clarisse, on the other, should not be overstated. Ulrich and Agathe are certainly more reflective and more circumspect than Clarisse but her original concern was no less positive for that. Even Walter, whom she torments, recognises her intense interest in the world and her refusal to behave like the vast majority of people who simply do nothing when, for example, the newspapers bring news of disasters happening all around. As Walter expresses it, 'she is better than we are in her demand that we should all change and take on a more active conscience, a conscience without end, eternal, so to speak' (916). Musil apparently intended that Ulrich, later in the novel, should follow the path of 'active conscience'. Certainly, under Agathe's gentle prompting, Ulrich seems to be preparing for action. Towards the end of the last chapter of the 1933 edition of Part III Musil wrote: 'In truth, [Ulrich] was erecting fortifications of thoughts against [Agathe] and knew that at a certain point there was a small bolt; if one drew this bolt back everything would be swamped and buried by feeling! And, in fact, he was thinking constantly about this bolt' (1038). Undoubtedly Musil was making a promise that the continuation of *The Man without Qualities* would see that 'bolt' drawn back.

Even before this point in the narrative, Agathe's presence has put an end to Ulrich's '"Leben [. . .] auf Urlaub"' (801) ('life [. . .] on leave') and has interrupted the leisurely rhythm of a self-indulgent reflective existence – a commitment to mathematical and philosophical research is scarcely compatible with passing judgement on Agathe's clothes which have transformed his whole house into a lady's dressing room: 'The doors between the rooms were open, his gymnastic equipment served as stands and supports, he was summoned from his writing desk to make a decision, like Cincinnatus from the plough' (937). It is in delicate detail such as this, and not only in the investigations into mysticism and incest, that the interest, and the value, of Musil's study of a love affair is to be found.

Where has Musil's massive project taken him by 1933 when the unfinished section of Part III appears? He has dealt the world of 'das Seinesgleichen' a doughty (though not fatal!) blow. He has reshaped the attitude of his hero and started him on his spiritual transformation – indeed he has firmly launched Ulrich into a search for the inner well-springs of authentic morality. In so doing Musil has committed himself to the writing of a whole new book, based on issues of daunting complexity. The sections of *The Man without Qualities* which had been published by 1933 are, of course, the only ones which bear Musil's (albeit grudging) seal of authorial approval, but the *Nachlaß* of the novel contains such important and fascinating material that it would be wrong to ignore it here.

### The 'Nachlaß' of 'The Man without Qualities'

All reflections on the *Nachlaß* of *The Man without Qualities* are necessarily speculative. As we saw above, very little of the material which Musil was working on in the last decade of his life reached the stage of a final, or even penultimate, draft. Clarisse seems firmly set on the path to madness – *Nachlaß*-chapters chart her attempts to see Moosbrugger (in some versions she does meet him, in some she even succeeds in arranging his escape, but Moosbrugger is recaptured after an interlude in which he is sheltered in a secret flat with Rachel, who was formerly Diotima's servant), her being sent to a sanatorium, her escape from there and journey to Italy in which she is embroiled in fantasies of liaisons with Nietzsche, Ludwig of Bavaria and the Pope,[24] her pursuit of a Greek homosexual and eventually her descent into utter insanity. (This aspect of the *Nachlaß* is so unwieldy that it appears that Musil considered dropping a large part of it in an attempt to finish the novel.)

Diotima and Arnheim, as far as we can tell, neither marry nor consummate their passion; they part, Diotima in scorn and anger at Arnheim's pusillanimity, Arnheim in sorrow at the sacrifice which business and 'Seele' force him to accept. In one chapter draft Diotima meets Ulrich at a party in which many of the women are dressed as men (another reminder of the theme of the hermaphrodite!); she has chosen to go as a hussar. Ulrich takes her to his home, makes love to her but, apparently, deserts her by the morning.[25]

The fate of another woman friend of Ulrich's, Gerda, is equally unhappy – her father, Leo Fischel, gives up his steady bank job and lives a precarious and incidentally promiscuous life as a stockmarket speculator; her fiancé, Hans Sepp, who is deeply unhappy as a conscript in the army, commits suicide; Gerda, more mature but now very much the spinster in manner and appearance, announces her intention to go off as a nurse to care for the wounded in World War I which has just started.

The men who pull the strings behind the 'Parallelaktion' – it gradually emerges that these are officials from the Foreign Ministry and the Ministry of War – plan to hold a conference on world peace at just about the time when World War I will break out! They have suppressed the resolution passed at the final meeting of the 'Parallelaktion' recorded in *The Man without Qualities*, Part III (1933) – this had proposed that, while everyone was free to give his life for his beliefs, whoever forces another to die for whatever cause is a murderer – and are moving towards a compromise in which assertions of their desire for world peace are backed up with voting money for guns for the Austro-Hungarian army!

As we have seen above, Musil does not rely only on the

interaction of the characters to make his work cohere; in the incomplete sections of his novel as in the completed ones there are many common themes and intellectual strands. Ulrich seeks 'the right way to live', others, like Meingast and Lindner, are as convinced that they have found it as the narrator is convinced that they have not. Meingast and Lindner both make propaganda – the former through philosophising, the latter through moralising – for visions of human behaviour which centre on wilfulness. Lindner makes 'will' the factotum of petty-bourgeois virtues, non-militant Christianity coexisting complacently with the heritage of the Classical world; for Meingast, 'will' is the reckless expression of human energy released from any civilising constraints, passion without rational reflection.[26] The reader gauges Ulrich's view of 'das rechte Leben' by reference to these two champions of extreme positions. Passages in later stages of the novel are concerned with the notion of genius – this is not only a recurrent topic of conversation between Ulrich and Stumm[27] but an obsession which Clarisse borrows from Nietzsche. As the reader works through the *Nachlaß*, these and many other important themes are subtly brought forward for consideration. But the overriding theme remains as it has been before, above all in Part III: love, ranging from unadorned sensuality to mysticism, is vital to the action and to the reflective fabric of the narrative. This leads us to consider the relationship between Ulrich and Agathe through which Musil develops the theme of love in the *Nachlaß* of *The Man without Qualities*.

There has been much argument, as we have seen, on the question of whether or not Ulrich and Agathe commit incest. I have pointed to the warnings about incest in Part III (1933) which indicate that, in 1933 and perhaps even later, Musil intended the relationship to become incestuous; on the other hand, as we have seen, I accept de Rougement's view that, at some time after 1933, Musil probably decided that his lovers should respect the unidentified constraint which held them back on the very threshold of this sin. One of the most fascinating of the *Nachlaß*-chapters, 'Mondstrahlen bei Tage' ('Moonbeams by day'), owes its beauty in part to the delicacy with which Musil traces the path of the lovers along the very edge of a precipice of illicit passion.

In the chapter preceding, 'Moonbeams by day', Agathe and Ulrich's intimacy deepens. The impetus for this is, in the first instance, sensual. Ulrich and Agathe are changing for an evening engagement when Ulrich, who is standing behind his sister, is suddenly held by the beauty of her body. Without being conscious of what he is doing, he sweeps her up in his arms. Agathe's response is described thus:

When Agathe got over her fright and felt herself not so much flying through the air as rather resting in it, suddenly released from gravity and, instead, guided by the gentle force of this gradual deceleration, there came about, through the agency of one of those coincidences over which no one has control, a strange sense of reassurance in this state, indeed a sense of transport beyond all earthly discomfort; with a movement that altered the balance of her body and which she would never have been able to repeat, she slipped off the last silk thread of compulsion, turned as she fell towards her brother and, falling, continued, as it were, to rise and, sinking down, lay, a cloud of happiness in his arms. (1082)

This event takes place in two contexts: it is undoubtedly something that happens in the physical universe, but, on another level, it involves 'a second nature which gently lamed all limbs and, at the same time, ensnared them with an inexpressible sensitivity' (1082–3). Ulrich and Agathe both know that they have spent 'a moment within that shared state [...], at whose border they had hesitated so long, which they had described so often to each other already and yet which they had always only seen from without' (1083). Their relationship has thereby entered a new dimension in which 'every prohibition was now a matter of indifference to them' (1083) – despite the strong urge to sexual fulfilment which they now both feel, something holds them back: 'the gestures of the flesh had become impossible for them and they felt an indescribable warning which had nothing to do with the precepts of morality' (1083). Still caught in an intense emotion they sit, exchanging a few quiet words; the narrator compares their mood to that of a moonlit night:

Not only do the external conditions melt away to take new shape in the nuptial couch of light and shade but the inner ones, too, move together in a new way [...] All assertions express only one single flooding experience. The night folds all contradictions in her shimmering motherly arms and at her breast no word is false and none true but each is the incomparable birth of spirit ['Geist'] from the dark, which the human being experiences with a new idea. Thus each event on moonlit nights possesses the nature of the unrepeatable. (1084)

This passage embodies the problem which Ulrich faces in his attempt to subject mystical experience to precise observation. To comprehend is to identify and label the parts from which the whole is composed. It is a movement from the amorphous to the individual form, from the unnameable totality to the named elements. In the passage quoted above, Musil makes his language go against the grain, unmaking distinctions, blurring contours, rubbing out identifiers, restoring the formless fullness of unmediated experience. We can imagine the ironic pleasure which Musil, the apostle of clarity, must have taken in fashioning this passage where words subvert, by simply being true to their nature, the purpose which they are here put to serve!

The above reflection sets the direction for the next chapter 'Moonbeams by day' which provides a commentary, largely through the medium of Ulrich's reflections, on the nature and significance of the experiences which Ulrich and Agathe have undergone. A recurrent theme of the chapter is the way in which language affects our view of the world.

### 'Moonbeams by day'

In the opening paragraph Musil sets, as an image, a statue in the midst of natural surroundings: 'there, in unexpected sensuous fulfilment, arises an island of significance, spirit ['Geist'] raised and precipitated from the fluid depths of existence!' (1087). I believe that, in choosing this image – though in his case the medium is not the wood, stone or other plastic material of the sculptor, but words – Musil has in mind his own activity as author, reshaping in literary form the experiences that he has shared with Martha in real life. This whole chapter is concerned with man as the maker of a world constructed largely from the words he finds to hand and the concepts and ideas which he fashions with them.[28] In fact, one has the sense that the narrator, throughout this chapter, is circling 'der andere Zustand' ('the other state'), which is the heart of the lovers' shared life, and conjuring up from memory and imagination descriptions, images, analogies and reflections which, though they do not exhaust that experience and indeed do not finally grasp it, are so many perspectives from which it can be glimpsed.

Through their mutual love, Ulrich and Agathe's senses are enhanced; their vision, for example, is more intense. It does not have the sharpness of a hunter fixing his eyes on his prey but possesses rather a heightened awareness of the balance between an individual object and the mysterious context in which all things are set – a context which itself is not a thing.[29] Musil captures this feeling in an image which is more powerful than any of the other perspectives on Ulrich and Agathe's relationship found in the chapter: 'the delight which they found in each other [. . .] was also a stimulation of the eye: colours and shapes which they pointed out to each other were disseminated and unfathomable yet stood out sharply like a garland of flowers floating on dark water' (1087). The beauty of the flowers, in which the brightness of visual perception finds a focus, is set off by the darkness of the deeper total mystery of the world – here glimpsed in the unfathomed waters on which they float. Altering position again a few lines further down, as if to shift the weight of an obsession, the narrator alights on the balancing of perception and feeling in an individual:

The impression belonged to the succinct realm of perception and atten- tion as well as to the inexact one of feeling; and it was precisely this that made them hover betweeen inner and outer as a breath pauses between breathing in and breathing out, and, in a curious contrast with its strength, made it difficult to distinguish whether it belonged in the physical world or merely owed its emergence to an intensified concern with inwardness.                                                    (1087–8)

Here again, as with the flowers floating on dark waters, there is the sense of the incommensurability of such experience, for the passage continues: 'Neither of them wanted to be specific for they were restrained by a kind of shame about reason' (1088). Reason is not suspended, but is restrained by other faculties.

Ulrich wanders through the garden and examines plants and flowers. But in his present state of mind he feels that nature does not allow herself to be held in any man-made inventory of names, species or other categories, and when he finds some plant or blossom which he does not recognise, '(he) still resigned himself [. . .] to being unable to identify in words a colour which was so palpably clear or to describe one of the shapes which, in such an unthinkingly urgent fashion, spoke for itself' (1088). This fact, he reflects, is 'probably the first mystery of daylit mysticism' (1089) which is the collective name which he has given to the new range of perceptual and emotional experience which he and Agathe are now meeting. Starting from this intense experience of the limita- tions of man's power to grasp the world of flowers and plants, Ulrich's thoughts shape themselves into an attack on all aspects of 'understanding' which predisposes to 'a kind of superficiality, [. . .] a clinging to the surface which was, moreover, expressed in the word "to grasp" and which was connected with the way that the original experiences were not understood singly but one with the next and were thereby necessarily linked more to the surface than the depths' (1088). In a passage in which he reflects on the impotence of a term like 'green' to express the multitude of shades and textures of the organic profusion which surrounds him, he appears to pick up the tone of the opening chapter of *The Man without Qualities* when he reflected on the inadequacy of the term 'red' as an element in a description. But, in fact, the direction of the reflection has shifted completely. In that earlier passage he attempted to qualify an attribute of the physical world, the quality of 'redness', in precise scientific language, in terms of a specific light-wavelength rather than in the imprecise language of a novelist.[30] Here, however, he finds orthodox scientific descriptions inadequate:

'I [. . .] could perhaps also measure the colour: I would estimate that it has a wavelength of 540 millionths of a millimeter; and thereby this green might seem to have been captured and nailed to a particular spot! But already it is eluding me – look here: there is after all something substantial about this basic colour which cannot be characterised with colour-words at all because it is different from the same green in silk or wool. And now we have reached once again the profound illumination that green grass is just grass-green!'                                                       (1089)

Science ultimately capitulates in the face of the phenomena of the world – but it takes a scientist to reach this conclusion!

At this point, Agathe seeks to confirm Ulrich's opinion with an image of the incommensurable from another source:

'I suggest you take a look at a mirror in the night; it is dark, black, you see virtually nothing at all; and yet this nothing is quite clearly something different from the nothing of other forms of darkness. You have an intuition of the glass, the doubling of the depth, somehow a vestigial capacity to shimmer and yet you still perceive nothing!'                     (1089–90)

Although loyalty to science stirs uneasily in Ulrich, he offers only token resistance to Agathe's image of human incomprehension. He contributes yet another observation to this discussion of the limits of understanding: the individual constantly sets the world around him into contexts of meaning with himself at the centre (and here the ghosts of Husserl and Heidegger stalk the text!), but, all of a sudden, these structures of relevance may slip and a man find himself standing helpless 'in the face of indescribable and inhuman, indeed revoked and shapeless creation!' (1090).

This suspension of the significance of the self, this unmediated confrontation with creation for which mankind was not responsible, leads to the question of the divine. Agathe, with her perfect recall of many of the things she has read, quotes a passage from one of the mystics: '"I know not where I am, nor seek I myself, nor will I know of it, nor have tidings thereof. I am steeped in the source of his love as if I were under the waters of the sea and could, on no side, see anything save water"' (1091). Perhaps the association of this passage with the image of the flowers floating on the water is not fortuitous.

Agathe faces Ulrich firmly with something which he has not really properly acknowledged before: that his interest in mystical experience is not merely an offshoot of his interest in psychology – it is something more than that. At this point in the narrative we find further evidence of the change which has taken place in Ulrich. He is no longer the sceptic of Part I and Part II, whose main concern was to hold the world at a safe intellectual distance from himself – in fact he has even changed since the moment at the end of Part III (1933) when he speculated on that 'Gedankenbollwerk' (1038) ('thought-fortifications') which he had set up against the influence of his sister. He wondered then about 'drawing back a bolt' in a 'door' in this 'Gedankenbollwerk' which he sensed would lead to a new way of living for him, a new openness. It is a significant advance for him to ask himself now: 'whether it was not possible to believe more than he had allowed himself to do' (1091). Ulrich is on the threshold of religious awe.

We should not underestimate this development. Indeed there are suggestions that Ulrich will try to build a bridge between science and theology. It is true that, in the past, Ulrich has turned his back on religion. But a new thought occurs to him now:

'What if precisely this ungodly way were none other than the contemporary path to God? Every time has taken a different thought-path in this direction, corresponding to her greatest spiritual powers; would it not be our fate then, the fate of an age of clever enterprising experience, to deny all dreams, legends and ingenious concepts only because, at the summit of our research into, and discoveries about, the world we shall turn to Him again and gain a relationship of dawning experience of Him?' (1092)

In the course of the few months of the action of the novel, Ulrich, the man of science, has changed his outlook to the point where he says that scientific method consists, apart from logic, 'in sinking into the depths of phenomena the concepts which have been gained at the surface through "experience" and [that it] explains the former by means of the latter' (1092); he continues: 'one makes earthly things barren and shallow in order to dominate them' (1092). In the wasteland of shallow scientific scepticism, even scientists start to see God: 'the desert has, since time immemorial, been a birthplace for visions of heaven' (1092).

Ulrich had earlier responded to the challenge posed by the self-devaluation of the world of 'Wirklichkeit' by the search for new meaning – a Promethean search which seems to involve him in a struggle with destiny itself. Quite suddenly his attitude to this undertaking changes, for he realises that he may not be struggling against, but side by side with, the power behind creation: 'For what if it were God Himself who devalues the world? Would it not suddenly by that fact regain sense and joy? And would He not necessarily devalue it by simply coming even the smallest step closer to it? And would not the only real adventure be simply to become aware of even an intimation of this?!' (1093).

This 'adventure' is, of course, a reference to Ulrich's relationship with Agathe. Agathe, through an empathy consolidated by many hours of discussions and days spent in close contact with her brother, intuitively grasps what is happening within him. Thus Musil lifts their love onto a transcendental plane (in the sense that it is to be seen to transcend sensual, emotional or even intellectual experience): '"He doesn't want it to become merely a love-story" [Agathe] thought; and added: "This is how I feel too." And immediately afterwards she thought: "He will love no woman after me, for this is not a love story any more; it is positively the last love-story there can be!"' (1094). Their love affair, by being given central significance in *The Man without Qualities*, symbolises the way out of the maze of 'das Seinesgleichen' – it is conceived as a path which leads mankind to a new relationship with itself, with the world, and with God.

When we apply this perspective to earlier sections of the novel we find evidence that Musil was trying to prepare the ground for this apparently radical shift in stance by his hero. Indeed there are times when it seems that Ulrich only needs a sufficiently powerful stimulus to reveal the core of belief within him.

William James compared the condition of a believer to a piece of iron that has been suspended within a magnetic field. If this field were changed the bar of iron 'might be [. . .] determined to different attitudes and tendencies. Such a bar of iron could never give you an outward description of the agencies that had the power of stirring it so strongly; yet of their presence, and of their significance for its life, it would be intensely aware through every fibre of its being.'[31] Surely this might serve as an analogy for Ulrich's state, too; however irreverent his tone may be, however insistent his demand for knowledge that is nothing less than objective, he can disguise neither from himself nor from some other people that he is impelled from within by a force that looks very much like a variety of belief. It was this sense that prompted Arnheim to say of Ulrich: ' "This man has soul ['Seele']!" ' (548).

There are moments in the novel when this part of Ulrich's character, which is usually hidden even from himself, is expressed with startling clarity. Shortly after his arrival in his home-town he sorts through the contents of his father's desk. (The desk itself is a symbol, for it seems that the countless hours the father has spent seated at it have impregnated it with ideas, desires and ambitions that depend on traditional values.)[32] There, at the back of a drawer, the very drawer which has contained his father's will, Ulrich finds obscene pictures and other pornographic material. The reader might expect Ulrich to be amused at this, to see it with detachment and pass it off with a wry comment about the gulf between the show of propriety and the secret world of private desire. In fact, the discovery touches a raw nerve and Ulrich reacts with revulsion. For the first time in the novel he is roused to anger at such hypocrisy: ' "There, together in the same drawer, lie the stern moral injunctions of the will and this filth!" ' (769). If we had no knowledge of Ulrich's past we might think that this outburst was either conventional moral disapproval or a show of annoyance for the benefit of Agathe who happens to be with him. But neither of these explanations holds water: with his record of adultery Ulrich is hardly in a position to condemn his father on this account, and his relationship with Agathe is remarkable for its total frankness on all matters, including sexuality.

The conclusion we must draw is that Ulrich's vituperative denunciation of his father's immorality and hypocrisy is an unpremeditated rejection of a whole way of life. Filed away neatly in a compartment of his father's desk he has found evidence of 'Arbeitsteilung' (509) ('division of labour') in the realm of feeling, an emotional orderliness which the narrator despises, and which he identified also in Arnheim. Ulrich is revolted by this distortion of sexual desire under the self-imposed pressures of bourgeois existence. He wants to get away from the mentality represented here, according to which morality reaches only as far as a man's public conscience and fear of being found out – the kind of morality which sees in the opinion of one's fellows a law as unswerving in its pursuit of open wrong-doing as the law of the land, but which is oblivious to any activity that is not seen to interfere with the life of the community. What Ulrich wants is a 'Gesetz des rechten Lebens [. . .], das ehern und natürlich ist' (825) ('law of the right way to live [. . .] which is hard as brass and natural'), something that reaches into the remotest and most private corners of human existence, which abolishes the distinction between the realms of public morality and private conscience, and brings the notions of crime and sin under the same roof. As we have seen, he searches for such a law in the proximity of 'der andere Zustand'.

His anger at this discovery of the pictures (which embody in blatant fashion the way that, in his father's life, the realm of 'Liebe' is corrupted by a form of 'Gewalt') prompts a personal confession of hitherto unparalleled frankness. He explains to Agathe how uncomfortable he feels within the code of conduct which society expects of him. He deplores its rigidity, its lack of subtlety: '"The morality which has been handed down to us is as if we had been sent out onto a swaying rope stretched across an abyss", he said "and given us no other advice but to keep our back straight!"' (770). He describes conventional morality as a form of repression, just as Arnheim did: '"I believe that all precepts of our morality are concessions to a society of savages"' (769). But the principles which Arnheim accepts Ulrich condemns: '"I believe that none are right"' (769). Thus far he has dealt in negatives; now, however, he puts forward the positive: '"Another meaning shimmers [behind the precepts of our morality . . .] A fire that is to melt them down"' (769). Without warning, Ulrich falls into the timeless imagery of faith.[33] He likens the force of authentic morality to a fire which consumes the dead wood of traditional precepts and from whose ashes arises the 'Gesetz des rechten Lebens [. . .], das ehern und natürlich ist' (825) ('law of the right way to live [. . .] that is hard as brass and natural'). Here Ulrich implies that there are certain actions which issue spontaneously from the soul of the individual; the law under which they fall is continuous with the force which shapes them. This force seems to be dictating the end of the relationship between Ulrich and Agathe.

## The end of the affair?

How can the feelings which Ulrich and Agathe experience be contained for long within a relationship without sexual fulfilment, without the sanction of legality or morality, but equally without the burden of a guilt to shield from the outside world (for it is clear that without corroborating evidence of wrongdoing – such as proof of incest between brother and sister – Hagauer will never be able to uphold the charge that Agathe altered her father's will). The relationship has no permanent focus and Ulrich and Agathe are at the mercy of emotions that tend to lead them apart – Agathe's interest in Lindner and Ulrich's in Diotima, for example. Musil's inner concern, the search for 'der andere Zustand', also points towards the end of the relationship of brother and sister. Incest would anchor it in guilt-burdened complicity – but then 'der andere Zustand' would elude them. The alternative – the deliberate avoidance of incest – would involve, given the constant strains and temptations of proximity, acts of steadfast purpose incompatible with spontaneity, and, again, 'der andere Zustand' would be lost. Ulrich and Agathe recognise this: '"[...] How [...] is one to hold fast to a feeling? How would it be possible to remain on the highest level of happiness if it were possible to reach it at all? We are preoccupied, basically, with this question alone [...]"' (1130).

These reflections are taken from a diary which Ulrich has started to write in secret. Though this is not the work of a creative writer but rather of a scientist preoccupied with the realm of feelings, it is an important step on his part. Agathe, having chanced upon Ulrich's writing, finds that in it a changed Ulrich appears before her; she recognises 'that, tentatively and emotionally, he is opening his arms to something' (1125) – she sees, that is to say, precisely the Ulrich who has responded inwardly to her presence in ways which as yet he has not expressed to her in words. The revelations in this secret writing, particularly those contained in Part III, Chapter 50, not only throw light on Ulrich's attitude, but unveil something of the basis of Musil's thinking in The Man without Qualities as a whole.

Almost with a touch of embarrassment, Ulrich has written here: '"[...] In my mind, next to the doubt and scorn, a primeval thought has settled: everything in the world is love, covered in ash but inextinguishable, love is the gentle, divine essence of the world! [...]"' (1123). It is evident that this thought is not a dogmatic pronouncement but rather a feeling of certainty that occasionally overwhelms him. Agathe has shown him places in the Bible which speak of God as 'Love' and this has set him reflecting on the relationship between this power and the world at large. He visualises God, the all-loving one, as the 'Eternal Artist' (1125) and sees His relationship to the world in the following way: '"[...] He loves creation for as long as he is making it, but His love turns away from the finished parts [...]"' (1125). In the storms of creative passion, the Creator turns His back on what He made earlier: ' " [. . .] What He has already created, even if it is good, grows cold for Him: it becomes so lovelorn that He can scarcely understand Himself in it any more and the moments are few and unpredictable when His love returns and feasts on what it has made [. . .]" ' (1125). What, then, of those facets of the created world which have cooled? Ulrich sees them as no longer under the reign of 'Liebe' but of 'Gewalt': ' "[. . .] And it is without doubt, violence ['Gewalt'] which keeps the world in motion and prevents it falling asleep, and not love! [. . .]" ' (1125).

From the passion of creation to the cold world of outer 'Wirklichkeit' is a surprisingly short step – for reality is the sum of things, originally conceived in passion but which passion has now abandoned. The universal law holds good for human creativity, too: the architecture of a town square, the design of a uniform, even the shape of a parasol all speak to the world with the firmness of erstwhile conviction – this is how a building, a uniform, a parasol must be! Though the passion of their origin does not survive the passage of time this is not so with the imperative embodied in their form; Ulrich expresses this as follows: ' "[. . .] Every distinct detail in which our environment finds expression 'speaks to us'. It means something. It shows that it has taken shape from an intention which is by no means ephemeral. It is true that it is only an opinion, but it pretends to be a conviction. It is merely a notion, but behaves as if it were unshakeable will [. . .]" ' (1128).

Let us recapitulate these ideas of Ulrich's since they articulate the testimony of the narrative as a whole. Love is the origin of all things: it is the expression of God, as the Artist-Creator, in His passionate relationship with what He is creating. But as He turns from that created thing and His attention focusses elsewhere, that passion cools and the thing grows cold. This sequence holds true for human beings, also – for in the human artist-creator a spark of the divine resides. For mankind, too, love is found in the passion of creation – it is present, also, as we saw earlier, in the 'fire' that is the origin of all authentic goodness. But love does not let itself be held fast in any form: when, for example, the passion of overwhelming insight cools to idea, and idea is absorbed into ideology, and eventually ideology petrifies in dogma, 'Gewalt' has taken the place of 'Liebe'; thereby spontaneous creativity is curbed and transformed into external pressures which act on the individual from without. This, then, is Musil's account of the twin elements that shape the history of civilisations – on the one hand, creativity conceived in 'Liebe', on the other, external pressure born of 'Gewalt'.

This 'Gewalt'–'Liebe' cosmology, as we have seen, can be discerned throughout the text as a base position to which other statements about the shape of things can be related – it stands, for instance, as the ultimate source of all those pairings which recur in the text: 'Moral und Ethik' ('morality and ethics'), 'Genauigkeit und Seele' ('precision and soul'), 'Eindeutigkeit und Gefühl' ('single-mindedness and feeling'), 'die zwei Bäume des Lebens' ('the two trees of life'), 'Möglichkeit und Wirklichkeit' ('possibility and reality') and others, too. In each of these pairs is reflected the dynamic balance central to Musil's perception of things: to 'Moral', for instance, which Musil sees as the deliberate subjection of human conduct to a system of regulations, with connotations of constraint and repression, corresponds the passion of 'Ethik', the spontaneous 'fire' (and Musil frequently signals this association in his imagery) that suffuses the life of the saint; 'Genauigkeit' is identified as, for example, the precision of the scientist, with overtones of understanding hard-won through scepticism and self-sacrifice, and counterbalances 'Seele' which is alive in the open-minded and open-hearted state of an innocence beyond all reason. The 'Gewalt'–'Liebe' polarity also underlines the division of the work into sections: Part I, and more so Part II, are concerned with the realm of 'Gewalt', the world, as the title of Part II expresses it, of 'Seinesgleichen geschieht'; Part III, on the other hand, takes the reader into the realm of 'Liebe', 'Ins Tausendjährige Reich' ('Into the Millennium'), as this is put in *its* title. It is possible to see, from the perspective of the 'Gewalt'–'Liebe' principle, how Musil sees the love of brother and sister as a response to the coldness of 'das Seinesgleichen' – how their relationship is a token of the potential of mankind to escape the nexus of externality.

But, as Ulrich says: '"[...] Feelings are [...] changeable and inconstant [...]. They become inauthentic when they last [...]"' (1129). For the relationship between Ulrich and Agathe to last it would have to change; the purity of the passion that informs it would have to be tainted. This, surely, is proof that Musil did not intend their relationship to be permanent.[34]

# EPILOGUE

Musil was in the tradition of dissenting authors such as Schiller, Brecht and Böll. He believed, as they did, that writing involved the changing of ingrained attitudes, or what we might call 'socio-psychic engineering'. However, in his lifetime, Musil did not have the reputation which would have been a prerequisite for revolutionary impact. In his declining years, as he eked out an existence in exile in Switzerland, Musil might have been excused if he had felt that he had failed. He certainly complained of neglect, but he never doubted that his works would be appreciated, if only after his death. In this, he has been proved right. The wide attention which Musil has received, above all in the last two decades, is a belated tribute to the worth of his creative works. This study has been an attempt to assess the most important of these works.

In the twenties, Musil is asked what he wants to achieve in this novel; he replies, with the confidence of an author who does not yet know that he will not be able to complete his literary project, that his aim is 'geistige [...] Bewältigung der Welt' (GWII, 942) ('conquest of the world by force of mind and spirit'). Since even the accumulated achievements of civilisation are a prison, Musil wants to contribute to mankind's release from the past, and to offer advice on a more rational and creative use of human potential in the future. *The Man without Qualities* records what it is like to be fettered by early twentieth-century attitudes; it documents the way men and women speak, think, feel and act; it recreates aspects of society's social, moral, political and scientific constitution, representing its habits and eccentricities in human case-studies. *The Man without Qualities* alienates readers from the spectacle of a world gone wrong by means of often brilliant satire – the 'Parallelaktion', for example, is an outstanding comic invention in its own right. The work is not only an inventory of what civilisation offered Musil's contemporaries, but a reminder of what it denied them. The creative intelligence at the heart of the work had a specific function for contemporary, and indeed later, readers – to warn against what was to be avoided, to point towards what might be won. Thus *The Man without Qualities* bears witness to a mind of extraordinary perception and sensitivity and of penetrating and creative moral concern.

To make space for creation, much needed to be destroyed; in this work, Musil was an iconoclast. He used satire to challenge the divine right of moribund institutions and to break the spell of self-importance that attached to insignificant personalities. Some passages of *The Man without Qualities* have the tone of a polemic against individuals – for example, Arnheim, Meingast, Feuermaul and Lindner are seen, as it were, as Musil's rivals in the struggle to attract the attention of the public. They, or to be precise, the real counterparts whom they represent, are false prophets, pointing contemporaries in the wrong direction. Musil demolishes them by judicious quotation from statements they have made, from books they have written, condemning them out of their own mouths and by means of their own texts, and showing how, in practice, they fall far short of what they preach. (The educational theorist cannot keep his own son in order; the sage, professing intimacy with the realm of the soul, cannot keep the love of the woman he loves.) With each of these figures, as with others less well-known but sometimes of greater importance to the narrative itself, Musil shifts the perspective out of the range of personal self-approval to some oblique and embarrassing angle: we secretly observe the poet as thinker, the business-man as lover, the aristo-crat as entrepreneur, the soldier as researcher, the engineer as bourgeois, the 'Salondame' as liberated woman. This multiplicity of angles, demanding of its author an unusual breadth of know-ledge and insight, presents many a telling perspective on the collective madness which has taken hold of contemporary civili-sation, the 'Seinesgleichen' of society on the brink of war.

As we have seen, *The Man without Qualities* is not only intended to alienate and destroy aspects of past and present but to shape the future: how does Musil attempt to achieve this? The first step is to win back the ground of the subject. This has been lost, in the field of ideas, to the march of a militant objectivity which is both superficial and insensitive; it has been lost in the field of morals with the sense that principles are written on tablets of stone rather than in the human heart; it has been lost in the field of science with the disappearance of the observer from the scope of what is observed. Musil counterattacks with his hero, the 'Mann ohne Eigenschaften', a name which expresses his protest against the world of externality.

Ulrich's wide-ranging talents are not put to specific use. In the eyes of the world he is a gifted wastrel – indecisive, passive, emotionally unstable, amoral, critical, lacking any career or sense of direction. From the author's perspective, Ulrich, with his lack of 'amour propre', is equipped to avoid the pitfalls of 'das Seinesgleichen'. Of liberal instincts, he seeks a code by which he might willingly be bound; he is, by turns, sceptical and passionate, a scientist who is fascinated by mystical experience, a prototype 'free spirit', whose inner eye turns away from the distractions of the actual towards the promise of the possible. Ulrich, at the outset overwhelmed by the loss of subjectivity, takes a path which he hopes will ultimately lead to his intellectual, emotional and moral centre.

The path is no easy one. It meanders through long detours. It passes through the purgatory of the 'Parallelaktion' with its revelations about the deceits which shape contemporary behaviour. It leads through the Moosbrugger-experiment which explores the way one human mind reaches out to the consciousness of another, using image and analogy as subtle psychic tools to assist the process (and this is surely more than a mere literary 'tour de force' – rather a significant step towards understanding human understanding itself). Finally, it leads the hero to his sister.

When Agathe appears, the novel moves decisively into the territory of the subject. Musil withdraws his hero from life in society into the intimacy of house and garden. Here, with few distractions, Ulrich studies the thoughts, impulses and emotions that teem in his brain. Having rejected what the world offers him – its habitual patterns of thinking, 'systems of feeling' and codes of behaviour – Ulrich focusses his mind on itself, trying to discover what, at its innermost core, it yearns for. Without abandoning the discipline of his scientific training, he reaches for the secret of the right way to live. Agathe is caught up in this search because she is Ulrich's double in feminine form and because she shares with him a love without reservation. When, in the long unfinished latter sections of the novel, Ulrich explores the vaults of inwardness, Musil makes the world of the subject available to the objective scrutiny of the reader.

In this part of the work, 'der andere Zustand' is glimpsed. Musil shows how experiences which are most commonly linked with mysticism and religion appear to the critical awareness of a respectful agnostic. Rational enquiry is brought to the very brink of meditation in passages which are sometimes even more demanding than the cerebral prose of *Acts of Union*. Musil is unwilling to compromise the search for the key to the human mind and heart, even when this search begins to run counter to the task of finishing the novel, leading it into apparently interminable dialogues and reflections. Such concessions to the plot as the forging of a codicil to the will or the 'journey to Paradise' which are part of earlier chapter drafts are evidently abandoned as diversions from the central quest. The result is a sequence of chapters which, though they move the work as a whole no nearer to any horizon and scarcely any closer to completion, capture, in words without precedent or parallel, the fervour of their author's unique enterprise.

# NOTES

## 1 Impressions of Robert Musil

1 In 'Erinnerung an Musil', in *Robert Musil – Leben, Werk, Wirkung*, edited by Karl Dinklage (Zürich, Leipzig, Wien, 1960), pp. 400–4, p. 403.

2 Hans Mayer, *Zur deutschen Literatur der Zeit* (Reinbek bei Hamburg, 1967), p. 138.

3 In 'Robert Musil in der geistigen Bewegung seiner Zeit', in *Robert Musil – Leben, Werk, Wirkung*, pp. 133–44, p. 140.

4 In 'Erinnerung an Robert Musil', in *Robert Musil – Leben, Werk, Wirkung*, pp. 364–76, pp. 367–8.

5 *Die Welt als Wille und Vorstellung*, in *Sämtliche Werke* (Wiesbaden, 1961), 2, p. 22.

6 See Karl Otten, 'Eindrücke von Robert Musil', in *Robert Musil – Leben, Werk, Wirkung*, pp. 357–63, p. 361.

7 As Frisé explains, Musil felt he should record as much as possible since anything might come in useful at some time! See Adolf Frisé, 'Die Tagebücher Robert Musils', in *Die neue Rundschau*, 85 (1974), 124–38, pp. 129–30.

8 See, for example, Tbi, 31, where Musil has written the word 'Clarisse' alongside three entries. The material here was evidently relevant to his work for MoE on this particular character.

9 See Tbi, 366 (entry on Liechtenstein) and Tbii, 227–9 (Anm.98, 100, 101).

10 See Tbi, 151 ('In the coffee-house in the evening I read an essay by E. Key which affected me deeply') and Tbii, 90, 'Anm.79'.

11 See, for example, two of Adolf Frisé's notes on the diaries, 158 and 159 (Tbii, 101–2) which trace the path from some of Musil's excerpts from Ellen Key's essay 'The Unfolding of the Soul through the Art of Living' (see Tbi, 163) to their location in the text of MoE where they are attributed to Diotima.

12 See – re Kerschensteiner – for example the entry beginning 'Goethean Man: see Georg Kerschensteiner' (Tbi, 572–3) and Tbii, 381–3, 'Anm.27ff'. See – re Foerster – for example reference to 'F. W. Förster' (Tbi, 575) and Tbii, 383–5, 'Anm.55' and Tbii, 1139–44 (appendix to 'Anm.55').

13 Musil invites critics to study his characters closely: 'If only critics, when faced with the figures in a book and with a creative writer, would ask themselves simply: what kind of people are they? [...] instead of concerning themselves with aesthetic laws which they don't understand' (Tb1, 451).

14 It is, of course, 'contemporary' in that it matches the course of Musil's own life; it does not match the chronology of the fictional narrative. Kaiser and Wilkins show that Ulrich 'ages', so to speak, with his creator over the many years of composition (see Ernst Kaiser and Eithne Wilkins, *Robert Musil – eine Einführung in das Werk* (Stuttgart, 1962), p. 25).

15 Quoted by Karl Otten, 'Eindrücke von Robert Musil', p. 358.

16 Frisé includes a draft of a scene where Moosbrugger is hanged in Tb11, 1065.

17 It often seems that Musil's first priority is the formulation of experience in language which is both vivid and precise, the second, to provoke thought and then, only in third place, the requirement of plot or character within the given work. In a review of the 1978 Frisé edition of Musil's works, Rolf Schneider goes as far as to deny that Musil possesses any creative imagination at all: 'The writer, Robert Musil, was a scientist who found himself by mistake in "belles lettres"; his precision was as great as his imagination was small [...]' (in 'Über die Neu-Edition von Robert Musil, "Gesammelte Werke", hrsg. von Adolf Frisé, Reinbek, 1978', in *Musil-Forum*, 4 (1978), 350–4, p. 354). However, what Schneider dismisses as 'lack of imagination' was, in reality, another aspect of Musil's passion for exact rendering of experience.

18 See also Musil's reflections looking back on that decision in Tb1, 918–19.

19 Musil's fellow-novelist, Alfred Döblin, gave a convincing account of this condition of moral inertia in his essay, *Wissen und Verändern* (Berlin, 1931).

20 See Franz Theodor Csokor, 'Gedenkrede zu Robert Musils achtzigstem Geburtstag', in *Robert Musil – Leben, Werk, Wirkung*, pp. 347–56, p. 355.

21 See David Luft, *Robert Musil and the Crisis of European Culture, 1880–1942* (Berkeley/Los Angeles/London, 1980), pp. 119–20; see also Armin Kesser's account of Robert Musil's apparent detachment as he listened to radio broadcasts on the advances of German armies in the early forties 'as if it was only a weather-forecast'; when asked to explain his attitude Musil replied: 'There's no point in protesting about the Flood' (in 'Begegnung mit Musil – Gespräche und Aufzeichnungen', in *Robert Musil – Leben, Werk, Wirkung*. pp. 183–6, p. 184).

22 Quoted in Tb11, 1259.

23 *A Proliferation of Prophets* (Manchester, 1983), p. 50.

24 See *Briefe* 1, 368.

25 See Peters, *Robert Musil – Master of the Hovering Life* (New York, 1978) on the paradoxes in Musil's interests, pp. 14–15.
26 See, on this aspect of Musil's interests: von Allesch, 'Robert Musil in der geistigen Bewegung seiner Zeit', p. 139; Fontana, 'Erinnerungen an Robert Musil', p. 337; Roth, 'Robert Musil im Spiegel seines Werkes', p. 29. David Luft and Carl Schorske both discuss the question of art as a substitute religion in Musil's life (in, respectively, *Robert Musil [. . .]*, p. 14, and *Fin-de-siècle Vienna*, Cambridge, 1981, pp. 8–9).
27 Musil read the collection of lectures by William James published as *The Varieties of Religious Experience* (London, New York, Bombay, 1902) – in one of the lectures on mysticism, XVII, James discusses Jakob Boehme's view of primal love, where God is nothingness, the void into which all created things fall. In the same lecture, James quotes Angelus Silesius:

| | |
|---|---|
| Gott ist ein lauter Nichts, | God is a Nothing pure, |
| ihn rührt kein Nun noch Hier; | Untouched by Now or Here; |
| Je mehr du nach ihm greiffst, | The more thou reachst for Him, |
| je mehr entwind er dir | The more He'll shrink from thee |

Musil's view seems to me to embrace both of these notions.

## 2 Musil from youth to maturity

1 See TbII, 55, Anm.129 and TbII, 862, AN84a.
2 See Sibylle Mulot, *Der junge Musil – seine Beziehung zu Literatur und Kunst der Jahrhundertwende* (Stuttgart, 1977), pp. 41–128.
3 *Die Welt von Gestern – Erinnerungen eines Europäers* (Frankfurt am Main, 1970), p. 39. (English translation, *The World of Yesterday: an Autobiography* (Lincoln, Nebraska, 1964).
4 Schorske, *Fin-de-Siecle Vienna*, pp. 226–36.
5 *Panorama of the Nineteenth Century* (New York, 1977), pp. 8–16 (original edition, *Panorama oder Ansichten vom 19. Jahrhundert*, Hamburg, 1955).
6 'Leutnant Gustl', in *Gesammelte Werke* (Berlin, 1922), 9 vols, I, pp. 261–302.
7 David Luft gives a valuable account of the liberal tradition in Austria with close reference to Musil's background, in *Robert Musil [. . .]*, pp. 23–62.
8 See, for example, the diary entry for 8 May 1902: 'Today I borrowed two big volumes of Nietzsche from the Franzenmuseum. Involuntarily holy mood, for how I once used to read him!' (TbI, 19); the twenty-two-year-old Musil looks back with awe on the effect on him of Nietzsche when he was even younger!
9 See, particularly, F. G. Peters, 'Musil and Nietzsche: a Literary Study of a Philosophical Relationship' (unpublished PhD. dissertation, University of Cambridge, 1972).

10 See Adolf Frisé's notes on Emerson and Musil's references to Emerson's works in Tb<small>II</small>, 25, Anm. 151.
11 'Self-Reliance' in Emerson, *Essays*, Everyman edition (London, 1906), pp. 29–56, p. 41.
12 'Self-Reliance', p. 42.
13 'History' in *Essays*, p. 16.
14 See Tb<small>I</small>, 168–9.
15 'Robert Musil in der geistigen Bewegung seiner Zeit', in *Robert Musil – Leben, Werk, Wirkung*, p. 133.
16 'Robert Musil in der geistigen Bewegung seiner Zeit', p. 134.
17 'Beitrag zur Beurteilung der Lehren von Ernst Mach' (doctoral dissertation, Friedrich-Wilhelm-Universität, Berlin, 1908).
18 Wolfdietrich Rasch, *Über Robert Musils Roman 'Der Mann ohne Eigenschaften'* (Göttingen, 1967), p. 13.
19 Hugo von Hofmannsthal, 'Ein Brief', *Gesammelte Werke*, edited by Herbert Steine (Frankfurt am Main, 1953), Prosa 2, pp. 7–20; see the discussion of the relevance of 'Ein Brief' to Musil's work in R. M. Paulsen, *Robert Musil and the Ineffable in Hieroglyph, Myth, Fairy-Tale and Sign* (Stuttgart, 1982), pp. 43–8.
20 See, on Musil's relationship to Mach, Manfred Requadt, 'Robert Musil und das Dichten "more geometrico" ', in *Text + Kritik*, 'Robert Musil', third edition, 1983, pp. 29–43, particularly pp. 36–43.
21 See GW<small>II</small>, 832, also in Tb<small>II</small>, 1193.
22 In 1904, Musil made extensive notes on the first volume of Husserl's *Logische Untersuchungen* shortly after it had been published, see Tb<small>I</small>, 119–31 passim.
23 *Husserl and the Search for Certitude* (New Haven and London, 1975).
24 In *Robert Musil, Konstanz und Entwicklung von Themen, Motiven und Strukturen in den Dichtungen* (Bonn, 1972), p. 45.

### 3 Musil's Works, 1906–1924

1 See Adolf Frisé's detailed information on this title in Tb<small>II</small>, 4–6, note 4.
2 Franz Kafka, 'Ein Landarzt', in *Gesammelte Schriften*, edited by Max Brod, 5 vols (New York, 1946), 1, pp. 134–9.
3 See 'Fragments du Narcisse', in *Œuvres*, edited by Jean Hytier, 2 vols (Paris, 1957), pp. 122–30.
4 See letter to Paul Wiegler, *Briefe* 1, 23–4.
5 See GW<small>II</small>, 62.
6 J. P. Stern compares Beineberg's ideas to those of Himmler and the S. S. Stern criticises Musil very sharply for failing to present clearly in the novel any moral context in terms of which Beineberg's behaviour would be unequivocally condemned. In so doing, Stern argues, Musil contributed to an ethos which Nazism was later to exploit. (See 'History in Robert Musil's "Törleß" ', in *Teaching the Text*, edited by Susanne Kappeler and Norman Bryson, London, 1983, pp. 35–55.) While I

recognise the force of Stern's argument, it is my view that Musil was right to publish this work in which the dilemma of the emerging intellectual is presented with unflinching immediacy, even though the work may thereby be open to the charge which Stern makes against it – the author, at this time in his development, was indeed unable to give an adequate moral evaluation of what happens in his novel. Musil felt – and I believe he was right – that it was important to identify and describe Törleß's psychic condition, however unpleasant it was and however far he, as author, may have stood from a proper appreciation of its causes, let alone from discovering any remedy.

7 See David Luft, *Robert Musil [. . .]*, p. 74.
8 See David Luft, *Robert Musil [. . .]*, p. 74.
9 See Dorrit Cohn, 'Psycho-Analogies: A Means for Rendering Consciousness', in *Probleme des Erzählens*, edited by Fritz Martini (Stuttgart, 1971), pp. 291–302, p. 291.
10 In the essay 'Geist und Erfahrung' (1921) which contains critical reflections on Spengler's *Der Untergang des Abendlandes*.
11 Many thinkers have remarked on this phenomenon: see, for example, C. G. Jung's observations on the ebbing of passion from what he calls the 'myth' of Christianity, in *Memories, Dreams, Reflections* (London, 1967), pp. 363–4.
12 In 'Der deutsche Mensch als Symptom'.
13 In 'Geist und Erfahrung'.
14 In 'Der "Untergang" des Theaters'.
15 See, for example, 'Der deutsche Mensch als Symptom' (GWII, 1392–1400).
16 In 'Geist und Erfahrung'.
17 See, for example, 'Der deutsche Mensch als Symptom' (GWII, 1392–1400).
18 In 'Der deutsche Mensch als Symptom'.
19 Musil's observations on mysticism are ecstatic and sober by turns: in 'Der deutsche Mensch als Symptom', Musil describes 'der andere Zustand' as 'Vereinigung mit Gott', ('uniting with God') (GWII, 1399); on the other hand, he defines mysticism itself (in 'Das hilflose Europa' (1922)) as simply 'thought being more deeply bedded-down into the realm of feeling' (GWII, 1092–3).
20 In 'Geist und Erfahrung'.

## 4 Introduction

1 See the very early studies of Robert (Musil), Bertha (Alice Charlemont) and Gustl (Gustav Donath) as children in about 1903 (TbI, 38–48, and TbI, 88–94).
2 See Adolf Frisé, 'Von einer "Geschichte dreier Personen" [. . .]', p. 431.
3 Ernst Kaiser and Eithne Wilkins give the following datings for the

sequence of novels: 'Der Spion', approximately 1918–21, 'Der Erlöser', 1921–3, 'Die Zwillingsschwester', 1924–8 (Kaiser and Wilkins in 'Monstrum in animo [. . .]', p. 84). However, the final date for 'Die Zwillingsschwester' should, according to Adolf Frisé, be brought back to early 1927 – see below in text.

4 It is significant that, as early as 'Der Erlöser', almost all the main characters of MoE are present (see Adolf Frisé, 'Von einer "Geschichte dreier Personen" '), pp. 438–9.

5 See Adolf Frisé, 'Unvollendet – unvollendbar? [. . .]', p. 92.

6 See the many references to a satirical novel *Das Land über dem Südpol*, later 'Ed' in *Tagebücher*, Heft 28, Heft 31, Heft 34, etc.

7 See Marie-Louise Roth, 'Robert Musil als Aphoristiker', in *Beiträge zur Musil-Kritik*, edited by Gudrun Brokoph-Mauch, pp. 289–320.

8 Only a few of these portraits can be examined below, but the editions of Musil's *Tagebücher* and *Briefe* by Adolf Frisé are a mine of important, and often fascinating, information on this aspect of MoE.

9 Henceforth, in referring to *The Man without Qualities* in my text, I understand those sections of the novel published in Musil's lifetime. All other sections of the novel which were left behind in proof or manuscript form I refer to collectively as 'MoE-*Nachlaß*'. It will be convenient, below, to refer to Musil's second volume of MoE, published in 1933, as 'Part III (1933)'.

10 See Musil's letter to Franz Blei on 25 December 1932, on the decision to publish an interim volume – *Briefe* I, 553.

11 See Adolf Frisé, MoE, 2047; see also Adolf Frisé, 'Unvollendet – unvollendbar? [. . .]', p. 88.

12 I follow Wolfdietrich Rasch, 'Zur Entstehung [. . .]', p. 65, who argues that, by concentrating on work on the Ulrich and Agathe scenes, Musil had not rejected all the material from other sub-plots in MoE; the Ulrich/Agathe scenes were simply those which demanded his attention at this particular point in the composition of the novel.

13 The MoE-*Nachlaß* is a field of specialised research on which opinions differ markedly. My own view is that, in the last few years of his life, Musil decided to revise the so-called 'Druckfahnenkapitel' (chapters which had actually been set up in print in 1938 by Bermann-Fischer and then withdrawn by Musil for revision – see MoE, 1045–1203); after an initial heavy revision of all these chapters, which are numbered 39 to 58, he decided on major surgery to the sequence again starting in the middle with Chapter 47. This involved extensive reshaping of the novel from Chapter 47 of Part III onwards as recorded in MoE, 1204–1239. In this re-writing he progressed only as far as Chapter 52 (i.e. the second chapter bearing this number in the MoE-*Nachlaß*). Thus, we might argue that, had Musil been given the opportunity to note down on the day of his death which chapters he considered more or less ready for publication ('more or less ready', not 'ready'!) he might have said (and it is important to stress that this is only a guess): Chapters 39–46 from

the 'Druckfahnenkapitel' – MoE, 1045–1095 – and, from the sequence, mentioned above, Chapters 47–52 – MoE, 1204–1239. The combined total being only fourteen chapters and, indeed, as Wolfdietrich Rasch properly reminds us, none of the MoE-*Nachlaß* can properly be treated as a final draft (see 'Zur Entstehung von Robert Musils Roman "Der Mann ohne Eigenschaften" ', in *Über Robert Musils Roman 'Der Mann ohne Eigenschaften'*, Göttingen, 1967, pp. 35–77, p. 75).

14  MoE, 1377–1381, for instance, provide clear examples of Musil's 'narrative housekeeping'.

15  In 1930, after the publication of the first volume of MoE which, of course, contained nothing of the 'Schwester'-theme Musil described the content of his work in the following reply to a questionnaire from a literary magazine: 'In it I want to expose well-known mistakes of the European ideology, mistakes which have still not been put right. Starting from the principle according to which ideas do, indeed, determine history but people don't seem to have any new ideas, the plot and style of this novel has an ironical and imaginary character. In addition, I am trying to describe the adventures of an individual who is so fettered by the advantages of scientific thinking that he does not renounce this thinking even though he is morally obliged to do so' (*Briefe* I, 471).

16  See, for example, Musil's notes on possible alterations to the plot of the novel in MoE, 1838–1839.

17  Perhaps one of the major difficulties which Musil faced in his declining years was the mental effort required to recreate the world of a much younger man. Wolfdietrich Rasch certainly feels that Musil found it hard to maintain the quality of his work towards the end of his life. In later years, says Rasch, 'it was only with the greatest difficulty that he could match the level of earlier parts of the novel, and the chapters written in Switzerland (i.e. after Musil emigrated from Austria in 1938 – PP) are, despite individual passages of high value, by no means among the best in the novel' ('Zur Entstehung [...]', p. 72). I would agree with this judgement, with the reservation that, though the later passages may lack the ironical dimension and the breadth of reference of the earlier ones, they do have a depth which, on occasions, transcends all earlier work.

18  Writing this work was, for Musil, an organic process. Even holidays are taken for the well-being of the novel; writing to a friend from the Tirol he says: 'The air has done my novel good' (*Briefe* I, 424); see also the letters to Franz Blei, 31 July 1939 (*Briefe* I, 449) and to Viktor Zuckerkandl, 1 February 1939 (*Briefe* I, 929–32).

19  On the question of the successive names of the hero of the novel, see Adolf Frisé, MoE, 2123.

20  See Wolfdietrich Rasch on this aspect of earlier versions of the novel, in 'Zur Entstehung von Robert Musils Roman [...]', pp. 37–8 and p. 51.

21  See 1926 talk by Musil, GWII, 941.

22 See Wolfdietrich Rasch, 'Zur Entstehung von Robert Musils Roman [...]', p. 41.

23 This view, if correct, would mean, however, that a later continuation of the novel by Musil would not have been consistent with sections of the novel as published in 1933 (see particularly the narrator's warning to the reader about the impending development of Ulrich and Agathe's relationship, MoE, 761).

24 In 'Zur Entstehung von Robert Musils Roman [...]', p. 63, Wolfdietrich Rasch suggests that it may have been Musil's intention to cut out a large part of later sections of the Clarisse material from the continuation of the work. If this assumption is correct it would represent a major sacrifice by Musil since the material in question is some of the most interesting in the MoE-*Nachlaß*.

25 In earlier drafts of the novel she masterminds a plan to free the imprisoned Moosbrugger and arranges a hiding place for him (see MoE, 1579–1597).

26 See Karl Corino, 'Musils Diotima: Modelle einer Figur', in *Literatur und Kritik*, No. 149/150, 1980, 588–98.

27 See MoE, 1579–1597.

28 Musil was not sure how to develop this theme. According to Ernst Kaiser, Musil wrote, in an undated note which was probably written about 1938–9: 'How is the question of the [will] to be resolved?' (in Ernst Kaiser, 'Die Entstehungsgeschichte [...]', p.22).

29 However, according to Wolfdietrich Rasch, the spying theme was probably dropped at some point in the mid-twenties (see 'Zur Entstehung von Robert Musils Roman [...]', pp. 59–60).

30 See, on this problem, for example, Ernst Kaiser, 'Zur Entstehungsgeschichte [...]', p. 27; Adolf Frisé, MoE, 2050; Elisabeth Castex, 'Zum neuesten Stand [...]', p. 55.

## 5 A critical approach to the structure

1 See Ernst Kaiser and Eithne Wilkins, 'Monstrum in animo [...]', pp. 84–5 and also the important page of plans for the 'Schlußteil', written on 6 January 1936, in MoE, pp. 1902–3.

2 Some draft material for the final sections of MoE can be found on the following pages: MoE, 1902–1907, MoE, 1930–1935, MoE, 1943.

3 Musil, in his diary in 1930, notes that he is revising Chapter 61, '[and] that is very time-consuming, but very important for the novel because now the [Ulrich]-problem will almost be ready up to the turning-point at the end' (Tb1, 700). See also below, pp. 156–9, 'A flaw in the design of *The Man without Qualities*?'.

4 One must preserve a sense of the limitations of one's own activity as a critic when quoting Ulrich's words to Diotima from Part II, Chapter 114: ' "[...] It is impossible to separate a thought in a book from the page which surrounds it [...]" ' (574).

5 See, for example: Günter Blöcker: '[the] narrative technique of seizing each concrete case, then exploding it in a shower of sparks of insight, typifies Musil's style of writing – a style characterised by a kind of abstract sensuousness' (in 'Robert Musil', in *Die neuen Wirklichkeiten: Linien und Profile der modernen Literatur*, third edition, Berlin, 1961, pp. 319–28); Walter Jens, who describes Musil as 'the first poet of the abstract' (in 'Der Mensch und die Dinge', in *Statt einer Literaturgeschichte*, fifth (revised) edition, Pfullingen, 1962, pp. 109–33); Maurice Blanchot: '[l'art musilien] conçoit précisément que, dans une œuvre littéraire, on puisse exprimer des pensées aussi difficiles et d'une forme aussi abstraite que dans un ouvrage philosophique, mais à condition qu'elles ne soient pas encore pensées. Ce "pas encore" est la littérature même, un "pas encore" qui, comme tel, est accomplissement et perfection' (in 'Recherches', in *La nouvelle revue française*, 6 (1968), 300–9 and 480–90, p. 488).

6 See MoE, 374.

7 Elsewhere the narrator demonstrates the same 'innervation' of ideas in Clarisse. In Part II, Chapter 97, for example, we read: '[Clarisse's] hand, when touched by Walter, immediately set in motion a current of intentions and assertions which flowed from head to toe, but which carried no words with it' (441).

8 Wolfdietrich Rasch argues: 'Doubling up of thought- and plot-motifs, repetition with modulation, variations, each of which throws light on the others, structure Musil's novel' (in 'Musil: "Der Mann ohne Eigenschaften" ', in *Der deutsche Roman: Vom Barock bis zur Gegenwart*, edited by Benno von Wiese, 2 vols, Düsseldorf, 1963, 2, pp. 361–419, p. 394). I prefer to use the term 'theme' rather than 'motif' since the former suggests something more substantially a part of the whole literary undertaking than the latter.

9 See MoE, 64 (in Part I, Chapter 17, 'Wirkung eines Mannes ohne Eigenschaften auf einen Mann mit Eigenschaften') ('Effect of a man without qualities on a man with qualities').

10 The narrator's sceptical attitude towards Diotima frequently makes itself felt. Part II, Chapter 22, is entitled 'The Parallelaktion, in the form of an influential lady of indescribable spiritual grace, is ready to devour Ulrich'. In the same chapter, Ulrich visualises Diotima as ' "a Hydra of beauty" ' (95).

11 See Part II, Chapter 26.

12 See MoE, 503–5.

13 In Part II, Chapter 86, the description of Arnheim's love for Diotima would not have been out of place in an account of the most intense of Ulrich's experiences of love: 'the events of reality were distant as sounds heard from a garden, [Arnheim] [. . .] imagined that soul ['Seele'] had overflowed its banks and was now, for the first time, truly present [. . .] [this was] just as physical an event as when, in the light of the morning, one sees the moon hanging, silent and pale in the sky' (386).

14 See, for example, Günter Graf, 'O. F. Bollnow: "Wahrhaftigkeit" und Robert Musil: "Ein Verkehrsunfall" ', in *wirkendes wort*, 17 (1967), 198–205; Rasch, 'Musil [...]', pp. 385–90; Helmut Arntzen, 'Robert Musil: "Der Mann ohne Eigenschaften" ' in *Der moderne deutsche Roman: Voraussetzungen, Strukturen, Gehalte* (Heidelberg, 1962), pp. 102–5; there are so many others that one begins to wonder how many readers get beyond the first chapter!

15 According to the *Oxford English Dictionary*, the word 'retina' is itself derived from the Latin 'rete', a net.

16 Friedrich Nietzsche, 'Jenseits von Gut und Böse', Zweites Hauptstück, paragraph 40 (in *Nietzsches Werke*, edited by Giorgio Colli and Mazzino Montinari, Berlin and New York, 1967 on, VI$_2$). See the comprehensive assessment of the influence of Nietzsche on Musil in F. G. Peters, 'Musil and Nietzsche – a Literary Study of a Philosophical Relationship' (unpublished Ph.D. dissertation, University of Cambridge, 1972).

17 Maurice Blanchot, 'Recherches', in *La nouvelle revue française*, 6 (1968), 300–9, p. 305.

18 It is very difficult to capture the quality of Musil's irony in any broad definition. Wolfdietrich Rasch, for example, who has made a notable contribution to Musil scholarship, is wrong, in my view, when he says that both the narrator and Ulrich experience their environment 'in the perspective of a total irony in which each detail is given with a degree of reservation' (in Rasch, 'Musil [...]', p. 382). This is not true of the way that both approach Moosbrugger, for example, where there is a complete absence of irony – though, of course, the people and institutions with which Moosbrugger comes into contact feel the full weight of such irony.

19 Ernst Mach, *Die Analyse der Empfindungen und das Verhältnis des Physischen zum Psychischen*, sixth edition (Jena, 1911), p. 15 (which was the oldest edition available to me).

20 Mach, *Die Analyse* [...], p. 2.

21 Richard von Mises, *Positivism* (Harvard University Press, Cambridge, Mass., 1951), p. 292 (original German version: *Kleines Lehrbuch des Positivismus*, The Hague, 1939). In the English version the term 'Gedankenexperiment' is retained.

22 See one of the 'classic texts' of Musil scholarship: Albrecht Schöne, 'Zum Gebrauch des Konjunktivs bie Robert Musil', in *Euphorion*, 55 (1961), 196–220.

23 One suspects that this, too, may relate to some intellectual experiment which Musil tried out himself, as a young man – see also below, p. 232, note 29.

24 See, below, Chapter 6, pp. 93–4, under the heading 'Systeme des Glücks' ('Systems of happiness').

25 See, for example, Musil's discussion of the frame of reference of the terms 'Moral' and 'Ethik' in his essay 'Das hilflose Europa', GWII, 1093.

26 See the exposition of the notion of 'Seele' in 'Der deutsche Mensch als Symptom', GWII, 1364–1400, p. 1384.

27 See above, Chapter 2, pp. 42–6, discussion of the essay 'Geist und Erfahrung'.

28 See above in this chapter, pp. 66–9, 'The theme of love', relating to MoE, 125.

### 6 An investigation of two major themes

1 Art, wrote Viktor Sklovskij, involves 'the technique of alienation' (see 'Kunst als Verfahren' ('Iskusstvo kak priëm'), in *Texte der russischen Formalisten*, edited by Jurij Striedter, 2 vols, I, Munich, 1966, pp. 2–35, p. 17). It opens his eyes to the familiar things around him and makes him see them anew. Musil here fulfils precisely this function: he makes the reader aware of the novel as a novel and aware, too, of the detailed operations of human consciousness. Eng. tr. in L. T. Lemon and M. J. Reis, ed. and tr., *Russian Formalist Criticism: Four Essays* (Lincoln, Nebraska, 1965).

2 Musil was fascinated by Honoré de Balzac, partly because Balzac presented in his novels a vision of 'Wirklichkeit' which was radically different from that of MoE. Erich Auerbach (in *Mimesis: the Representation of Reality in Western Literature*, Princeton, 1953) examines this aspect of Balzac's work. Balzac both gives expression to, and relies on, a nineteenth-century collective Parisian point of view – without the author appearing to be aware of this at all. Balzac's 'Gedankenexperimente', to use von Mises' term again, are carried out in ignorance of the hypotheses on which they rest, the network of shared attitudes to, and assumptions about, the contemporary world. 'Such a life's work', Musil continues in his diary, 'would not be driven by the same motive power today. In its place belongs the subjective-philosophical formula for living' (TbI, 342).

3 See Marshall McLuhan, *The Gutenberg Galaxy* (Toronto, 1962).

4 See below, sub-section entitled 'Systeme des Glücks'.

5 Here the reader follows the movements of Ulrich's consciousness. In other sections of the work the narrative is focussed on the consciousness of other characters. In this respect, as Erhard von Büren explains, MoE is different from Musil's earlier prose works: 'Whereas, up till this work, the narrator depicted "reality" mainly from the point of view of a single person, through the refraction of a single consciousness, [in MoE] he places himself alternately into the experiences of a broad range of different people. In so doing he changes his point of view either from one chapter to the next, or indeed within one and the same chapter' (*Zur Bedeutung der Psychologie im Werk Robert Musils*, Zurich, 1970, p. 80).

6 MoE, Part II, Chapter 83.

7 Musil provides various explanations of this term; see, for example, TbI, 401, *Briefe* I, 471 and MoE, 1844.

223

8 Here again the influence of Nietzsche can be detected; the argument of *Die Geburt der Tragödie* is constructed around the premise that mankind, through acts of creative imagination in which the artist plays an essential part, transforms this world of otherwise unbearable suffering into an aesthetic spectacle (see *Nietzsches Werke*, $III_1$).

9 This idea seems to be derived from Nietzsche – see, for example, 'Nachgelassene Fragmente', in *Nietzsches Werke*, VIII, 3, pp. 144–5.

10 See, for example, Joseph Strelka who refers quite simply to 'Ulrich-Musil' and 'Musil-Ulrich' ('Robert Musil', in *Kafka, Musil, Broch*, Vienna, Hannover, Berne, 1959, pp. 36–64, p. 50 and p. 53 respectively).

11 This is made explicit in the final chapter of MoE where Ulrich, talking of the 'thousand-year-long religious war' (1038), anticipates what he describes as the next 'mass disaster' (1038). The narrator comments: 'Ulrich was predicting fate and had no inkling that he was doing so' (1038).

   The narrator's retrospective viewpoint is evident, too, in subtler details. An intriguing example is found in MoE, Part II, Chapter 23. Arnheim's real life counterpart is Walther Rathenau; in 'Parallel-aktion'-circles, rumour has it that Arnheim intends to go into politics and, indeed, hopes to become a minister. Arnheim, like Rathenau, is a Jew and is disadvantaged in Wilhelmine society which discriminated against Jews. Tuzzi, Diotima's husband, is therefore sceptical that Arnheim's ambition can ever be fulfilled; 'In the opinion of Section-Head Tuzzi this was [...] quite out of the question unless it was preceded by a world-wide catastrophe' (96). Walther Rathenau did indeed become German Foreign Minister – after the Great War!

12 Hans Wolfgang Schaffnit emphasises Musil's isolation: 'It is essential, in any understanding of Musil's creative work [to realise] that Musil had no orientation towards a public for whom he was writing' (*Mimesis als Problem*, Berlin, 1971, p. 3).

13 See MoE, Part I, Chapter 4, 'Wenn es Wirklichkeitssinn gibt, muß es auch Möglichkeitssinn geben' ('If such a thing as a sense of reality exists, then a sense of possibility must exist also.')

14 This desire was, in fact, manifest in the scene in the Hofburg, where Ulrich, to his own intense embarrassment, blurted out a plea on Moosbrugger's behalf to Graf Stallburg.

15 Part II, Chapter 86, which deals with Arnheim, is followed, without transition, by Chapter 87 which deals with Moosbrugger.

16 See MoE, 101.

17 See MoE, 404.

18 See MoE, 268.

19 See MoE, 224.

20 See above, in this chapter, pp. 91–3, 'Seinesgleichen geschieht'.

21 See MoE, 374.

22 See MoE, 386.

23 See MoE, 492.
24 See MoE, 587.
25 See below, pp. 148–66, 'Ulrich as Man without Qualities'.
26 See MoE, 636.
27 See MoE, 616.
28 See MoE, 774.
29 See Part III, Chapter 23, 'Bonadea oder der Rückfall' ('Bonadea or the relapse').
30 See MoE, 1135.

## 7 Moosbrugger – a study in applied subjectivity

1 See *Briefe* I, 954.
2 Karl Jaspers, *Einführung in die Philosophie* (Munich, 1953), p. 12.
3 Karl Corino, ' "Zerstückt und durchdunkelt". Der Sexualmörder Moosbrugger im "Mann ohne Eigenschaften" und sein Modell', in *Musil-Forum*, 10 (1984), 105–19.
4 See, for example, long entries on Husserl in Heft 24, Tb1, 115–35.
5 Edmund Husserl, 'Phänomenologische Psychologie', in *Gesammelte Werke*, edited by Walter Biemel (The Hague, 1962), 10, p. 107. A further reference to this edition is given after the quotation in the text below.
6 See Husserl, 'Phänomenologische Psychologie', paragraph 37, pp. 187–92.
7 Frank Kermode, 'A Short View of Musil', in *Puzzles and Epiphanies*, second (revised) impression (London, 1963), pp. 91–107 (p. 100).
8 Musil explores the technique of imaginative newspaper reading elsewhere in the text – see MoE, 712.
9 See above, Chapter 6, sub-section 'Seinesgleichen geschieht', dealing with Musil's use of the theatre as an analogy for 'Wirklichkeit'.
10 S. S. Prawer points to 'Musil's ability to suggest physical analogies for states of mind that have never been properly described' ('Robert Musil and the "Uncanny" ', in *Oxford German Studies*, 3 (1968), 163–82, p. 176); Dorrit Cohn invents the curious but apt name of 'psycho-analogies' for the similes employed by Musil in *Acts of Union* ('Psycho-Analogies: a Means for Rendering Consciousness', in *Probleme des Erzählens*, edited by Fritz Martini, Stuttgart, 1971, pp. 291–302, p. 291).
11 'Rede zur Rilke-Feier', GWII, 1229–1242.
12 Quoted by F. C. Happold in *Mysticism* (Harmondsworth, 1963), p. 28.
13 Ulrich's father is a lawyer of this old school and is strongly influenced by Classical thought; he stubbornly resists the attempts of a colleague, Professor Schwung, to introduce into legal theory a somewhat more advanced and more scientifically up-to-date version of human motivation as revolutionary nonsense (nonsense, in other words, that has its origin in the French Revolution) – see MoE, Part II, Chapter 74,

entitled 'Das 4. Jahrhundert v. Chr. gegen das Jahr 1797 [...]' (MoE, 316) ('The 4th Century B.C. versus the year 1797').

14 Moosbrugger has murdered more than one girl (see MoE, 69).

15 Marie-Louise Roth writes of 'The anchoring [of Musil's thought] in Gestalt psychology' (in *Robert Musil: Ethik und Ästhetik*, Munich, 1972, p. 52); Wolfgang Köhler, a leading exponent of this school of psychology, shows that the visual data that the eye receives are transformed by the brain into meaningful images (see *Gestalt Psychology*, London, 1930, pp. 56–64). Something in Moosbrugger seems to have inhibited this transformation of data into recognised things.

16 As he attempts to come to terms with Clarisse's inner life – which is no less original and no less unpredictable than Moosbrugger's – the narrator wonders about the suitability of words to convey what she feels: 'why look for words for something which does not lie on the thoroughfare of words' (443).

17 See, for example, Max Wertheimer – another leading member of the 'Gestalt'-school – on 'associationism' (*Productive Thinking*, London, 1961, pp. 8–11). We shall see below how, on the night when he commits murder, Moosbrugger gets caught up in such thinking-in-associations, which proves in his case to be a dangerous substitute for self-critical reasoning.

18 Erhard von Büren has traced some of the ideas which are central to the portrayal of Moosbrugger to Eugen Bleuler, *Lehrbuch der Psychiatrie* (Berlin, 1916) (see von Büren, *Zur Bedeutung der Psychologie* [...], pp. 120–3); Musil takes the squirrel-example direct from Bleuler's text (see Bleuler, *Lehrbuch* [...], p. 334).

19 See, for example, Sartre: 'Faute de savoir [se servir des mots] comme signe d'un aspect du monde, [le poète] voit dans le mot, l'image d'un de ces aspects. Et l'image verbale qu'il choisit pour sa ressemblance avec le saule ou le frêne n'est pas nécessairement le mot que nous utilisons pour désigner ces objets' (*Qu'est-ce que la littérature?*, pp. 19–20).

20 See MoE, 70–1.

21 Musil's account of Moosbrugger's difficulties with language are clearly derived from Bleuler's description of the way the epileptic becomes tongue-tied before a fit (see Bleuler, *Lehrbuch* [...], p. 336).

22 Moosbrugger, we are told, 'did not deny his deeds, he wanted them to be understood as casualties of a great conception of life' (72). Is this Musil's hint at the potential, and the dangers, of what one might call the Expressionist vision of man?

23 Booth, *The Rhetoric of Fiction* (Chicago, 1961), pp. 388–9.

24 See, for example, Hellmuth Mielke's strong condemnation on moral grounds of *Young Törless* (in *Der deutsche Roman*, fourth (revised) edition, Dresden, 1912, p. 330).

25 Kurt Michel, 'Die Utopie der Sprache', in *Akzente*, 1 (1954), 23–35, p. 24.

26 Ernst Kretschmer, *Medizinische Psychologie* (Stuttgart, 1963), (first edition, Leipzig, 1922).

27 See Karl Popper, 'Indeterminism is Not Enough', in *Encounter*, 40 (1973), 20–6, p. 21.

28 Musil describes the predicament of someone like Moosbrugger in the following way: 'The criminal who has been caught in the moral force-field of his deed can only move like a swimmer pulled along by a fast-flowing river' (251–2). Nietzsche expressed a similar idea: 'The criminal who knows the full flow of circumstances does not find his deed so far removed from all order and comprehension as do his judges and critics' (in 'Der Wanderer und sein Schatten', in 'Menschliches, Allzumenschliches', in *Nietzsches Werke*, IV₃, paragraph 24, p. 197).

29 In MoE, Part II, Chapter 32, Musil argues that a great deal could be done to prevent crimes such as the one which Moosbrugger is about to commit 'if society itself could only summon up half of the moral energy which it demands of such victims' (121).

30 Wilhelm Braun argues: 'Moosbrugger cannot escape [the prostitute] for she represents his suppressed sexual desires' (in 'Moosbrugger Dances', in *Germanic Review*, 35 (1960), 214–20). Although I must acknowledge my debt to Professor Braun for his fine work on Musil, I can find nothing in the account of Moosbrugger which convinces me that this is the only possible explanation for Moosbrugger's confusions.

31 John Wilson, 'Freedom and Compulsion', in *Mind*, 67 (1958), 60–9, p. 61. There are further references below in the text to this article.

32 Ulrich considers it inevitable that 'the state will kill Moosbrugger in the end because, given that theory is at such an unfinished stage, it is simply the most obvious, the cheapest and safest thing to do' (245).

33 See note 13 above.

34 In an essay 'Das Unanständige und Kranke in der Kunst', Musil argued: 'Art seeks knowledge; it represents the obscene and sick by means of its relationship with what is decent and healthy, which means simply: it extends its knowledge of the decent and healthy' (GWII, 980).

35 In response to Bonadea's urging him to use his influence at the 'Parallelaktion' to help Moosbrugger, Ulrich indicates his own indecision on the question of Moosbrugger's innocence or guilt: ' "Will you go in now?" Bonadea asked.
"And prevent the injustice which is to be inflicted on Moosbrugger? No, I don't even know if injustice is really being done to him! [...]" ' (580).

36 Georg Lukács, 'Die Gegenwartsbedeutung des kritischen Realismus', in *Essays über Realismus*, in *Gesammelte Werke* (Neuwied and Berlin, 1971), 4, pp. 457–603.

37 Lukács argues that the interdependence in bourgeois society of the eccentric and the average is demonstrated by the phenomenon of Moosbrugger: 'How deep this movement goes, how intimately it is linked with the *Weltanschauung* that is fundamental to creativity is shown by an interesting statement in Musil's great novel. It goes: "Wenn die Menschheit als Ganzes träumen könnte, müßte Moos-

brugger entstehen." ("If humanity were to dream as an entity, Moos-brugger would emerge"). This Moosbrugger is a semi-idiotic sex-murderer' ('Die Gegenwartsbedeutung [...]', p. 483). I do not think that Musil's portrait of Moosbrugger allows one to conclude that he is even half-way to being an idiot – ideological blindness on Lukács's part seems to have made him see Moosbrugger, in general, and this quotation from MoE in particular, in too narrow a perspective.

38 Ulrich, is also (as I argued above, Chapter 5, sub-section entitled 'The observer in *The Man without Qualities*') a 'man in a mask'.

39 See Kaiser and Wilkins, 'Monstrum in Animo', in *Deutsche Vierteljahres-schrift für Literaturwissenschaft und Geistesgeschichte*, 37 (1963), 78–119.

40 See note 35 above.

41 The way the narrator intervenes to explain what Bonadea feels in his terms rather than hers is clearly expressed: 'they are stage-eyes, a stage-moustache, the buttons which are opened before one's eyes are costume-buttons [...] Bonadea did not quite use the same words, and *indeed only part of her thinking about them was carried out in words at all*' (259) (my emphasis).

42 This is similar to Bonadea's reaction to Ulrich's admittedly ambigu-ous remark (referring to the impending arrival of his sister) which he evidently hopes will be taken as a broad hint that he wants to curtail the relationship with his mistress: ' "I have resolved that, for a long period, I shall love no woman in any other way than as if she were my sister" ' (891). Bonadea replies sharply: ' "But you are per-verse!" ' (892).

43 S. Körner argues along similar lines in his book on Kant: 'We usually regard a person as responsible for his action if he could have chosen not to perform it' (in *Kant*, Harmondsworth, 1955, p. 156).

44 But in fact she knows that this is an illusion spawned by her desire: 'As if in an illuminating flash of lightning, Bonadea understood that this was an involuntary continuation of the lost shoe' (266).

45 See MoE, 645.

46 What happens to Bonadea here seems not entirely involuntary. See also MoE, Part II, Chapter 115: '[Bonadea] remembered that, when talking about this murderer, Ulrich had said that we possess a second psyche ['Seele'] which is always innocent, and a person who is respon-sible in law could always choose another course of action, the person who is not responsible, could never do so' (577). She sees that this notion can be modified to excuse her extra-marital adventures; the narrator tells us: 'She derived from this something like the following conclusion: that she wanted to be not responsible in law and would then be innocent' (577).

47 See MoE, Part II, Chapter 122, where Ulrich reflects that men use Moosbrugger 'to reinstate their morality' (653), in other words, they see that he is tried and condemned but they do so 'after sating themselves

on him' (653) – after they have vicariously satisfied their appetite for violence by reenacting his crime in imagination.

## 8 Ulrich as the 'Man without Qualities'

1 See MoE, Part I, Chapter 2.
2 See Annie Reniers-Servrankx on Musil's discussion of the use of a telescope, in *Robert Musil – Konstanz und Entwicklung [. . .]*, pp. 41–6.
3 In an article in 1913 Musil wrote: 'Österreich könnte ein Weltexperiment sein' ('Austria could be a world-experiment') (in 'Politik in Österreich', GWII, 992–4, p. 993).
4 The narrator makes use of the relationship between Diotima and Ulrich to draw attention to the hiatus between mind and body. When Diotima first meets Arnheim in private, his presence overwhelms her and the narrator informs us that 'the wonderful dream of a love *in which body and soul ['Seele'] are completely one*, shone through Diotima' (my emphasis) (183). Ulrich takes up this theme but sets it on its head; he seems both to have an intuitive grasp of Diotima's feelings and to wish to pour cold water on her plans when he says: ' "It is [. . .] my conviction [. . .] that thinking is one thing and real life another" ' (274). The next chapter but one (Part I, Chapter 68), which is interpolated between Chapter 67, 'Diotima and Ulrich' and Chapter 69, 'Diotima and Ulrich. Continuation', is entitled 'A digression. Do people have to coincide with their bodies?' In this chapter the tension between the two is presented as a mixture of physical attraction and spiritual incompatibility: 'He had held her gentle hand in his [. . .] and they had looked into each other's eyes; they had both certainly felt antipathy, but thought that they might yet merge so utterly one into the other that they melted away. [. . .] *In this way, two heads direct a dreadful coldness towards each other while, beneath, the bodies flow unresisting and glowing, one into the other*' (284) (my emphasis). In their last meeting in the novel as published, they seem to achieve for a fleeting moment a kind of union. Here again Ulrich grasps Diotima's hand and kisses it: 'And, although this hand-kiss was only a gallant jest, it shared with an act of infidelity that bitter vestige of pleasure at having leant so close to another person that one drank from them like a beast and one's own image was no longer reflected from the water' (815). Ulrich-Narcissus, watching his reflection in the pool of another person's eyes, stoops low and, even as he disturbs the reflection, comes into another kind of contact with her; there is here a suggestion, however slight, of a harmony that embraces mind and body.
5 F. G. Peters, 'Musil and Nietzsche [. . .]', p. 75.
6 Husserl was preoccupied with similar problems. Mathematics, in Husserl's view the supreme science, has put at men's disposal what he called: 'a marvellous technique for making inductions of such power,

probability, exactness and calculability that they could never even have been dreamt of before' ('Die Krisis des europäischen Menschentums und die Philosophie', in *Gesammelte Werke*, 6, pp. 314–48, p. 343). But this technique does not bring the benefits that it might bring. For, according to Husserl, the scientist tends to become so engrossed in the apparently objective realm of his scientific pursuit that he loses sight of the social context into which his reasearch must fit and, indeed, often neglects the significance of his own existence as 'the working subject' (p. 343). Science floats free of its human base. Considered in its own terms, science is a model of rationality; but since scientific development runs on apace without regard to the needs of man, at root it is irrational. A profound human crisis ensues.

7 See MoE, 64.

8 In MoE, Part II, Chapter 40, the theme of 'Geist' and its elusiveness is explored at length; see, particularly, MoE, 152–5.

9 David Hume, *A Treatise of Human Nature*, edited by T. H. Green and T. H. Grose, 2 vols (London, 1886), I, Part IV, Section VI, 'Of personal Identity', p. 534.

10 Descartes' *Discours de la méthode pour bien conduire sa raison* [...] (in *Œuvres et Lettres*, edited by Alain Bridoux, Paris, 1953) also throws light on the moral dimension of Ulrich's misguided attitude. Descartes makes it clear that moral issues lead beyond the reach of mere thought. Indeed this seems so self-evident to Descartes that he compresses the notion into a single phrase 'Les problèmes de la vie ne souffrant souvent aucun délai' (p. 142). This philosopher, the arch-advocate of the rational approach, insists that there are many times when it is simply impossible to think out what one is to do next; moral matters, Descartes argues, are pressing obligations, they take a man out of his intellectual depth, and he must then simply swim, or sink.

11 See Peter Nusser's account of such narrative elisions in *Musils Romantheorie* (The Hague and Paris, 1967), pp. 61–74.

12 See my argument in 'On Reading Robert Musil's "Der Mann ohne Eigenschaften" ', in *Sprachkunst*, 9 (1978), 88–100, pp. 95–7.

13 See Husserl, 'The Thesis of the Natural Standpoint and Its Suspension', in *Phenomenology – The Philosophy of Edmund Husserl and Its Interpretation*, edited by Joseph Kockelmans (New York, 1967), pp. 68–79, p. 78.

14 One is strongly reminded of the argument in Kleist's essay, 'Über das Marionettentheater', in *Sämtliche Werke und Briefe*, edited by Helmut Sembdner, 2 vols (first edition, München, 1951, edition consulted sixth, revised, 1977), I, 338–45.

15 See, for example, in MoE, Part II, Chapter 40: 'Ulrich [...] thought [...] of the strange experience of "Geist" as of a lover by whom one is betrayed throughout the whole of one's life without loving her any the less' (155–6).

16 Sibylle Bauer presents Ulrich's notion that the world is no more than

'an image, an analogy, a figure of speech' (357) as the fundamental assumption beneath his moral philosophy (see Bauer, 'Ethik und Bewußtheit', in: Sibylle Bauer and Ingrid Drevermann, *Studien zu Robert Musil*, Cologne, 1966, pp. 47–51). She disregards or overlooks the way in which the hero, in the course of the work, comes to reject this notion.

17 He continues this theme in a later conversation with her in MoE, Part II, Chapter 114. He says: ' "[...] Let us try to love each other, as if you and I were the figures, created by a writer, who meet on the pages of a book. So let us, at any rate, leave aside the whole fatty structure which rounds out reality." ' (573).

18 In fact, in MoE, Part II, Chapter 74, we find a letter from Ulrich's father urging the hero to use his influence at the 'Parallelaktion' to support a particular legal argument. The father, of course, wants his son to protect the redundant traditional line of legal thinking on the question of moral responsibility – and it is precisely this attitude which Ulrich feels ought to be changed. But the father's letter serves to remind the reader of Ulrich's potential for effective social action, and, by extension, is an indictment of his inactivity.

19 See MoE, Part II, Chapter 97, where Clarisse reflects: 'in Ulrich [...] [there was] something [...] devilish that was bound up with the easy-going gait of the world. He had to be freed. She had to go and get him' (444).

20 In earlier versions of the novel the hero's preoccupation with, and willingness to experiment with, the notion of irresponsibility seems to have been much stronger still, amounting to obsession, as Kaiser and Wilkins demonstrate in 'Monstrum in Animo', in *Deutsche Vierteljahresschrift für Literaturwissenschaft und Geistesgeschichte*, 37 (1963), 78–119.

21 Ulrich is not allowed to forget Moosbrugger. In Part II, Chapter 115, Bonadea also tries to persuade Ulrich to intercede for the murderer.

22 The narrator does not conceal his delight at Ulrich's embarrassment over mentioning this psychopath in such august company. The painful pause which follows upon Ulrich's words is amplified in the following image: 'A few words like this, scattered in the right place, can be beneficial as a sprinkling of garden manure, but in this place they had the effect of the little pile of dirt that one has inadvertently trodden in and brought into the room on one's shoes' (85–6).

23 See MoE, 176.

24 Joseph von Allesch was a colleague of Wolfgang Köhler, one of the founding fathers of Gestalt-psychology – thus, through his friend, Musil had direct access to this movement.

25 Johannes von Allesch, 'Robert Musil in der geistigen Bewegung seiner Zeit', in *Robert Musil: Leben, Werk, Wirkung*, edited by Karl Dinklage (Zurich, Leipzig, Vienna, 1960), pp. 133–44, p. 133.

26 Ulrich does not always appear to have confidence in his undertaking –

on at least one occasion he speaks of the 'Urlaub vom Leben' with some irony (see MoE, 256).

27 F. G. Peters points to the change in Musil's attitude to science between the time when he wrote *Tonka* in the early years of this century and the time when he wrote MoE in which the scientific attitude fails as the basis of an existential experiment (see *Robert Musil – Master of the Hovering Life*, New York, 1978, p. 146).

28 See the discussion of these 'utopias' in Ulf Schramm, *Fiktion und Reflexion: Überlegungen zu Musil und Beckett* (Frankfurt, 1967), pp. 93–105, and in Elisabeth Albertsen, *Ratio und Mystik im Werk Robert Musils* (Munich, 1968), pp. 67–70.

29 An entry in his diary in 1905 seems to indicate that Musil was trying out in his own life something like the 'Utopie der Exaktheit': 'All thoughts on the "science of the human being" should be entered here' (TbI, 86).

30 David Pears, *Wittgenstein* (London, 1971), p. 21.

31 Musil appears to have departed from strict 'scientific' practice in his 'Gedankenexperiment' at the point where we read that Ulrich, relinquishing the analogy between life and a scientific hypothesis in favour of the notion of life as a kind of essay, did so 'later, when his intellect grew sharper' (250). Here he comes down unequivocally in favour of one existential option; elsewhere, with the exception I discuss earlier in this chapter (see above, pp. 156–9), the narrator does not show his hand in such an overt manner.

32 Although Musil seems not to have had much to do with existentialism this version of morality reminds one strongly of existentialist thinking.

33 See MoE, 801.

34 Renate von Heydebrand is one of the critics who do see this development: 'The decisive difference between Ulrich and the other figures [...] is that, with respect to fundamental design, they are static [...]. While he is dynamic [...]. Ulrich [...] is not fixed, he responds to the changing situations and grows with his experiences' (in *Die Reflexionen Ulrichs in Robert Musils Roman 'Der Mann ohne Eigenschaften'*, Münster, 1966, p. 2).

35 Hamburger, *From Prophecy to Exorcism* (London, 1965), p. 98.

36 J. P. Stern examines the way in which Dostoevsky has the hero of his novel, *The Idiot*, attempt an 'imitatio Christi' in a modern context – see the section entitled 'The testing of the prince', in *On Realism* (London, 1973), pp. 5–19.

37 See MoE, Part III, Chapter 12.

38 Peter Nusser, *Musils Romantheorie*, p. 66.

39 Walter Sokel captures precisely the attitude of the mature Ulrich when he states: 'The human being determines himself by realising possibilities in what he or she does'; he points out the role which Agathe, Ulrich's sister, plays in this context: 'Agathe is not only the embodiment of Ulrich's ideal of the person of possibility and the being without characteristics but also of the urge within himself towards active

realisation of possibilities' (in 'Agathe und der existenzphilosophische Faktor im "Mann ohne Eigenschaften" ', in *Beiträge zur Musil-Kritik*, edited by Gudrun Brokoph-Mauch, pp. 111–28, p. 116a).

40 Most critics overlook this and tend to stress the reflective side of Ulrich's make-up. M.-L. Roth, for example, states: '[Ulrich] sets in opposition to the world of reality a world of possibility [. . .] He sees the world as a laboratory, as a "große Versuchsstätte an, wo die besten Arten, Mensch zu sein, durchgeprobt und neue entdeckt werden müßten" ("great experimental station where the best ways of living ought to be tested and new ones discovered") (MoE, 152)' (in 'Robert Musil im Spiegel seines Werkes. Versuch einer inneren Biographie', in *Robert Musil: Leben, Werk, Wirkung*, edited by Karl Dinklage, Zurich, Leipzig, Vienna, 1960, pp. 13–48, p. 34). This, I believe, is a description of the Ulrich who carries out the 'Urlaub vom Leben' experiment, not the mature Ulrich of later stages of the novel. Rolf Schneider states categorically that Ulrich remains an incorrigible intellectual: 'Ulrich never changes. He is an intellectual principle dressed up with a few biographical features. He doesn't bring anything about [. . .] because he doesn't want to and, according to the fiat of the author, is not supposed to' (in *Die problematisierte Wirklichkeit – Leben und Werk Robert Musils*, Berlin, 1975, p. 96).

41 Hans Mayer (in 'Erinnerungen an Robert Musil', in *Neues Forum*, 14 (1967), 169–75) records that Musil once told him of a meeting which he, Musil, had had with Walther Rathenau (around whom, as we saw above, Musil built the character, Arnheim). Just as Arnheim does in the scene with Ulrich, so then Rathenau had put an arm around Musil's shoulder. This gesture made Musil feel intensely angry, since he evidently felt that it was patronising.

42 See Nietzsche's aphorism: 'We are still drawing conclusions from judgments which we consider wrong, from teachings in which we no longer believe – through our feelings' (in 'Morgenröte', in *Nietzsches Werke*, v₁, paragraph 99, p. 87).

43 This leave-taking from abstract thought may be a parallel to Musil's own decision, explained in a letter to Professor Alexius Meinong in 1909, to turn down the offer of a post in philosophy in order to devote himself to creative writing. See *Briefe* 1, 63–4.

44 See MoE, 661.

45 See Ulf Eisele's discussion of Ulrich as a frustrated literary man in *Die Struktur des modernen deutschen Romans* (Tübingen, 1984), pp. 114–17.

46 See MoE, 662.

47 See my article ' "Der Mann ohne Eigenschaften" – The Wrong Title?', in *Musil-Forum*, 5 (1979), 184–98.

## 9 *The Man without Qualities* from the narrator's perspective

1 In Part II, Chapter 116, the 'Gewalt'–'Liebe' principle is discussed in detail; it is represented, in symbolical metamorphosis, in the 'two trees of life' which are part of the narrator's commentary on Ulrich's thinking, and in Ulrich's proposal for a 'Generalsekretariat der Genauigkeit und Seele' ('General Secretariat of Precision and Soul').

2 Hume distinguishes between 'impressions' and 'ideas': 'those perceptions, which enter with most force and violence, we may name impressions; and under this name I comprehend all our sensations, passions and emotions, as they make their first appearance in the soul. By ideas I mean the faint images of these in thinking and reasoning' (David Hume, *A Treatise* [...], 1, Part I, Section 1, p. 311). In the same section he introduces a fundamental proposition: 'That all our simple ideas in their first appearance are deriv'd from simple impressions, which are correspondent to them, and which they exactly represent' (p. 314).

3 See, particularly, MoE, Part II, Chapter 72.

4 Both Kretschmer (in *Medizinische Psychologie*, passim) and William James (in *The Varieties of Religious Experience*, New York, 1902, Lectures VI and VII) point to the way in which the mentally sick provide insights into the working of the healthy brain.

5 That Musil associates sex with violence is confirmed by a powerful image: 'the gentler feelings of male abandon are rather like the growling of a jaguar over a piece of meat, and any interruption is taken very badly' (40).

6 Something of the narrator's vision of love in its natural state is intimated in a few words in MoE, Part II, Chapter 68: 'The pure pleasure that two people take in each other, this simple and most profound of the feelings of love which is the natural wellspring of all others' (284). Love in this pristine form is contrasted with bourgeois sexuality.

7 The narrator makes much of Arnheim's fastidiousness. He asks us, for example, to imagine Arnheim throwing himself at Diotima's feet 'without regard to his trousers and his future' (510). The implication is that it is not only a fear of total commitment to the relationship but also the fear of creasing his clothes that stops Arnheim short.

8 See Stefan Howald, *Ästhetizismus und ästhetische Ideologiekritik* (Munich, 1984), p. 258.

9 See, for example, Stefan Zweig, 'Eros Matutinus', in *Die Welt von Gestern* (Stockholm, 1941), pp. 74–99.

10 See MoE, 105.

11 See MoE, 110–11.

12 See MoE, 201.

13 See, for example, MoE, 774.

14 See MoE, 334.

15 See also above, discussion of Musil's use of 'Seele', pp. 82–3, subsection entitled 'Language and the structure of MoE'.

16 In 'Jenseits von Gut und Böse', in *Nietzsches Werke*, VI₂, Hauptstück V, paragraph 188, p. 110.

17 See MoE, 187.

18 See section referred to in Note 15 above.

19 His presentation of Arnheim recalls his merciless exposure of Ulrich's father who flatters those who are likely to bring him advantage, but who is able to persuade himself that his conduct is irreproachably moral. See MoE, Part II, Chapter 3.

20 John Jones describes our present notion of personal identity as follows: 'we see action issuing from a solitary focus of consciousness – secret inward interesting – and in which the status of action must always be adjectival: action qualifies: it tells us what we want to know about the individual prompting it' (John Jones, *On Aristotle and Greek Tragedy*, London, 1962, p. 33). This oversimplified notion of identity is, of course, challenged in MoE. But, the narrator argues, despite the universal flux Arnheim is still able to make his actions 'adjectival' (to borrow John Jones' term) by forcing them to 'qualify' – to expound and demonstrate – principles which the narrator exposes as ignoble.

21 There is further evidence of Arnheim's pessimistic outlook in MoE, Part III, Chapter 38. Groups have formed at a meeting of the 'Parallelaktion' and, the narrator observes with delicate irony, 'around the War Minister, people were speaking of peace and love, around Arnheim, talk centred, for the moment, on the view that German benevolence flourished best in the shadow of German strength' (1022–3). The discussion going on around him bears the imprint of Arnheim's influence.

22 See, for example, the confrontation in MoE, Part II, Chapter 118, where Clarisse, as she resists Walter's amorous advance, flings out the accusation ' "Instead of achieving something yourself, you would like to reproduce yourself in a child!" ' (609).

23 See MoE, 444–445.

24 See MoE, 909.

25 A similar juxtaposing of 'fire' and 'wall' images is used to convey the sensation of falling in love in MoE, Part II, Chapter 46. Here Arnheim and Diotima experience 'something like the noiseless blazing of the world around the four walls' (188).

26 Here, again, we find 'Seele' expressing two different ideas: first it represents the individual unspoilt, then the individual corrupted.

27 Karl Bapp notes that Nietzsche acknowledged he was deeply indebted to Heraclitus (in *Aus Goethes griechischer Gedankenwelt*, Leipzig, 1921, p. 1).

28 Heraclitus formulated this as follows: 'We step, yet do not step, into the same rivers, we are, and are not' (quoted in Hermann Diels, *Fragmente*

*der Vorsokratiker*, seventh edition, edited by Walther Kranz, Berlin, 1951, paragraph 49a).

29 This notion is most clearly expressed in a fragment which comes complete with its own (Ancient) commentary: 'The universe is governed by lightning [. . .] By "lightning" [Heraclitus] understands the eternal fire. He also says that this fire is endowed with reason and is the cause of the overall governance of the world' (Diels, *Fragmente [. . .]*, paragraph 64).

30 Fire, argued Heinrich Gomperz, one of the leading exponents of Heraclitus's teaching earlier this century, is identical with soul (see Heinrich Gomperz, *Philosophical Studies*, edited by D. S. Robinson, Boston, 1953, p. 102).

31 Diels, *Fragmente* [. . .], paragraph 30.

32 Diels, *Fragmente* [. . .], paragraph 102; see also paragraph 58: 'And Good and Evil is one.'

33 Karl Popper, *The Open Society and its Enemies*, fourth (revised) edition, 2 vols (London, 1962), I, Chapter 2, pp. 11–17.

34 J. P. Stern describes this quality as Musil 'peeling the onion'. In MoE, he argues, 'every man depends on his job, every social position on choice or graft, every ethical system on its social setting, every event on its interpretation. Every word is a metaphor and thus points to some other thing which it is not, every philosophy is a joke but every joke is a serious matter' ('Viennese Kaleidoscope', in *The Listener*, 1 November 1962, 722–3, p. 723).

## 10 Ulrich and Agathe

1 See Tb1, 167, where Musil comments on Ellen Key's views on the distinctions between man and woman.

2 See MoE, 645.

3 Martin Buber's anthology of mystical writings, *Ekstatische Konfessionen* (Jena, 1909) had a profound influence on MoE – see Dietmar Goltschnigg, *Mystische Tradition im Roman Robert Musils – Martin Bubers 'Ekstatische Konfessionen' im 'Mann ohne Eigenschaften'* (Heidelberg, 1974).

4 Opinions on this matter have differed strongly, indeed acrimoniously at times. What is clear is that Musil himself was uncertain whether or not the relationship of Ulrich and Agathe should stop short of incest or not.

5 See Tb1, 953.

6 In a typical remark in a letter, Musil describes Martha as 'mein musikalischeres zweites Ich' (*Briefe* I, 716) ('my more musical second "I"').

7 Walter Sokel demonstrates how Agathe tends to project Ulrich's ideas into deeds: 'Agathe represents not only the embodiment of Ulrich's moral views but the tendency to realise them, to translate them into

action. As such she represents the actual "existentialist" motive force in the novel' (in 'Agathe und der existenzphilosophische Faktor im "Mann ohne Eigenschaften"', in *Beiträge zur Musil-Kritik*, edited by Gudrun Brokoph-Mauch, pp. 111–28, p. 116).

8 See MoE, 707.

9 Hagauer's attitude to his pupils, for example, is governed by an unfeeling rationality. See, for example, his correcting of a pupil's Shakespeare translation, MoE, 704.

10 See Raymond Furness, 'The Androgynous Ideal: its significance in German Literature', in *Modern Language Review*, 60 (1965), 58–64.

11 See MoE, 908.

12 See MoE, 933.

13 See, for example, the conclusion drawn first by Bonadea (MoE, 891–2) and later by Stumm (MoE, 930–1) about their relationship.

14 In *Myths of Love* (London, 1963); subsequent references in the text are to this edition.

15 See '(Anders–Agathe) Reise' ('(Anders–Agathe) Journey') MoE, 1651–75. Anders is, of course, an earlier name for the hero of the novel.

16 In his account of this section of MoE, de Rougement stresses the aesthetic – Musil's sense of the proportions of a tale of passion – at the expense of the moral, namely Musil's wider and, indeed, overriding concerns in writing MoE to find a new ethical context for modern mankind.

17 There are several others: a statement, from Chapter 24 'Agathe is really there': 'There is no such thing as an inner prohibition about looking upon a blood relative with male love; this is only custom, or otherwise it is supported, in a roundabout way, by morals and hygiene' (897); Agathe's sardonic amusement at Lindner's offer of assistance in her anguish: 'Agathe laughed at the very idea that this man felt he had lived through her affliction which, had he known about it, would have filled him with revulsion' (968); Agathe's sensual arousal at the sight of Ulrich in his nightshirt (see MoE, 942).

18 Clarisse takes over as the instigator of Moosbrugger's escape – see MoE, 1584 – from one of Ulrich's 'forerunners', the hero of an earlier version of the novel.

19 MoE, 436–7.

20 See MoE, 786.

21 See also above Chapter 9, pp. 175–6, 'Wilfulness'.

22 See MoE, 832.

23 See MoE, 660–1.

24 See MoE, 1768.

25 See MoE, 1615–21.

26 Meingast is, in some ways, Ulrich's antithesis: he scorns all concern with matters of truth and falsehood, with understanding and explaining things, and believes that men should be uninhibited in their action – see MoE,

918. His views are echoed by Clarisse: ' "If everything is to be explained, human beings will never change anything in the world" ' (1009).

27 See MoE, 1253–71.

28 See Helmut Arntzen on this aspect of this chapter, in *Musil-Kommentar zum Roman 'Der Mann ohne Eigenschaften'* (Munich, 1982), pp. 127–8.

29 I am reminded of Jaspers' 'Das Umgreifende' ('The encompassing') (see *Einführung in die Philosophie*, pp. 28–37), which seems to be a philosophical equivalent to the notion which Musil expresses with his image of the flowers floating on unknown depths – see below in the text of this section; Jean Molinos is also struck by the affinity of Jaspers' and Musil's thought (in 'Doubles – sur la logique de Musil', in *l'Arc*: '*Robert Musil*', No. 74 (1978), pp. 63–74, p. 68.

30 See the opening chapter of the novel, MoE, 9.

31 James, *The Varieties of Religious Experience*, Lecture III, p. 56.

32 In Part III, Chapter 3, Ulrich is in his father's study working on his mathematical research project. The impression of the father's personality is preserved in the room which he has arranged and in which he has spent so many hours: 'Ulrich sat in the middle at the writing desk, [...] [on] the walls hung portraits of his ancestors [...]; the man who had lived here, had used the shell of their lives to make the egg of his own: now he was dead and his household effects stood there in such sharp relief that it was as if a file had been used to rasp him from the room' (687). Ulrich has consciously broken with his father's ways; but here, in this room, a tradition that he cannot ignore makes itself felt.

33 See, for example, Blaise Pascal who, on the night of 23 November 1654, felt the presence of God in the most immediate and powerful way; the image of fire is central to his record of his experience; see *Pensées*, in *Œuvres Complètes* (Paris, 1954), pp. 1079—1358, Pensée 457, p. 1217.

34 Musil seems to have planned, from the earliest years of the conception of the novel, that Ulrich and Agathe's relationship would fail. In a talk on the novel in 1926 he said: 'Brother and twin sister: the "I" and the "non-I" feel the inner discord of their shared life, they dissolve with the world, they flee. But this attempt to hold on to, to fix, the experience, is a failure. Absoluteness cannot be preserved. I assume from this that the world cannot continue to exist without evil, it brings movement into the world. Good, on its own, brings rigidity' (GWII, 940). A similar conviction is still evident much later: see, for example, Musil's note, written probably during the Thirties: 'U[lrich] Ag[athe] is really an attempt at anarchy in love. Which, even there, ends negatively.' (1876).

# SELECTED BIBLIOGRAPHY

### Works by Musil

*Gesammelte Werke*, edited by Adolf Frisé, 2 vols (Reinbek bei Hamburg, 1978) (revised edition, 1981) (This edition is also available in paperback, in nine volumes, with identical pagination.)

*Tagebücher*, edited by Adolf Frisé, 2 vols (Reinbek bei Hamburg, 1976)

*Briefe*, edited by Adolf Frisé, 2 vols (Reinbek bei Hamburg, 1981)

*Beitrag zur Beurteilung der Lehren von Ernst Mach* (doctoral dissertation), Friedrich-Wilhelm-Universität, Berlin, 1908 (also available in book form, Reinbek bei Hamburg, 1980)


### Translations of Musil's work into English by Ernst Kaiser and Eithne Wilkins:

*Young Törless* (London, 1971)

'The Perfecting of a Love', in *Botteghe Oscure*, XVIII (Rome, 1956)

'The Temptation of Quiet Veronika', in *Botteghe Oscure*, XXV (Rome, 1960)

*Tonka and Other Stories* (London, 1965)

*Five Women* (New York, 1966)

*The Man without Qualities* (London, 1953, 1954, 1960)


### Other translations into English:

*On Mach's Theories*, translation of Musil's doctoral dissertation by G. H. von Wright (Munich/Vienna, 1982)

*The Enthusiasts*, translation of *Die Schwärmer* by Andrea Simon, introduced by Martin Esslin (New York, 1982)

'The German Personality as a Symptom', translation of 'Der deutsche Mensch als Symptom' by Ian David Hays, in *Austrian Philosophy: Studies and Texts*, ed. J. C. Nyiri (Munich, 1981), pp. 173–200

*Selected Writings* (including *Young Törless*, *Three Women*, 'The Perfecting of a Love' and other writings), edited by Burton Pike, Continuum Publishing Company (New York, 1986)

239

# Bibliography

*Forthcoming translations:*

*The Man without Qualities*, new tr. by Sophie Wilkins (Knopf)
*Selected Essays*, tr. by David Luft and Burton Pike (University of Chicago Press)

## Bibliographies

Thöming, Jürgen C., *Robert-Musil-Bibliographie* (Bad Homburg v.d.H./ Berlin/ Zürich, 1968)
Thöming, Jürgen C., 'Kommentierte Auswahlbibliographie zu Robert Musil', *Text + Kritik*, No. 21/22 ('Robert Musil'), second edition, 1972, 73–87
King, Lynda J., 'Robert Musil Bibliography 1976/1977', *Musil-Forum*, 4 (1978), 104–16
Mae, Michiko, 'Robert-Musil-Bibliographie 1977–1980', *Musil-Forum*, 6 (1980), 239–58
'Robert-Musil-Bibliographie 1980–1983', *Musil-Forum*, 9 (1983)
Arntzen Helmut, *Musil-Kommentar sämtlicher zu Lebzeiten erschienener Schriften außer dem Roman "Der Mann ohne Eigenschaften"*, (Munich, 1980), pp. 279–310
*Musil-Kommentar zum Roman "Der Mann ohne Eigenschaften"* (Munich, 1982), pp. 450–90

## Secondary literature on Musil or with extensive references to his work

Albertsen, Elisabeth, *Ratio und Mystik im Werk Robert Musils* (Munich, 1968)
'Ea oder die Freundin bedeutender Männer. Porträt einer Wiener Kaffeehaus-Muse', *Musil-Forum*, 5 (1979), 21–37 and 135–53
Allemann, Beda, *Ironie und Dichtung*, second edition (Pfullingen, 1969)
Alt, Peter-André, 'Ironie und Krise – ironisches Erzählen als Form ästhetischer Wahrnehmung', in *Thomas Manns "Der Zauberberg" und Robert Musils "Der Mann ohne Eigenschaften"* (Frankfurt am Main, 1985)
Arntzen, Helmut, 'Robert Musil: "Der Mann ohne Eigenschaften"', in *Der moderne deutsche Roman: Voraussetzungen, Strukturen, Gehalte* (Heidelberg, 1962)
*Satirischer Stil* (Bonn, 1960)
*Musil-Kommentar sämtlicher zu Lebzeiten erschienener Schriften außer dem Roman "Der Mann ohne Eigenschaften"* (Munich, 1980)
*Musil-Kommentar zu dem Roman "Der Mann ohne Eigenschaften"* (Munich, 1982)
'Symptomen-Theater. Robert Musil und das Theater seiner Zeit', *Literatur und Kritik*, No. 149/50 (1980), 598–606
Aspetsberger, Friedbert, 'Zu Robert Musils historischer Stellung am

# Bibliography

Beispiel des Romans "Der Mann ohne Eigenschaften"', *Sprachkunst*, 4 (1973), 231–47

'"Der andere Zustand" in its contemporary context', in *Musil in Focus* (London, 1982), pp. 54–73

Aue, Maximilian, 'Musil und die Romantik. Einige grundsätzliche Überlegungen', in *Sprachästhetische Sinnvermittlung*, ed. Farda and Karthaus, 125–34

Auernhammer, Achim, 'L'Androgynie dans "L'Homme sans qualités"', in *L'Arc*: '*Robert Musil*', No. 74 (1978), 35–40

Bauer, Sibylle, 'Ethik und Bewußtheit', in Sibylle Bauer and Ingrid Drevermann, *Studien zu Robert Musil* (Cologne, 1966)

Baur, Uwe and Dietmar Goltschnigg, *Vom "Törleß" zum "Mann ohne Eigenschaften"* (Munich/Salzburg, 1973)

Baur, Uwe, 'Zeit und Gesellschaftskritik in Robert Musils Roman "Die Verwirrungen des Zöglings Törleß"', in *Vom "Törleß [. . .]*, ed. Baur and Goltschnigg, pp. 19–45

Baur, Uwe and Elisabeth Castex, *Robert Musil. Untersuchungen* (Königstein, Taunus, 1980)

Baur, Uwe, 'Sport und subjektive Bewegungserfahrung bei Musil', in *Robert Musil. Untersuchungen*, ed. Baur and Castex, pp. 99–112

Bausinger, Wilhelm, *Studien zu einer historisch-kritischen Ausgabe von Robert Musils Roman "Der Mann ohne Eigenschaften"*, (Reinbek bei Hamburg, 1964)

Beard, Philip H., 'The "End" of "The Man without Qualities"', *Musil-Forum*, 8 (1982), 30–45

Berghahn, Wilfried, *Robert Musil – in Selbstzeugnissen und Bilddokumenten* (Reinbek bei Hamburg, 1963)

Böhme Hartmut, *Anomie und Entfremdung – Literatursoziologische Untersuchungen zu den Essays Robert Musils und seinem Roman "Der Mann ohne Eigenschaften"*, (Kronberg/Ts., 1974)

'Der Mangel des Narziß – Über Wunschstrukturen und Leiberfahrungen in Robert Musils "Der Mann ohne Eigenschaften"', in *Sprachästhetische Sinnvermittlung*, ed. Farda and Karthaus, pp. 45–85

Bouveresse, Jacques, 'La science sourit dans sa barbe . . .', in *l'Arc*: '*Robert Musil*' No. 74 (1978), 8–31

Braun, Wilhelm, 'Musil's "Erdensekretariat der Genauigkeit und Seele", a Clue to the Philosophy of the Hero of "Der Mann ohne Eigenschaften"', *Monatshefte*, 46 (1954), 305–6

'Musil and the Pendulum of the Intellect', *Monatshefte*, 49 (1957), 109–19

'Musil's Siamese Twins', *Germanic Review*, 33 (1958), 41–52

'Moosbrugger Dances', *Germanic Review*, 35 (1960), 214–20

'An Interpretation of Musil's Novelle "Tonka"', *Monatshefte*, 53 (1961), 73–85

'The confusions of Törleß', *Germanic Review*, 40 (1965), 116–31

Brokoph-Mauch, Gudrun, editor, *Beiträge zur Musil-Kritik* (Bern/Frankfurt am Main, 1983)

241

# Bibliography

Büren, Erhard von, *Zur Bedeutung der Psychologie im Werk Robert Musils* (Zurich/Freiburg i. Br., 1970)

Castex, Elisabeth, 'Probleme und Ziele der Forschung am Nachlaß Robert Musils', *Coloquia Germanica*, 10 (1976–7), 267–79

'Die Bedeutung der Wiener Forschungsarbeit am Musil-Nachlaß für Literaturwissenschaft und Edition', in *Robert Musil. Untersuchungen*, ed. Baur and Castex, pp. 1–9

'Die Wiener Robert Musil Nachlaß-Dokumentation – Ansatz, Methode und editorische Perspektiven', *Philologie und Kritik*, ed. Freese, pp. 53–66

'Zum neuesten Stand der Musil Editions-Forschung und Rezeption', *Musil-Forum*, 7 (1981), 53–64

Cohn, Dorrit, 'Psycho-Analogies: A Means for Rendering Consciousness', in *Probleme des Erzählens*, ed. Fritz Martini (Stuttgart, 1971)

Corino, Karl, 'Törleß ignortus', *Text + Kritik*, No. 21/22 'Robert Musil', second edition, 1972, 61–72

'"Der Zaubervogel küßt die Füße". Zu Robert Musils Leben und Werk in den Jahren 1914–16', in *Robert Musil – Literatur, Philosophie, Psychologie*, ed. Strutz and Strutz (Munich/Salzburg, 1984), pp. 143–72

'Musils Diotima. Modelle einer Figur', *Literatur und Kritik*, No. 149/150, 15 (1980)

*Robert Musils "Vereinigungen" – Studien zu einer historisch-kritischen Ausgabe* (Munich/Salzburg, 1974)

'Zwischen Mystik und Theaterleidenschaft – Robert Musils Brünner Jahre (1898–1902)', in *Robert Musil und die kulturellen Tendenzen seiner Zeit*, ed. Strutz and Strutz, pp. 11–28

'Ein Mörder macht Literaturgeschichte. Florian Grubatscher, ein Modell für Musils Moosbrugger', in *Robert Musil und die kulturellen Tendenzen seiner Zeit*, ed. Strutz and Strutz, pp. 130–47

Daigger, Annett, 'Tonka, une héroine de l'Homme sans qualités', in *Sud: 'Robert Musil'* (Marseille, 1982), pp. 133–37

Danner, Karl-Heinz, editor, *Internationales Symposium zu Fragen der Robert-Musil-Forschung* (Saarbrücken, 1974)

Dinklage, Karl, editor, *Robert Musil: Leben, Werk, Wirkung* (Vienna and Reinbek bei Hamburg, 1960)

(with Elisabeth Albertsen and Karl Corino), *Robert Musil – Studien zu seinem Werk* (Reinbek bei Hamburg, 1970)

Eibl, Karl, *Robert Musil. Drei Frauen. Text, Materialien, Kommentar* (Munich/Vienna, 1978)

Eisele, Ulf, 'Robert Musil – "Der Mann ohne Eigenschaften"', in *Die Struktur des modernen deutschen Romans* (Tübingen, 1984), pp. 114–50

Farda, Dieter P. and Ulrich Karthaus, editors, *Sprachästhetische Sinnvermittlung. Robert Musil Symposium, Berlin, 1980* (Frankfurt am Main, 1982)

# Bibliography

Fischer, Ernst, 'Das Werk Robert Musils: Versuch einer Würdigung', *Sinn und Form*, 9 (1957), 851–901

Fourie, Regine and Wolfgang Freese, 'Robert Musil: Ausgaben und neuere Forschung', *Acta Germanica*, 14 (1981), 213–32

Frank, Manfred, 'Auf der Suche nach einem Grund – über den Umschlag von Erkenntniskritik in Mythologie bei Musil', in *Mythos und Moderne*, ed. Karl-Heinz Bohrer (Frankfurt am Main, 1983), pp. 318–62

Franke, Hans-Peter, editor, *Materialien zu Robert Musil "Die Verwirrungen des Zöglings Törleß"* (Stuttgart, 1979)

Freese, Wolfgang, editor, *Philologie und Kritik* (Munich/Salzburg, 1981)
'Zur neueren Musil-Forschung. Ausgaben und Gesamtdarstellungen', *Text + Kritik*, No. 21/22, 'Robert Musil', third edition, 1983, 86–148
and Regine Fourie, 'Robert Musil: Ausgaben und neuere Forschung', *Acta Germanica*, 14 (1981) 213–32

Frisé, Adolf, *Plädoyer für Robert Musil. Hinweise und Essays 1931 bis 1980* (Reinbek bei Hamburg, 1980) (new, extended edition, 1987)
'Unvollendet–unvollendbar? Überlegungen zum Torso des "Mann ohne Eigenschaften"', *Musil-Forum*, 6 (1980), 79–104
'Der Zeitgenosse Robert Musil', *Literatur und Kritik*, 16 (1981), 381–91
'Von einer "Geschichte dreier Personen" zum "Mann ohne Eigenschaften". Zur Entstehung von Robert Musils Romanwerk', *Jahrbuch der deutschen Schillergesellschaft*, 26 (1982), 428–44
'Erfahrungen mit Robert Musil', *Musil-Forum*, 8 (1982, 16–29)

Furness, Raymond, 'The Androgynous Ideal: Its Significance in German Literature', *Modern Language Review*, 60 (1965), 58–64

Gargani, Aldo, 'Wittgenstein's "Perspicuous Representation" and Musil's "Illuminations"', in *Robert Musil und die kulturellen Tendenzen seiner Zeit [. . .]*, ed. Strutz and Strutz, pp. 110–19

Goltschnigg, Dietmar, *Mystische Tradition im Roman Robert Musils – Martin Bubers "Ekstatische Konfessionen" im "Mann ohne Eigenschaften"* (Heidelberg, 1974)

Graf, Günter, 'O. F. Bollnow: "Wahrhaftigkeit" und Robert Musil: "Ein Verkehrsunfall"', *wirkendes wort*, 17 (1967), 198–205

Gumtau, Helmut, *Robert Musil* (Berlin, 1967)

Hamburger, Michael, 'Explorers: Musil, Robert Walser, Kafka', in *A Proliferation of Prophets* (Manchester, 1983), pp. 244–72

Henninger, Peter, *Der Buchstabe und der Geist* (Frankfurt am Main, 1980)
'Der Text als Kompromiß. Versuch einer psychoanalytischen Textanalyse von Musils Erzählung "Tonka"', in *Psychoanalytische und psychopathologische Literaturinterpretation*, ed. Bernd Urban and Winfried Kudszus (Darmstadt, 1981)

Heydebrand, Renate von, *Die Reflexionen Ulrichs in Robert Musils Roman "Der Mann ohne Eigenschaften"* (Münster, 1966)
editor, *Robert Musil* (Darmstadt, 1982)

# Bibliography

Hickman, Hannah, '"Lebende Gedanken" und Emersons "Kreise"', in *Robert Musil. Untersuchungen*, ed. Baur and Castex, pp. 139–51

'Der junge Musil und R. W. Emerson', *Musil-Forum*, 6 (1980), 3–13

*Robert Musil and the Culture of Vienna* (London/Sydney, 1984)

Hochstätter, Dietrich, *Sprache des Möglichen – stilistischer Perspektivismus in Robert Musils "Mann ohne Eigenschaften"* (Frankfurt am Main, 1972)

Holmes, Allan, *Robert Musil, "Der Mann ohne Eigenschaften": An examination of the relationship between the author, narrator and protagonist* (Bonn, 1978)

Howald, Stefan, *Ästhetizismus und ästhetische Ideologiekritik* (Munich, 1984)

Huber, Lothar and John J. White, editors, *Musil in Focus – Papers from a Centenary Symposium* (London, 1982)

Huber, Lothar, 'Satire and Irony in Musil's "Der Mann ohne Eigenschaften"', in *Musil in Focus*, ed. Huber and White, pp. 99–114

Hüppauf, Bernd, 'Von Wien durch den Krieg nach Nirgendwo: Nation und utopisches Denken bei Musil und im Austromarxismus', *Text + Kritik: 'Robert Musil'*, Nos. 21/22, third edition, 1983, pp. 1–28

Kaiser, Ernst, 'Die Entstehungsgeschichte von Robert Musils Roman "Der Mann ohne Eigenschaften"', *studi germanici* (new series), 4 (1966)

Kaiser, Ernst and Eithne Wilkins, *Robert Musil: Eine Einführung in das Werk* (Stuttgart, 1962)

Kappeler, Susanne and Bryson, Norman, editors, *Teaching the Text* (London/Boston/Melbourne/Henly, 1983)

Karthaus, Ulrich, 'Musil-Forschung und Musil-Deutung. Ein Literaturbericht', *Deutsche Vierteljahrsschrift für Literaturwissenschaft und Geistesgeschichte*, 39 (1965), 441–83

Kermode, Frank, 'A Short View of Musil', in *Puzzles and Epiphanies*, second (revised) impression (London, 1963), pp. 91–107

Krusche, Dieter, 'Robert Musil: "Vereinigungen"', in *Kommunikation im Erzähltext*, 2 vols (Munich, 1978), I, pp. 137–53

Kühn, Dieter, *Analogie und Variation: Zur Analyse von Robert Musils Roman "Der Mann ohne Eigenschaften"* (Bonn, 1965)

'Sätze und Ansätze (Musils Tagebücher)', *Neue Rundschau*, 88 (1977), 610–18

Kühne, Jörg, *Das Gleichnis: Studien zur inneren Form von Robert Musils Roman "Der Mann ohne Eigenschaften"* (Stuttgart, 1970)

Laermann, Klaus, *Eigenschaftslosigkeit: Reflexionen zu Robert Musils Roman "Der Mann ohne Eigenschaften"* (Stuttgart, 1970)

Luft, David S., *Robert Musil and the Crisis of European Culture, 1880–1942* (Los Angeles, 1980)

Mae, Michiko, 'Robert Musils Novellentheorie', *Beiträge zur Germanistik*, edited by the Germanisten-Vereinigung at the University of Kanazawa, I (1980), 25–43

# Bibliography

'Robert Musils Novellenband "Vereinigungen" in der Kritik seiner Zeit. Ein Beitrag zur historischen Rezeptionsanalyse', *Doitsu Bungaku*, edited by the Japanische Gesellschaft für Germanistik, 44–55

Magnou, Jacqueline, 'Grenzfall und Identitätsproblem oder die Rolle der Psychopathologie in den literarischen Praxis und Theorie Musils anhand der Novellen: "Vereiningungen"', in *Sprachästhetische Sinnvermittlung*, ed. Farda and Karthaus, pp. 103–16

'Situation de Törleß, *Sud*: *'Robert Musil'* (Marseille, 1982), pp. 112–28

Mayer, Hans, 'Erinnerung an Robert Musil', in *Zur deutschen Literatur der Zeit* (Reinbek bei Hamburg, 1967), pp. 137–54

Meister, Monika and Paul Stefanek, 'Die Schwärmer in Wien', *Musil-Forum*, 8 (1982), 137–50

Michel, Kurt Marcus, 'Die Utopie der Sprache', *Akzente*, 1 (1954), 23–35

Militzer, Gerti, 'Internationales Robert-Musil-Sommerseminar 1982 in Klagenfurt', *Musil-Forum*, 8 (1982), 163–7

Molino, Jean, 'Doubles – sur la logique de Musil', *l'Arc*: *'Robert Musil'*, No. 74 (1978), pp. 63–74

Moser, Walter, 'Musil à Paris', *Critique*, Nos. 433–4, June/July 1983, pp. 459–76

Müller, Götz, *Ideologiekritik und Metasprache* (Munich/Salzburg, 1972)

'Zur Entwicklungsgeschichte von Robert Musils Roman "Der Mann ohne Eigenschaften". Folgerungen aus der neuen Edition', *Zeitschrift für deutsche Philologie*, 98 (1979), 524–43

'Isis und Osiris. Die Mythen in Robert Musils Roman "Der Mann ohne Eigenschaften"', *Zeitschrift für deutsche Philologie*, 102 (1983), 583–604

Mulot, Sibylle, *Der junge Musil: Seine Beziehung zur Literatur und Kunst der Jahrhundertwende* (Stuttgart, 1977)

Nagonowski, Egon, 'Robert Musils "Vinzenz", der Dadaismus und das Theater des Absurden', *Il teatro nella Mitteleuropa* (Gorizia, 1980), 195–204

Neuenfels, Hans, *Robert Musil – "Die Schwärmer"* (Reinbek bei Hamburg, 1985)

Nusser, Peter, *Musils Romantheorie* (The Hague/Paris, 1967)

Paulson, Ronald M. *Robert Musil and the Ineffable: Hieroglyph, Myth, Fairy Tale and Sign* (Stuttgart, 1982)

'Myth and Fairy-tale in Robert Musil's Grigia', in *The Turn of the Century – German Literature and Art 1890–1915*, ed. Gerald Chapple and Hans H. Schulte (Bonn, 1981), pp. 135–48

Payne, Philip, 'Moosbrugger and the Question of Free Will', *New German Studies*, 3 (1975), 139–54

'Musil erforscht den Geist eines anderen Menschen – zum Porträt Moosbruggers im "Mann ohne Eigenschaften"', *Literatur und Kritik*, Nos. 106–107 (1976), 389–404

'Feuer als Kern von Musils Ethik im "Mann ohne Eigenschaften"', *wirkendes wort*, 28 (1978), 36–45

245

# Bibliography

'On Reading Robert Musil's "Der Mann ohne Eigenschaften"', *Sprachkunst*, 9 (1978), 88–100

'"Der Mann ohne Eigenschaften" – The Wrong Title for Robert Musil's Work?', *Musil-Forum*, 5 (1979), 184–98

'Robert Musil, von innen gesehen. Betrachtungen zu den Tagebüchern', *Musil-Forum*, 6 (1980), 227–38

'Robert Musil's Diaries' in *Musil in Focus*, ed. Huber and White, 131–43

'Robert Musils Briefe an die Nachwelt', *Neue Zürcher Zeitung*, 26/27 June 1982, pp. 67–8

*Robert Musil's Works, 1906–1924 – a Critical Introduction* (Frankfurt am Main/Bonn/New York, 1987)

Peters, Frederick, G., *Musil and Nietzsche: a Literary Study of a Philosophical Relationship* (PhD. dissertation, University of Cambridge, 1972)

*Robert Musil – Master of the Hovering Life* (New York, 1978)

Pike, Burton, *Robert Musil: An Introduction to his Work* (New York, 1961), (reissued in 1972)

Pott, Hans-Georg, *Robert Musil* (Munich, 1984)

Pütz, Heinz-Peter, 'Robert Musil', in *Deutsche Dichter der Moderne*, ed. Benno von Wiese (Berlin, 1965)

Rasch, Wolfdietrich, *Über Robert Musils Roman "Der Mann ohne Eigenschaften"* (Göttingen, 1967)

Reinhardt, Stephan, *Studien zur Antinomie von Intellekt und Gefühl in Musils Roman "Der Mann ohne Eigenschaften"* (Bonn, 1969)

Reiss, Hans, 'Musil and the Writer's Task in the Age of Science and Technology', in *Musil in Focus*, ed. Huber and White, pp. 41–53

Reniers-Servrankx, 'L'Homme sans qualités de Musil: interpretations et problèmes d'interpretation', *Études germaniques*, 26 (1971), 231–9

Reniers-Servrankx, Annie, *Robert Musil – Konstanz und Entwicklungen von Themen, Motiven und Strukturen in den Dichtungen* (Bonn, 1972)

Requadt, Manfred, 'Robert Musil und das Dichten "more geometrico"', *Text + Kritik: 'Robert Musil'*, third edition, No. 21/22 (1983), pp. 29–43

Rocek, Roman, '"Der Mann ohne Eigenschaften" – ein Roman ohne Ende', *Musil-Forum*, 7 (1981), 143–53

Roseberry, Robert L., *Robert Musil: ein Forschungsbericht* (Frankfurt am Main, 1974)

Roth, Marie-Louise, *Robert Musil: Ethik und Ästhetik. Zum theoretischen Werk des Dichters* (Munich, 1972)

'Robert Musil-Forschung. Situation und Symptome', in *Nachlaß- und Editionsprobleme bei modernen Schriftstellern*, ed. Marie-Louise Roth, Renate Schröder-Werle and Hans Zeller (Berne, 1981), pp. 23–9

'Robert-Musils Essayismus', *Arbeitskreis Heinrich Mann* special number, ed. Peter-Paul Schneider (Lübeck, 1981), pp. 248–55

editor, *L'Herne: 'Robert Musil'* (Paris, 1981)

# Bibliography

'Robert Musil als Aphoristiker', in *Beiträge zur Musil-Kritik*, ed. Gudrun Brokoph-Mauch, pp. 289–320

(with Renate Schröder-Werle, Hans Zeller, co-editors), *Nachlaß- und Editionsprobleme bei modernen Schriftstellern* (Bern/Frankfurt am Main/Las Vegas, 1981)

Schaffnit, Hans Wolfgang, *Mimesis als Problem: Studien zu einem ästhetischen Begriff der Dichtung aus Anlaß Robert Musils* (Berlin, 1971)

Schelling, Ulrich, *Identität und Wirklichkeit bei Robert Musil* (Zürich, 1968)

Schmidt, Jochen, *Ohne Eigenschaften – eine Erläuterung zu Musils Grundbegriff* (Tübingen, 1975)

Schneider, Rolf, *Die problematisierte Wirklichkeit, – Leben und Werk Robert Musils – Versuch einer Interpretation* (Berlin, 1975)

Schöne, Albrecht, 'Zum Gebrauch des Konjunktivs bei Robert Musil', *Euphorion*, 55 (1961), 196–220

Schönwiese, Ernst, *Literatur in Wien zwischen 1930 und 1980* (Vienna and Munich, 1980)

Schramm, Ulf, *Fiktion und Reflexionen: Überlegungen zu Musil und Beckett* (Frankfurt, 1967)

Schröder, Jürgen, 'Am Grenzwert der Sprache. Zu Robert Musils "Vereinigungen"', *Euphorion*, 60 (1966), 173–87

Schröder-Werle, Renate, 'Musil-Edition zwischen Anspruch und Wirklichkeit – zur Entwicklung der Musil-Philologie', in *Nachlaß- und Editionsprobleme bei modernen Schriftstellern*, ed. Marie-Louise Roth, Renate Schröder-Werle and Hans Zeller (Berne, 1981), pp. 30–44

'Probleme einer künftigen Musil-Edition. Bestandsaufnahme und Lösungsvorschläge', in *Philologie und Kritik*, ed. Freese, pp. 13–52

Sokel, Walter H., 'Kleist's Marquise of O., Kierkegaard's Abraham, and Musil's Tonka: Three Stages of the Absurd as the Touchstone of Faith', *Wisconsin Studies in Contemporary Literature*, 8 (1967), 505–16

'Musils "Mann ohne Eigenschaften" und die Existenzphilosophie', in *Sprachästhetische Sinnvermittlung*, ed. Farda and Karthaus, pp. 97–102

'Agathe und der existenzphilosophische Faktor im "Mann ohne Eigenschaften"', in *Beiträge zur Musil-Kritik*, ed. Gudrun Brokoph-Mauch, pp. 111–28

Stefanek, Paul, 'Musils Posse "Vinzenz" und das Theater der Zwischenkriegszeit', *Maske und Kothurn. Vierteljahrsschrift für Theaterwissenschaft*, 26 (1980), 249–70

Stefanek, Paul and Monika Meister, '"Die Schwärmer" in Wien', *Musil-Forum*, 8 (1982), 137–50

Stern, Joseph Peter, 'Viennese Kaleidoscope', *The Listener*, 1 November 1962, pp. 722–3

'Die Wiener "Wirklichkeit" im Roman "Der Mann ohne Eigenschaften"', *Literatur und Kritik*, No. 149–50, 1980, 525–31

# Bibliography

' "Reality" in "Der Mann ohne Eigenschaften" ', in *Musil in Focus*, ed. Huber and White, 74–84

'History in Robert Musil's "Törleß" in *Teaching the Text*, ed. Kappeler and Bryson, pp. 35–55.

Stopp, Elisabeth, 'Musils "Törleß" – Content and Form', *Modern Language Review*, 63 (1968), 94–118

Strelka, Joseph, 'Robert Musil', in *Kafka, Musil, Broch* (Vienna, Hannover and Berne, 1959)

Strelka, Joseph, 'Claudine und Veronika – zur weiblichen Doppelfigur von Robert Musils "Vereinigungen" ', in *Probleme der Moderne: Studien zur deutschen Literatur von Nietzsche bis Brecht*, ed. B. Bennett, A. Kaes, W. J. Lillyman (Tübingen, 1983)

Strutz Josef and Johann Strutz, editors, *Robert Musil und die kulturellen Tendenzen seiner Zeit* (Munich/Salzburg, 1983)

*Robert Musil – Literatur, Philosophie und Psychologie* (Munich/ Salzburg, 1984)

Swales, Martin, 'Narrator and hero – Observations on Robert Musil's "Törleß" ', in *Musil in Focus*, ed. Huber and White, 1–11

Thöming, Jürgen, C., 'Musil-Chronik', *Text + Kritik: 'Robert Musil'*, Nos. 21/22 (1983), third edition, pp. 149–152

Tissot, Christiane, 'Tonka – Visions', *Sud*, special no. (1982) *'Robert Musil'*, pp. 141–9

Trommler, Frank, *Roman und Wirklichkeit: eine Ortsbestimmung am Beispiel von Musil, Broch, Roth, Doderer and Gütersloh* (Stuttgart/ Berlin/Cologne/Mainz, 1966)

White, John J., ' "Berühmt und unbekannt": Robert Musil's Collected Letters in Adolf Frisé's New Edition', *German Life and Letters*, 37 (1984), 232–49

Wilkins, Eithne and Ernst Kaiser, 'Monstrum in Animo', *Deutsche Vierteljahrsschrift für Literaturwissenschaft und Geistesgeschichte*, 37 (1963), 78–119

Wilkins, Eithne, 'Musils unvollendeter Roman "Die Zwillingsschwester" ', *Colloquia Germanica*, 10 (1976/7), 220–36

Willemsen, Roger, ' "Man nimmt Franz Blei zu leicht!" – Robert Musil und "Das große Bestiarium der Literatur" ', in *Robert Musil und die kulturellen Tendenzen seiner Zeit*, ed. Strutz and Strutz, pp. 120–9

*Das Existenzrecht der Dichtung. Zur Rekonstruktion einer systematischen Literaturtheorie im Werk Robert Musils* (Munich, 1984)

*Robert Musil – vom intellektuellen Eros* (Munich/Zurich, 1985)

Williams, Cedric E., 'Robert Musil', in *The Broken Eagle – the Politics of Austrian Literature from Empire to Anschluß* (London, 1974)

Zeller, Hans, 'Vitium aut virtus? Philologisches zu Adolf Frisés Musil-Ausgaben, mit prinzipiellen Überlegungen zur Frage des Texteingriffs', *Zeitschrift für deutsche Philologie – special number*, *Probleme neugermanistischer Edition*, 101 (1982), 210–44

Zeller, Rosmarie, 'Zur Komposition von Musils "Drei Frauen" ', in

# Bibliography

*Beiträge zur Musil-Kritik*, ed. Gudrun Brokoph-Mauch (Berne/ Frankfurt am Main, 1983), pp. 25–48

'Robert Musils Auseinandersetzung mit der realistischen Schreibweise', *Musil-Forum*, 6 (1980), 128–44

Zima, Pierre V., 'Musil', in *L'ambivalence romanesque. Proust, Kafka, Musil* (Paris, 1980), pp. 207–318

# INDEX

# Index

# Index

'Wissenschaft', *see* science
'without qualities'
  as contemporary condition of
    mankind, 64–6, 95
  as epithet for Ulrich, 64, 148–66
Wittgenstein, Ludwig, 23
*The Woman from Portugal*, 191
words, *see* language
'World Secretariat of Precision and
  Soul', 104–5, 109–10, 112–13

Wotruba, Fritz, 3
writer, *see* Dichter

*Young Törless*, 15, 19, 27–31, 46, 50,
  51, 193, 216–17 n.6

'Zurechnungsfähigkeit'
  ('accountability'), *see under* law
Zweig, Stefan, 16
*Die Zwillingsschwester*, 49

WITHDRAWN

Gramley Library
Salem College
Winston-Salem, NC 27108